Spain
&
Franco

1949-59

Spain & Franco

1949-59

Edited by J. Lee Shneidman

Professor of History
Adelphi University (Garden City, N.Y.)

FACTS ON FILE, INC.   NEW YORK, N.Y.

Spain
&
Franco
1949-59

Library of Congress Catalog Card No. 72-92855
ISBN 0-87196-180-6
9 8 7 6 5 4 3 2 1
PRINTED IN
THE UNITED STATES OF AMERICA

Contents

i

Economic Reform, Political Stagnation (1959)

Index

FOREWORD

FOR MORE THAN $1/3$ OF A CENTURY the reins of government in Spain have been held by a single man—Francisco Franco y Bahamonde, a career army officer widely described as a dictator, who runs a monarchless country that he has declared to be a kingdom.

Many observers complain that there is incredibly little accurate knowledge and atrocious misinterpretation of the situation and of recent events in Franco's Spain. The purpose of this book is to provide a factual account of developments involving Franco and Spain during the crucial period 1949–59 when Spain emerged from its postwar isolation and made a serious effort to restore its economy. Much of the material recorded in this book is quite controversial, but, as in all books in the FACTS ON FILE series, great efforts were taken to present all pertinent facts without bias.

Some of the material in this book appeared in one form or another in other FACTS ON FILE publications; some was gathered by the editor in Spain between 1957 and 1971; some of the information came from individuals who, because of their positions or for other obvious reasons, must remain nameless. The editor would like to express his gratitude to the Adelphi University Faculty Committee on Grants in the Humanities for its financial support for some of his trips to Spain. He would also like to express his gratitude to his wife, Dr. Conalee Levine-Shneidman, who, both in the U.S. and in Europe, helped entertain the various unnamed individuals.

1

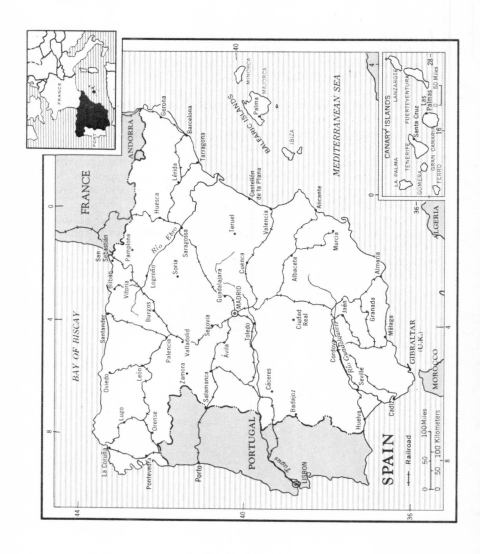

The People & the Land

Spain, whose population increased from 28 million in 1950 to 30.9 million in 1960, is considered by some of its inhabitants to be a country of at least 3 separate nations. The Basques (inhabiting the northern provinces of Vizcaya, Álava, Guipúzcoa and Navarra) and the Catalans (of Catalunya, or Catalonia) regard themselves as individual nations within Spain. In addition there are the Castilians of central Spain, the Galicians of the northwest and the Andalusians of the south. Spain is a Roman Catholic country; only about .1% of the population practice other religions.

Mainland Spain dominates the Iberian Peninsula, which it shares with Portugal. In 1972 the 195,988 square miles of the Kingdom of Spain included the Spanish mainland, the Balearic Islands, the Canary Islands, the North African cities of Ceuta and Melilla and 3 small islands off the coast of Morocco. The west African province of Spanish Sahara was under Spanish jurisdiction as well. In 1949 Spain also owned the west African colony of Ifni and the Equatorial colonies of Spanish Guinea and Fernando Poo and held administrative jurisdiction over parts of Morocco.

High plateaus and mountain and river barriers that divide the country into separate compartments are Spain's most obvious topographical features. The country is divided into 5 general topographic regions:

(1) The northern coastal belt of Galicia, Asturias and the Basque provinces is a mountainous region with fertile valleys and thick forests. The coast, from Rio Minho north to La Coruña (or Corunna) and then east to Gijón, is cut by deep fjords, while from Gijón to the French frontier the coast is dotted with little bays that provide excellent harbors for fishing fleets. There are several good ports along this coast: Vigo, La Coruña, Gijón, Santanter and Bilbao. The rugged Cantabrian mountains that form the southern boundary of the region, however, prevent full utilization of the ports because, until the 1960s, communication between the coast and the interior was difficult. This region is the center of Spain's coal and iron mines.

(2) Catalunya (Cataluña) and the Ebro valley in the northeastern region have Spain's largest port, Barcelona, and highest mountains, with peaks reaching 11,420 feet (Mount Mulhacen). The area is the center of the Spanish textile industry and is the most industrialized part of the country.

3

(3) The Levante, the southeastern coastal belt, has the 2d most fertile area in the peninsula and the largest lake, La Albufera. The northern part of the area is rugged and contains the highest peaks: Penagolsa (5,500 feet) and El Conador (4,300 feet). Even though the province has a long coastline, there are few ports. Alicante, on the sea, is a man-made port. Valencia, the chief city of the region, is on the Turia River.

(4) Andalucía covers the southern part of the country. With the exception of the flat and fertile plain of the Rio Guadalquivir, Spain's most fertile area, the region is mountainous. The southern coast is cut from the rest of the region by the rugged Sierra Nevada mountains, which are frequently snow covered in July, when temperatures on the neighboring plain of Almería reach 100°F. The chief city of the region is Sevilla.

(5) The central plateau, or Mesta, with an average altitude of 2,200 feet, dominates central Spain. The region is bounded in the north by the Cantabrian Mountains and in the south by the Sierra Morena mountains. The Mesta is cut by the Duero, Tagus and Guadiana rivers and the Gredos and Guadarrama mountains. Madrid, capital of Spain, is in the center of this region. The area north of Madrid is arid and appears lunar. The area to the south is flat and fertile.

Nearly ¾ of Spain is dry and has less than 20 inches of rainfall annually. Northwestern Spain, however, has a climate like England's with slight variations in temperature and plentiful rainfall, and the coastal regions in the east and south have a typically Mediterranean climate, with long dry spells and warmer temperatures.

History

During the period 1000–500 BC, Celtic tribesmen, who crossed the Pyrenees from France, and Phoenician and Greek merchants, who crossed the Mediterranean from the Middle East, invaded Iberia and conquered the native Iberian population. By 500 BC the Celts had occupied the central plateau, the Phoenicians had established cities on the southern coast and the Greeks had taken root on the eastern coast.

With the destruction of Phoenician independence (*circa* 580 BC) by Babylon, most Phoenician holdings fell to Carthage, which had originated as a Phoenician colony. During the period 500–330 BC, Greeks and Carthaginians fought for mastery of Iberia while the Celtic and Iberian peoples slowly merged as the Celtoiberians. With the defeat of the Greeks by Alexander of Macedon (*circa* 335 BC), the isolated Iberian Greeks found it increasingly difficult to defend themselves from

Carthaginian imperialism and turned to Rome for aid. As a result of 3 Roman-Carthaginian wars that ended with the destruction of Carthage in 202 BC, the Romans occupied not only the Greek and Carthaginian cities but also Celtoiberian villages. The Celtoiberians had at first welcomed the Romans as liberators from Carthaginian control, but when the Romans refused to leave Iberia, the Celtoiberians revolted. By 133 BC Rome had subdued all the Celtoiberians and dominated the entire peninsula except the region of the Basques, whose origins are unknown.

During the period 133 BC-19 AD, Iberia was a battleground for forces striving to control the Roman Republic. Native Celtoiberians were forced into the contending armies and became Romanized, while many Romans who had lost power in Rome fled to Iberia and established bases. A result was a growing Roman population in Iberia and a gradual Romanization of the natives. By 100 AD, with the exception of the Basques, the native population had been Romanized. Under Rome, the population became Christian.

Iberia was one of the more prosperous areas of the Roman Empire until 409 AD, when the first Germanic invaders crossed the Pyrenees. For 100 years various Germanic tribes (Suevii, Vandals, Alans and Visigoths) fought for mastery of Iberia. The Alans were destroyed, the Vandals fled to North Africa, the Suevii were restricted to the northwestern corner, and the Visigoths dominated. The Basques, however, maintained their independence.

The Muslims invaded Iberia in 711. By 713 the entire peninsula except the extreme northern coast (protected by the Cantabrian Mountains) and the Basque lands were conquered. During the period 750-1000, Muslim Spain was the most prosperous area of Western Europe and had great centers of learning. The Reconquest—the ouster of the Muslims—took until 1492, when the last Muslim stronghold, Granada, capitulated.

In 1150 Iberia was dominated by 2 civilizations: Christian and Muslim. Each civilization had several political entities. Among the Christians were the kingdoms of Portugal, Castile, León, Navarra and Aragon, the counties of Catalunya (Barcelona, Urgel, Roussillon, Ampurias, etc.) and the lordship of Albarracin. Muslims ruled the kingdoms of Sevilla, Toledo, Badajoz, Granada, Mallorca and Valencia. But by 1300, Muslim Spain (al-Andalus) was reduced to the small kingdom of Granada, while Christian Spain was divided among the kingdoms of Portugal, Castile (which was permanently united with León) and Navarra and a collection of states known as the Crowns of Aragon, which included the kingdoms of Aragon, Valencia and Mallorca and the counties of Catalunya. The Crowns was a loose confederation of states, each with its own social, political and economic structure, united only in the person of the sovereign.

Each state had a Cortes (parliament) that effectively limited royal power. The royal power was also limited by customs (frequently set down in charters) and traditions (usually understood but not written). In the kingdom of Aragon, royal authority was almost non-existant; in Catalunya, royal power could be exercised only with the approval of the merchant-dominated Cortes; in Navarra, the royal family, which was French, hardly bothered to visit the kingdom and preferred to act as French nobles; in Castile, royal authority was limited by the landed aristocracy and the urban centers.

In each state the Church held large tracts of land, exercised independent jurisdiction and had military forces at its disposal.

Iberia was divided into several linguistic groups by 1300. Except for the Basques, in Navarra and the portions of Castile bordering Navarra, and for the Muslims, in Granada, all Iberians spoke dialects of a Romance language that had been heavily influenced by the long period of German and Arabic occupation. The Germanic influence, however, varied. The extreme northwest had been the last stronghold of the Suevii tribe; the northeast had been influenced by the Germanic tribe called the Franks (who had invaded Iberia in 785 and conquered Catalunya by 830); the rest of the peninsula was influenced by the Visigoths, without other Germanic influences. The Suevii-Visigothic mixture was the basis of the Luso-Galician language, which became modern Portuguese and the Galician dialect of Spain; the Frankish-Visigothic mixture produced Catalan; from the pure Visigothic developed the Leonese-Castilian-Aragonese languages, which became modern Castilian, or Spanish.

To the men of the Middle Ages "Spain," like "Iberia," was a geographic expression indicating the entire peninsula. There was no individual called the "king of Spain."

The Castilian Kingdom faced a serious problem in the 2d half of the 15th century: There was no male heir. The wife of King Enrique IV (1454-74) had a daughter (allegedly sired by a lover) who was betrothed to King Afonso V of Portugal. Enrique also had a half-sister, Isabella, who had married Fernando, heir to the Crowns of Aragon. The Cortes of Castile had to choose a queen who was married to a foreign sovereign. In 1475 the Cortes, meeting in Segovia, chose Isabella and Aragon. The marriage of Fernando and Isabella had not united the 2 kingdoms. Isabella was queen of Castile (and after 1492, of America) while her husband ruled the Crowns of Aragon, which by that time included the kingdoms of Aragon, Valencia, Mallorca, Sardinia and Sicily (of which Malta was a part) and the principality of Catalunya. Their marriage, however, did permit the 2 states to unite for the conquest of Granada, which, in 1492, was appended to the Castilian kingdom.

Isabella died in 1504. Her eldest daughter, Juanna La Loca (Joan the Mad) became queen of Castile and the overseas territories. Fernando, ruler of the Crowns of Aragon, remarried. But this marriage produced no heir, so Juanna became ruler of the Crowns when Fernando died in 1516.

Juanna's husband, Philip of Hapsburg, had died in 1506, leaving his lands in Burgundy and the Netherlands to his oldest son, Charles. Because Juanna's insanity made her unfit to rule, the Castilian Cortes invited Charles to Castile. The Aragonese, however, did not want Charles as king and attempted to place Charles' brother Fernando on the throne of the Crowns. Charles, supported by the Church of both Castile and the Crowns of Aragon, ordered his brother to leave Iberia for Germany, and Fernanuo complied. Charles arrived in Castile in 1517 and secured the allegiance of the Castilian Cortes. He then visited each of the Iberian portions of the Crowns of Aragon and won the support of the individual Cortes. Charles' paternal grandfather, Holy Roman Emperor Maximilian, died in 1519, and Charles went to Germany to claim the imperial title.

Charles had the largest empire Europe had known since the fall of Rome. From his mother (who remained in a padded cell until her death in 1555) he inherited: Castile (which included most of the kingdom of Navarra, conquered by Fernando in 1512 and given to Castile in 1515); the American lands and claims to various territories in the Pacific; the Crowns of Aragon to which Fernando had added the kingdom of Naples and various North African territories. From his father, Charles inherited Burgundy and what is now the Netherlands, Belgium, Luxembourg and several departments of northern France. From his grandfather he inherited Austria and a claim to the title "Holy Roman emperor." But Charles found it impossible to govern and defend so vast an empire. He spent most of his life fighting the French, the Ottoman Turks, the Barbary pirates and the Protestant German princes. Tired and defeated, Charles abdicated in 1555. He gave his Italian, French, Dutch, Iberian and overseas kingdoms to his son Philip, Charles' brother Fernando, who had become king of Bohemia and Hungary, was granted Austria and the Imperial title.

Despite Charles' failure in his various wars, Hapsburg power plus the wealth from the American silver mines was sufficient to alter the constitutional structure of the Iberian states. With his American wealth and his ability to appropriate half of the Church's revenues (Hapsburg power in Italy prevented effective papal opposition to such appropriations), Charles began to by-pass the Cortes. Gradually these bodies lost all say in foreign affairs and could do little to prevent royal action.

Philip II (1556–98), like his father, ruled a collection of independent states. In 1580 he inherited the kingdom of Portugal. Although Philip was called "king of the Spains," each state remained independent: *e.g.*, a citizen of Aragon was a foreigner in Castile. Because the kingdom of Castile with its American possessions was the single most powerful state in Philip's empire, people began to look on Castile as Spain and the Castilian language as Spanish.

The growing identification of Spain with Castile was resented by the Portuguese and Catalans. As Philip III (1598–1621) and Philip IV 1621–65) began to concentrate their energies on serving Castilian interests above the interests of the Catalans and Portuguese, resentment became opposition. In 1640 the Catalans and Portuguese revolted. Lacking the force to defeat both revolutions, Philip IV concentrated his force against Catalunya. Portugal achieved independence, but Catalunya was conquered. The conquest, however, did not change the constitutional structure of Catalunya, which was still one of the territories of the Crowns of Aragon.

With the end of the Spanish Hapsburg dynasty in 1700, various European powers fought the War of the Spanish Succession to prevent the Spanish empire from falling to either the Austrian Hapsburgs or to the legal heir, King Louis XIV of France. After 15 years of war, the European powers agreed on a compromise: Philip, grandson of Louis XIV, would become king of Spain and the non-European Spanish territories, while Emperor Charles VI of the Holy Roman Empire would receive Spain's European lands in Italy and Belgium. England received Gibraltar, Menorca (Minorca) and some Spanish and French territory in America. During the war the Catalans had supported Charles and not Philip. When Philip conquered the province in 1707, he abolished Catalunya's constitutional structure.

Philip V, the first Spanish Bourbon, brought to Spain many French ideas about government. He implemented many of the absolutist concepts of Louis XIV. The internal divisions between Castile and the Crowns of Aragon were abolished; the separate rights and privileges and legal and economic institutions were abolished; the various Cortes were no longer called. All of Spain was ruled from Madrid. (The Basques maintained some local rights considered too unimportant for the Bourbon kings to object.) The political unification of Castile and the

Crowns of Aragon into the new kingdom of Spain did not, however, mean a cultural-linguistic unification. The Basques and the Catalans maintained their identities and objected to rule from Madrid.

Philip (who died in 1746) and his sons Fernando VI (1746–59) and Carlos III (1759–88) supported internal economic development by resorting to high tariffs and subsidizing industry. They engaged in massive public works. To pay for the economic improvements, they increased taxation; and much of the additional revenue came from America. During the 18th century the Spanish Bourbons were allied with France in war against England. As a result of these wars Spain lost several colonies in America. But during the American Revolution, Spain was able to retake Menorca and Florida from England.

When the French Revolution started, Spain joined the forces opposed to the French Republic. After a series of military defeats and a French offer to help Spain conquer Portugal, Spain made peace with France and allied with France in war against England and Portugal. Spain again suffered military defeat. In 1808 Napoleon tricked both Carlos IV (1788–1808, died 1819) and his son Fernando into abdicating and appointed his own brother Joseph as king of Spain. The Spanish people did not accept Joseph and revolted. With the aid of the Duke of Wellington, the Spanish forced the French to leave the country by 1813. In America, the Spanish drove out not only the pro-French but also those loyal to Spain.

By 1830 all that remained of the once vast Spanish empire was Cuba, Puerto Rico, the Philippines, a few outposts in Africa and several groups of islands and atolls in the Pacific. During the mid-19th century Spain attempted vainly to reconquer some of its colonies by minor wars with the Dominican Republic (occupied 1861–5), Mexico (1861), Peru 1864–5) and Chile (1865–6), but it made no lasting gains. A brief war with Morocco (1859–60) resulted in the grant to Spain of the uninhabited area of Sidi Ifni. The Spanish-America War of 1898 forced Spain to surrender Cuba, Puerto Rico, Guam and the Philippines to the U.S. At the same time Spain sold its Pacific islands to Germany.

According to historians, one reason for the rapid decline in Spanish power after 1815 was its government's instability. When the Spanish revolted against Joseph Bonapart in 1808, many of the revolutionary leaders had proposed that Spain be a united country ruled by the Cortes, with the king serving as a symbol. These individuals, who began to be called *liberales* (the English term liberal is of Spanish derivation), wrote a constitution in 1812 that expressed these ideas. King Carlos IV's son, Fernando VII, refused to accept the constitution and, having the support of the aristocracy and the Church, reestablished

absolute rule. The army leadership, which had accepted the liberal constitution, revolted in 1820. The king called on France for aid, and a
French army reestablished absolute rule.

Fernando VII voided the anti-female Salic Law and proclaimed his
3-year-old daughter Isabella heiress to the throne June 20, 1833. This
was protested by the king's brother Carlos Maria Isidro, who declared
that he was the legitimate heir and that he intended to fight for the
throne. Since Carlos was generally regarded as favoring an absolute
government, Queen Maria Cristina, mother of Isabella, promised to re-
activate the 1812 constitution if the Liberals would support Isabella II.
When Fernando died in the fall of 1833, Isabella was proclaimed queen
by the army in Madrid, but Carlos was proclaimed king by the Basques
and Catalans. The result was a civil war that devastated much of northern Spain. The First Carlist War ended Aug. 1839 with victory for Isabella and defeat for the Carlists. Having won the war, Maria Cristina,
who had acted as regent for her daughter abrogated the 1812 constitution. The army revolted, and the queen-regent fled Spain. For the next
35 years, even though there was a constitution and a Cortes, real power
was in the hands of the military. Whenever the government did not
follow army instructions there was a coup (as in 1840, 1843, 1854,
1856, 1857, 1866, 1868, 1869, 1873, 1874 and 1875), sometimes 2
within a year, i.e., Jan. 2, and Dec. 29, 1874.

Queen Isabella II Oct. 10, 1846 married her cousin Francisco de
Asis (1822–1902), duke of Cadiz, the eldest son of Francisco de Paula,
who was the young brother of King Fernando VII and Carlos "V." The
queen and her husband disliked each other. When Isabella gave birth to
a son in Nov. 1857, there was considerable speculation as to the father
(it was rumored that Francisco could not sire an heir). A young army
lieutenant named Antonio Puig Molto and an American dentist's assistant named McKeon were suddenly removed from the palace to avoid
embarrassment to Francisco. Many Spaniards, however, called the infant not Alfonso but "Puigmoltejo."

Carlos "V" had died Mar. 10, 1855. The new Carlist "king" was
his son Carlos "VI," Count of Montemolin. In Apr. 1860 Carlos invaded Spain from France by way of Mallorca, but the invasion was a
fiasco. The "king" and his young brother Fernando were captured,
brought before Isabella II, to whom they renounced their claims, and
then permitted to leave the country.

In Sept. 1868 an army coup forced Isabella II and her lover, Carlos
Marfori (son of a pastry cook), to flee. The Liberals ultimately elected
Amadeo of Savoy as king. But after 2 years of being ignored by the

populace, Amadeo left the country. A republic was proclaimed Feb. 1873.

Meanwhile the liberal views of Carlist "King Juan," brother of Carlos "VI" had alienated the Carlists. The "king" abdicated in Oct. 1868, and his son, Carlos, was proclaimed Carlos "VII." With the establishment of the Spanish Republic, the Carlists revolted. Once again the base of Carlist strength was in the Basque and Catalan provinces.

Unable to defend the republic, the Liberals invited the English-educated son of Isabella II to return to Spain as Alfonso XII. Carlos "VII" established his capital in Barcelona and by the winter of 1873 was within striking distance of Madrid. But after 2 years of fighting, the Carlists were defeated. Carlos fled to Paris in Mar. 1876. With the death of Carlos "VII" June 17, 1909, his claim passed to his son Jaime, who, since 1896, had distinguished himself as an officer in the Russian army. On becoming "king," he announced that he had no intention of starting a new civil war to establish his rights. "King Jaime II," who died in Paris in Oct. 1931, kept his word, and Carlism became a political rather than a revolutionary force in Spain.

Alfonso XII reestablished law and order by working with the various parties in the Cortes. To prevent further turmoil, the king and the politicians agreed that every 2 years there would be a shift in government. To insure this, the leading parties agreed that all elections would be rigged.

Alfonso XII died in 1885, leaving 2 daughters and a pregnant wife, Maria Cristina of Austria. In theory, the heir was the 5-year-old Princess Mercedes, but if the queen gave birth to a son, he would be king. 6 months after Alfonso's death the queen did bear a son—Alfonso XIII. Some politicians wanted to proclaim ex-Queen Isabella II as regent (Isabella died in 1904), but the Cortes decided to entrust the regency to Maria Cristina. The Cortes paid little attention to the regent and ruled; every 2 years there was a rigged election and a new party took power.

A Spanish-French secret treaty Oct. 3, 1904 guaranteed Spain an unspecified zone of influence in Morocco. France forced the sultan of Morocco Mar. 30, 1912 to sign the Treaty of Fez, which established a French protectorate over Morocco. The first article of the treaty required France to reach an understanding with Spain over the latter's zone of influence. The kingdom of Morocco was divided into 3 spheres of influence: The French Protectorate of Morocco (153,870 square miles), the Spanish Protectorate (30,000 square miles) and the international zone of Tangier. The Spanish zone was divided into 2 sections:

The southern portion, variously known as Cape Juby, Tarfaya or Trans Wadi-Draa, was a 12,700-square-mile wasteland with a population of less than 10,000. The Spanish did not occupy the territory until 1915. The 17,398-square-mile northern zone, called Spanish Morocco, was fertile and had a population of about a million.

During World War I German agents stirred up a rebellion in Morocco. The French Resident, Gen. Louis Lyautey, having the full support of Thami el-Glaoui (born 1878), pasha of Marrakesh, who commanded a private army of 100,000 Berber warriors, easily defeated the German-inspired nationalist rebels, who fled north into Spanish Morocco. In the Spanish zone, meanwhile, Abd el-Krim (born 1882) of the Khatibi family organized 50,000 Rifs to fight the Spanish. The Spanish, who usually charged in formation against Rif tribesmen hidden behind rocks and armed with German machine guns, were driven from the countryside. By 1921 the Spanish held only a few coastal towns and the interior capital of Tetuan. In July 1921 a Spanish army under Gen. Manuel Fernández Silvester attempted to open an interior highway but was wiped out at An-Nwal (Annul) by Abd el-Krim's forces. This disaster had serious repercussions on the Spanish government.

Alfonso XIII had objected to corrupt Cortes elections because they excluded him from any say in appointing the cabinet, but all his attempts to make a deal with the political bosses were rejected. The king then turned to the army, whose officers felt that the politicians were not giving them enough money to fight the Rifs. In theory the army was under the control of the war minister, who frequently was a civilian; in practice the army obeyed only the general staff. Alfonso began to deal with members of the general staff without informing the war minister. It was the king who had authorized Gen. Fernández Silvester's campaign even though the cabinet had ordered only defensive action. When reports of the disaster reached Spain, there were riots, and the Cortes demanded an inquiry into the king's activities. For 2 years the country was in turmoil. A Cortes report blaming the king for the defeat was suppressed in 1922.

Various groups began organizing a coup by mid-1923. The government learned that Gen. Miguel Primo de Rivera, military governor of Barcelona, planned a coup. War Min. Niceto Alcala Zamora prepared an order relieving the general of his command, but Alfonso refused to sign the order. Alcala Zamora resigned. Foreign Min. Santiago Albo learned by Sept. 12 that the revolt was to take place within 24 hours and that the revolutionists planned to arrest him. He resigned and fled the country. Primo de Rivera, leading the garrison at Barcelona, proclaimed a revolution. The garrison at Zaragoza announced its support.

The king, meanwhile, was motoring in northern Spain and could not be reached. When the king returned to Madrid Sept. 14, he refused to permit the cabinet to call on the garrisons at Valencia and Madrid to supress the revolt. The Catalans, however, who had been preparing their own coup, used Primo de Rivera coup's as an excuse to revolt in Barcelona. By Sept. 20 Primo de Rivera was in command of Barcelona, had received pledges of loyalty from the various garrison commanders throughout Spain and had abolished the constitution. Primo de Rivera ruled Spain as a military dictator from Sept. 20, 1923 to Dec. 3, 1925.

Beside the unresolved Moroccan rebellion, Primo de Rivera faced a severe economic depression. During World War I both the Allies and Central Powers had needed Spanish coal, iron and textiles. These industries, therefore, had been expanded. With the growth of industry came a rapid expansion of labor organizations: The Socialist UGT (Unión General de Trabajadores), the Anarchist CNT (Confederación Nacional del Trabajo) and the Catholic Consejo Nacional de las Corporaciones Católicas Obreras. These 3 organizations were frequently more opposed to each other than to either industry or the government. With the end of the war, the demand for Spanish goods declined, and many workers were thrown out of work. Starting in 1920 the UGT and CNT organized strikes and demonstrations in Catalunya and the Basque provinces. These actions frequently had the support of Catalan and Basque nationalists. When Primo de Rivera took power, he reached an understanding with UGT leader Francisco Largo Caballero to end UGT support of strikes in return for certain benefits.

Angered by the understanding with UGT and by the failure to resolve the Moroccan rebellion a group of conservative officers led by Gen. Valeriano Weyler y Nicolau, 86, organized a coup. Primo de Rivera discovered the plot in mid-1925 and exiled the leaders. To still further criticism from the military, the dictator (1) signed a military alliance in which France July 26, 1925 promised cooperation against the Rifs, and (2) ended his personal dictatorship Dec. 3 by appointing a cabinet of military men with himself as premier.

A Franco-Spanish army attacked Abd el-Krim in the Rif May 7, 1926. Abd el-Krim surrendered to France May 26 and was exiled to Réunion in the Indian Ocean.

The Moroccan victory solved no internal problems, and the army was called on to put down an attempted coup in Barcelona Nov. 2, 1926. In the face of growing demands for the restoration of the Cortes, Primo de Rivera summoned a consultative assembly to write a new constitution. The assembly met May 31, 1927, but most of the country's politicians refused to attend.

Conservative Party leader José Sánchez Guerra, supported by 18 artillery garrisons, staged a coup in Jan. 1929 and was defeated. The garrison at Ciudad Real revolted Jan. 29 and also was defeated. Riots broke out at Madrid University in Mar. 1929, were supressed, and the university was closed Mar. 17. In the face of growing unrest Alfonso XIII suggested that Primo de Rivera resign. The dictator initially refused but failed in an effort to win the General Staff's support. Primo de Rivera, very ill, then resigned Jan. 28, 1930 and died Mar. 16.

Alfonso asked Gen. Damaso Berenguer Jan. 30, 1930 to form a new government, but the king refused to call the Cortes. The military garrison at Jaca revolted Dec. 12 and demanded the establishment of a republic. This rebellion was suppressed with difficulty. Alfonso then announced Feb. 8, 1931 that the constitution would be restored, that Cortes election would be held in March and that Gen. Berenguer had resigned. The king asked various conservative politicians to form a government, but they refused until all the liberal and republican politicians in prison were released. Alfonso agreed provided that the Cortes election be delayed until after municipal elections, and the various politicians accepted this provision. The municipal elections were held Apr. 12. With the exception of Cádiz, every Spanish provincial capital voted republican majorities. Alfonso left the country Apr. 14 without abdicating, and Niceto Alcala Zamora was proclaimed president of the Spanish Republic.

The Republic faced revolts from both Right and Left for 5 years: Gen. José Sanjurjo seized Sevilla Aug. 10, 1932; an Anarchist uprising in Barcelona Jan. 8, 1933; a Syndicalist uprising in Barcelona Dec. 9-20, 1933; a general strike in Barcelona in Apr. 1934; a general strike throughout Spain Oct. 5, 1934; a Catalan nationalist uprising in Barcelona and Socialist UGT (Unión General de Trabajadores) demonstrations in the Asturias Oct. 6, 1934. The country was also plagued by almost daily murders of political leaders. But during most of this time the bulk of the army remained loyal to the Republic.

The election of Feb. 16, 1936 caused many army officers to reconsider their position. The Left Popular Front polled 4.8 million votes out of a total of 9.28 million cast and seated 277 deputies out a total of 441 elected. Manuel Azaña, known for anti-clerical and anti-military views, was appointed premier Feb. 19, 1936. Among his first acts were the granting of political autonomy to Catalunya and the confiscation of Church and aristocrats' property. When Pres. Alcala Zamora attempted to frustrate some of these plans, the Cortes Apr. 10 removed him from office. Azaña was elected president May 10. Communists and Socialists then began to take command of important army posts and refused to use troops to stop rioters from burning churches.

A revolt was started July 17, 1936 by army officers stationed in Morocco. It spread the next day to mainland Spain. By Mar. 31, 1939 the revolutionists ruled Spain. Through a series of accidental deaths, Gen. Francisco Franco had become leader of the revolutionists and head of the new government.

Franco & the Civil War

Francisco Paulino Hermengildo Teodulo Franco y Bahamonde (or Baamonde) Salgado Prado was born at a little past midnight Dec. 4, 1892 in the port city of El Ferrol (now called El Ferrol del Caudillo) to Nicolás Franco y Salgado Araujo, a paymaster in the Spanish navy, and his wife, Maria del Pilar Teresa Bahamonde y Pardo de Andtade. Francisco was the 2d of 5 children: Nicolás was older, and Pilar, Ramón and Paz were younger.

Both the Franco and Bahamonde families had a long tradition of serving in the navy, and Francisco's parents wanted Francisco to follow that tradition. When the time came to enroll in the Naval Academy, the government, faced with a financial crisis, canceled all entrances. Francisco, therefore, went to the Military Academy at Toledo Aug. 29, 1907. Graduating July 13, 1910, Franco joined the regular army, was sent to Morocco Feb. 24, 1912 and saw his first action May 14. He was wounded June 29, 1916, returned to Spain to recuperate and then was sent to Oviedo for garrison duty. There he met Carmen Polo y Martínez Valdes. Because of her father's objections to the young man, the 2 were not married until Oct. 16, 1923.

In the meantime Franco had distinguished himself in Morocco. By 1922 he was the youngest lieutenant colonel in the Spanish army, in 1925 the youngest colonel, in 1926 the youngest general. Franco returned to Spain in 1926 and began a private study of communism and Marxism.

During the period 1926–36 Franco refused to take part in plots and counterplots organized by various civilian and military groups. His younger brother Ramón, who had become an internationally known aviator, became involved in various republican organizations, and Franco's friends participated actively in various monarchical organizations. Gens. Emilio Mola Vidal, José Millan Astray and José Sanjurjo actively plotted against the Republic after 1931. Franco, accordingly to many accounts, knew about the anti-government activities of his friends.

Francisco Franco y Bahamonde

War Min. José María Gil Robles appointed Franco chief of the Central General Staff May 17, 1935. Franco was sent to London Jan. 25, 1936 to represent the Republic at the funeral of King George V, and Premier Manuel Azaña appointed Franco military commander of the Canary Islands Feb. 21.

Historians do not agree as to when Franco decided to cast in his lot with the generals who sought to overthrow the Republic. It is known that on the evening of Feb. 17, 1936, the day after the Left's election victory, Franco rejected a proposal by Gens. Joaquín Fanjul Goñi, Manuel Goded Llopis and Angel Rodríguez del Barrio to attempt a coup. Hugh Thomas asserted in *The Spanish Civil War* that Franco changed his mind sometime in Mar. 1936, but Brian Crozier said in *Franco* that he did not do so before June. Crozier reported that Franco agreed to help overthrow the government only after he had seen forged Communist documents calling for the murder of the General Staff and the establishment of a Communist government in Spain. Franco, then in the Canary Islands, was an active conspiratory by June 23. The revolt began at 5 p.m. July 17, 1936. Within days Spanish Morocco and parts of northwestern Spain had joined the rebels. Franco left the Canary Islands for Casablanca, where, dressed as an Arab, he boarded a plane for Tetuan, capital of Spanish Morocco. He arrived July 19 and took command of all revolutionary forces.

Franco was one of several generals who shared in the leadership. The others included Gens. Emilio Mola Vidal, who planned the revolt, José Sanjurjo, Manuel Goded Llopis, Miguel Cabanellas y Ferrer, Alfredo Kindelán and Gonzálo Queipo de Llano. When the revolt started Sanjurjo was declared head of state and Mola was entrusted with the formation of a cabinet. Sanjurjo was killed July 20 in an airplane crash in Portugal. Goded was captured the same day in an attempt to occupy Barcelona and was shot as a traitor Aug. 13. The revolutionists, who called themselves Nationalists, met in Burgos July 24 and established the Junta of National Defense with Cabanellas as president but with Mola as the effective leader.

Franco, still in Tetuan, was neither consulted nor appointed to the junta. Franco flew to Sevilla July 28, conferred with Queipo de Llano and he returned to Tetuan that evening. Franco Aug. 6 again flew to Sevilla, where he remained and established his headquarters. Mola flew to Sevilla and conferred with Franco Aug. 13. It was during this conference, authorities suggest, that Franco joined the junta. Franco and Mola went to Burgos Aug. 16 to plan military operations against Republican-held Madrid.

When the revolt started the Falange and Carlist groups announced their complete support for the Nationalist cause.

The Falange had been founded Oct. 29, 1933 by José Antonio Primo de Rivera y Saenz de Heredia, son of the former dictator Gen. Primo de Rivera. Its basic philosophy, announced by José Antonio (as he was called to distinguish him from his father), included: (1) a united Spain (no autonomy for Basques or Catalans); (2) no political parties; (3) an end to capitalism and labor unions and the establishment of a syndical economic organization following the Italian model. In Feb. 1934 the Falange united with the radical anti-clerical and anti-monarchist Juntas de Ofensiva Nacional-Sindicalista (JONS), led by Ramiro Ledesma Ramos. The new organization, called Falange Española de las Juntas de Ofensiva Nacional-Sindicalista, adopted as its symbols the yoked arrows and the red and black flag of JONS, and it adopted JONS' slogans.

The new organization attracted a diverse following. Intellectuals like Dionisio Ridruejo were attracted to the romanticism of José Antonio's nationalistic and elitist concepts, while former Communists and Anarchists were attracted to Ledesma's call for violence. During 1934 the student arm of the new organization, Sindicato Español Universitario (SEU), established by JONS in Mar. 1933, engaged in bloody battles with the Socialist student group Federación Universitaria Española (FUE). Several members of both organizations were killed in the battles; others were ambushed and murdered.

José Antonio did not approve of violence at this time, and he forced the expulsion of Ledesma Jan. 16, 1935. Most of the original JONS membership, however, remained, and the organization kept its name although most people called it the Falange. As a political force the Falange counted for little. It had fewer than 10,000 members, and in the Feb. 16, 1936 elections it polled fewer than 40,000 votes out of 9.28 million cast. Not one member of the Falange was elected to the Cortes. The new government, however, considered the Falange a subversive force and José Antonio was arrested in Madrid Mar. 14.

Gen. Emilio Mola, seeking political allies for his planned revolt, had approached the Falange. According to observers José Antonio's view on violence had been changed by the murder of at least 70 Falangists. José Antonio opened negotiations with Mola May 29, 1936 through a secret agent. In secret messages to his followers José Antonio informed them of this but indicated his distrust of the generals and other Rightists. The government decided to send José Antonio to a prison in Alicante lest he attempt to break out of the Madrid jail, so he was moved to the provincial jail June 5. Mola and José Antonio had also opened negotiations with the Carlists. In secret letters from Alicante, José Antonio told his followers that he did not like Carlism but that the Carlists were among the few honest politicians in Spain.

José Antonio sent word to his followers June 24 to prepare for an insurrection. He ordered the Falange June 29 to cooperate with the military and the Carlists in an insurrection but to maintain its separate identity.

Several Falange groups started revolts in Madrid and Valencia July 11 and 12, but when Gen. Mola refused to give the signal for the army revolt, the Falangists suspended the struggle and went underground. José Antonio sent word to Mola July 14 that unless the army revolted within 72 hours, he would proceed alone. Mola replied July 16 with the exact hour of the army revolt.

When the revolt started, José Antonio was in Alicante jail. An attempt to free him failed. He was tried for treason Nov. 13, was found guilty, and was shot Nov. 20, 1936.

The Falange militia led by José Antonio Girón and Luis González Vicen tried vainly to maintain its independence. Most of the militia was untrained and the Nationalist officers, who had expressed opposition to Falangist ideas, refused to train them. The militia was abolished in Dec. 1936, and its members joined the regular army.

The Carlists had joined the revolt in the outspoken hope of restoring the Carlist branch of the royal family. When the revolt started, "King Alfonso Carlos," 88, announced his support. (Alfonso Carlos, brother of Carlos "VII," had been proclaimed "king" by the Carlists Oct. 1931, following the death of "King Jaime II.") The Carlists in Navarra joined the Nationalists and prepared to have Alfonso Carlos crowned, but the "king" was killed by a car in Vienna Sept. 28, 1936. His death ended the Carlist branch of the royal family and temporarily deprived the Carlists of a leader.

The Junta of National Defense Oct. 1, 1936 appointed Franco "generalissimo of the national land, sea and air forces," and "head of the government of the Spanish state."

How this coup came about is not clear. The 2 leading movers of the coup, according to historians, were Nicolás Franco, Franco's older brother, and Gen. Alfredo Kindelán. They suggested to Franco that he assume supreme command of the Nationalist forces. Franco, according to both Kindelán and Nicolás Franco (who told the story to various historians), refused. Kindelán, with the support of Nicolás (who was not present), met Sept. 12 with the junta in Salamanca. Supported by Gens. Emilio Mola and Luis Orgaz y Yoldi, Kindelán called for the commissioning of a generalissimo to direct the war. Junta Pres. Miguel Cabanellas y Ferrer, 75, objected. Mola threatened to quit the junta if "within 8 days a generalissimo" were not named, and the Junta then agreed to appoint a generalissimo.

After the meeting, Nicolas Franco ordered that 100 Falangists and

100 Carlists appear at Salamanca Sept. 29 to greet Franco with shouts of "Long live the generalissimo and caudillo" when Franco arrived at the next meeting of the junta. The 200 supporters arrived but Franco did not. (Francisco Franco Salgado y Araujo, who was Franco's secretary and cousin, later showed Brian Crozier documents to prove that Franco was not in Salamanca Sept. 29. Several participants in the events, including Kindelán in his *Mis Cuadernos de Guerra*, have ascribed different dates to these events with the result that some historians have said Franco was present at the meeting and was hailed by the 200 supporters.) At the junta meeting, Kindelán proposed that Franco be named generalissimo and chief of state. Mola and Cabanellas had no objections to Franco's appointment as generalissimo but refused to accept him as chief of state. Kindelán proposed then that the wording be "head of the government of the Spanish state and will assume all the powers of the new state." The opposition accepted the change. Back in Burgos Sept. 30, Cabanellas signed the decree, and it was proclaimed Oct. 1.

Historians agree that while the Oct. 1 decree established a unified Nationalist military command under Franco's control, it did not end political opposition to Franco's rule. Opposition came from the Carlists, the Falange and some members of the military who supported Gen. Mola.

The Carlist opposition, according to observers, created a special problem for Franco. Franco later told Gen. Wilhelm von Faupel, Hitler's *chargé d'affairs* in Nationalist Spain, that he had needed the 40,000 Carlist troops, called *Requetes*, and, therefore, had not been free to alienate them by executing the Carlist leadership. Manuel Fal Conde, chief Carlist leader, had been in Vienna attending Alfonso Carlos' funeral when Franco's coup took place. On returning home, he complained to the Carlist organization and privately objected to Franco's assumption of power. In order to maintain the independence of the *Requetes*, Fal Conde Dec. 8, 1936 announced the establishment of a Carlist-controlled Royal Military Academy. Franco summoned Carlist leader Tomás Domínguez Arévalo, Conde de Rodenzo, to Burgos and informed him that he objected to the formation of the academy. Franco then told Gen. Fidel Dávila to go to Carlist headquarters and inform the Carlists that he, Franco, considered the academy to be proof that the Carlists planned a coup against the National government. Franco ordered Fal Conde to leave Spain within 48 hours. The Carlists then agreed to drop plans for the academy, and Fal Conde, left for Lisbon Dec. 20.

The Carlists, looking for a new claimant to the throne, had turned to the descendants of Carlos' young brother, Francisco de Paula. But Francisco's eldest son, Francisco de Asis, had married Isabella II, and his heir was Alfonso XIII. The Carlists claimed, however, that Francisco de Asis could not consumate the marriage and that Isabella's children, therefore, were not Francisco's. Besides, claimed the Carlists, Francisco de Paula was not the son of Carlos IV but the son of the then Spanish Premier Manuel Godoy, with whom Queen Maria Louisa, wife of King Carlos IV, was alleged to have had an affair. (Many historians refute this claim since Godoy at one point planned to have his daughter marry Francisco de Paula.) The next in line were the Neapolitan branches of the Bourbon family, but Prince Alfonso, claimant to the throne of the defunct kingdom of 2 Sicilies, had died in 1934 and left only daughters, the eldest of whom, Mercedes, had married Don Juan, the heir of Alfonso XIII. The younger Neapolitan branch was excluded on the ground that its male members were either too liberal or had tainted blood because a member had married a Jewess. The next in line were the heirs of Philip of Parma, the youngest son of King Philip V of Spain (the first Spanish Bourbon). Philip V had granted his son the Duchy of Parma in 1748. The claimant to the defunct Duchy of Parma was Francis-Xavier, whom the Carlists chose as the new regent of Spain.

According to material in Carlist archives in Sevilla, Francis-Xavier had been active in gathering financial support for the *Requetes* before the Civil War. It was, in part, through his efforts that the *Requetes* were so well armed when the revolt began. When, in the spring of 1936, Gen. Mola had established contacts with Carlist leaders, the Carlists had chosen Fal Conde and Francis-Xavier as their spokesmen with the military rebels. After the death of Alfonso Carlos, Francis-Xavier was proclaimed regent of Spain until the new Carlist king could be found. Franco announced in July 1937 that the new "monarchy would be different in constitution and person" from the old monarchy. In Dec. 1937 Francis-Xavier was making a tour of *Requetes* troops at the front when he received word from Franco to leave the country. According to the archives material, Francis-Xavier went to Burgos, where he met Franco. In the interview the regent told Franco that he would continue to work for the future of Spain but a Spain that did not include Franco. Francis-Xavier then went to Paris.

Franco, meanwhile, had organized another coup, and Franco Apr. 19, 1937 ended the independence of both the Carlist and Falange political organizations.

The Falange National Council met in Valladolid in Sept. 1936 to create a directing body to lead the Falange should José Antonio fail to escape from jail. The council established the Junta de Mando with Manuel Hedilla Larrey as acting *jefe*. (Until the execution of José Antonio Nov. 20, the council refused to consider any other national leader.) During the first 3 months of the Civil War, the Falange had greatly expanded in membership. According to Stanley Payne in *Falange*, many former Communists and Anarchists as well as Christian Democrats had joined. (1,000 Málaga citizens joined the Falange Feb. 11, 1937, the day after Málaga fell to the Nationalist forces. Total Falange membership had been only 10,000 in Feb. 1936.)

Franco's brother-in-law, Ramón Serrano Suñer, suggested to Franco in Mar. 1937 that he take control of the Falange. Serrano Suñer, a close friend of José Antonio, had not joined the Falange but had many contacts within both the Falange and the Christian Democratic Party. Serrano Suñer's suggestion was discussed by Franco Apr. 11 with Gen. Wilhelm von Faupel, Hitler's *chargé d'affairs* in Nationalist Spain. Von Faupel agreed that something had to be done to give Franco a political base on which to rule Nationalist Spain.

Hedilla, meanwhile, had attempted to reach an understanding with exiled Carlist leader Fal Conde. Negotiations collapsed when the Falange refused to accept Francis-Xavier as king and the Carlists refused to accept a regency dominated by Falangists to rule during the minority of Francis-Xavier's son Hugo Carlos.

The Falange National Council met in Salamanca Apr. 18 in order to elect a new national *jefe*. Hedilla was elected *jefe nacional*, but, according to Stanley Payne (in *Falange*), he received only 10 of the 22 votes cast; 8 votes were blank and the other 4 were for 4 other Falangists. That night Hedilla visited Franco to discuss the governance of Spain, but Franco refused to discuss political matters.

Franco, Apr. 19, delivered a radio message announcing the uniting of the Falange and the Carlist organizations by the creation of a new party, *Falange Española Tradicionalista y de las Juntas de Ofensiva Nacional-Sindicalista* (FET), of which he would be the *jefe*. The announcement took both the Falange and the Carlists by surprise. To prevent a Falange coup, Hedilla was arrested Apr. 25, tried for treason and sentenced to death. At the last minute Franco, at the request of von Faupel and Serrano Suñer, commuted the sentence to life imprisonment. Other Falange leaders who did not pledge loyalty to Franco were arrested. Among them were: Ricardo Nieto, *jefe* of Zamora province, Sandro Dávila, Agustín Aznar, commander of the Falange militia, and Rafael Garceran Sánchez. Falange propaganda chief Vicente Cadenas fled to Italy.

Carlist leaders were not informed officially of the dissolution of their organization until Apr. 30.

Franco made FET the only legal party in Nationalist Spain and entrusted it with the governance of the civil sector. While Franco was titular leader of FET, a functioning leader to oversee the daily operations was named. The nominee was Raimundo Fernández Cuesta, an old friend of José Antionio. Fernández Cuesta, however, was in a Republican jail. A deal was made with the Republicans, and Fernández Cuesta arrived in Nationalist territory Oct. 1937. Socialist Party leader Indalecio Prieto y Tuero, who had had many conversations with José Antonio and who had examined José Antonio's papers found in Alicante, was convinced, according to Stanley Payne (in *Falange*), that the Falange would never stay loyal to Franco. Prieto persuaded the Republican government to release Fernández Cuesta on the chance that he would organize the old Falange members in a coup against Franco.

FET, called Falange by everyone, began to function as the civil administration. Old Falangists like Dionisio Ridruejo and José Antonio Girón then began to call themselves Joseantonioistas to distinguish themselves from the new Falangists, who comprised the overwhelming majority.

A final threat to Franco's rule ended June 3, 1937 when Gen. Emilio Mola died in a plane crash. According to von Faupel, Franco felt "relieved by the death of Mola."

Having established control over the Nationalist forces, Franco's overriding task was to win the Civil War. The Spanish Civil War, in one way or another, affected all the world powers. It has been estimated that Germany supplied Franco with $200 million in aid; Italy gave Franco $400 million; the USSR and various Communist organizations gave the Republic $410 million. Beside the money, Germany supplied 16,000 troops and considerable war material; Italy supplied 50,000 troops, 763 planes and 91 ships and submarines; the USSR supplied 2,000 troops, 240 planes and 740 tanks. Some 40,000 foreigners fought on the side of the Republic. Many of these foreigners, like Clement Attlee, André Malraux, Klement Gottwald, Palmiro Togliatti, Tito (Josip Broz) and Walter Ulbricht, became government leaders after World War II.

The Republican government, which still held Madrid, capitulated Mar. 28, 1939. The most devastating conflict in Spanish history ended with Franco as Spain's unquestioned leader.

There are no accurate figures on the cost of the war to Spain. The Finance Ministry reported Aug. 5, 1940 that the Nationalists had spent $2¼ billion to fight the war; Republican figures are unavailable. It was estimated that it would require about $430 million to repair the war damage. The loss of life was high. 320,000 people died in battle and another 300,000 in air attacks and because of lack of medical

supplies; a million people were wounded. Tens of thousands left Spain
rather than live under the Franco government. Many of the exiles were
Spain's leading intellectuals and professionals. Their departure left the
country with a shortage of doctors, teachers and technicians.

World War II

The start of World War II Sept. 1, 1939 created what many
authorities agree was a serious problem for Spain: how to remain a
non-belligerent without forcing either the Axis (Germany, Italy and
Japan) or the Allies (Britain, France and later the U.S.) to invade
Spain for strategic reasons.

The Anti-Comintern Pact, signed by Spain Feb. 20, 1939, had
linked Spain with Germany, Italy and Japan. The pact was not made
public until Apr. 7, i.e., until after the final surrender of the Republican
forces. Brian Crozier reported in *Franco* that Franco, against the advice
of Foreign Min. Count Francisco Gómez Jordana Sousa, 63, had also
signed a friendship treaty with Germany Mar. 31. Authorities agree that
Franco had no intention of committing Spain to war by these treaties.
Franco's brother-in-law, Interior Min. Ramón Serrano Suñer, had informed Italian Gen. Gastone Gambara in March and Italian Foreign Min.
Count Galiazzo Ciano in July that Spain needed 5 years of peace before
it could fulfill the military obligations of the treaty. Ciano visited
Franco at San Sebastián July 19 and was told that Spain could not
engage in war.

The signing of the Nazi-Soviet pact Aug. 20-1 "shocked, outraged
and bewildered the Spanish," Brian Crozier reported in *Franco*.
Hitler's attack on Catholic Poland was, according to Crozier, "incom-
prehensible" to Franco. Franco tried Sept. 3 to act as mediator to end
the conflict. When he failed, Franco ordered Spain to be neutral in
the conflict. At this point Hitler had no intention, according to
observers, of seeking Spanish aid. In a letter to Mussolini Mar. 8, 1940,
the German dictator said he understood Franco's need to remain
neutral.

Spain needed to rebuild and therefore needed favorable trade
treaties. Such treaties were signed with Portugal and Germany in
Dec. 1939, with France in Jan. 1940 and with Britain in Mar. 1940.
The British advanced $19.2 million to Spain under their treaty.

The German blitzkrieg against Denmark and Norway in Apr. 1940
and against Belgium, the Netherlands, Luxembourg and France in
May–June 1940, the Italian declaration of war against the Allies
June 10, 1940 and the capitulation of France June 22 altered the

nature of the war. Franco's first act in this new situation, according to ex-Republican diplomat Salvador de Madariaga in *Spain*, was to order Col. Antonio Yuste Segura June 14 to seize control of the international city of Tangier and to place it under Spanish control. The British protested Dec. 15 after the Spanish had permitted 2 Italian submarines to use Tangier as refuge Nov. 3–Dec. 13, but Spain rejected the protest.

Franco, meanwhile, was moving from strict neutrality to non-belligerency, *i.e.*, support of the Axis without entering the war. Franco July 18, 1940 had demanded the retrocession of Gibraltar and had announced that 2 million Spaniards were ready to fight to reclaim their national territory.

Hitler and Franco met Oct. 23, 1940 in Hendaye, France. Franco had prepared for this meeting by appointing his openly pro-Axis brother-in-law Ramón Serrano Suñer Oct. 17 as foreign minister. According to reports, Franco was calm throughout the meeting, but Hitler was in a rage. Hitler requested that Spain permit German troops to cross Spain to attack Gibraltar. Franco responded that he had no objections to getting into the war provided that Germany first supplied Spain with food and war material. As for the attack on Gibraltar, that would be done by Spanish troops, Franco said. He insisted that Gibraltar, Morocco and parts of Algeria go to Spain. Hitler, however, refused to promise Franco the French African territories, and the meeting ended.

Authorities agree that Spain could not wage war effectively in 1940. There were 507,903 unemployed; 200,000 people were in prison. In a radio message Dec. 31, 1939 Franco had said that Spain needed immediately 500,000 tons of wheat, 120,000 tons of vegtables and rice and 180,000 tons of sugar. By Apr. 1940, Serrano Suñer told a reporter that Spain needed 2 million tons of wheat. The Sept. 1940 harvest was poor, and Spain faced starvation.

Spain needed foreign money to buy food. One way it took to earn this money was to buy oil and sell it to the oil-starved Axis. The French government protested to the U.S. June 14, 1940 that 21 U.S. ships were bringing oil to Spain. (In June, Spain bought 446,000 barrels of oil, a total equal to about ¼ of all its 1939 oil purchases.) When the Allies showed the U.S. State Department figures to prove that Spain could not possibly use so much oil, the U.S. announced that Spanish oil purchases would be curtailed. Spain threatened to confiscate the U.S.-owned Spanish Telephone Co., but even though the U.S. did not back down, the Spaniards did not carry out their threat.

Spain asked the U.S. Sept. 7, 1940 for a $100 million loan to buy U.S. goods. U.S. Amb.-to-Spain Alexander C. Weddell, according to Herbert Feis in *The Spanish Story*, said the U.S. should agree just to keep Spain neutral. The U.S. replied Sept. 19 that it was considering the Spanish request but that U.S. acceptance depended on Spain remaining at peace. Weddell informed Franco Oct. 4 that the U.S. might send a Red Cross ship to Spain. Nothing came of this plan because of the appointment of Serrano Suñer as foreign minister and the Hitler-Franco meeting.

By Nov. 1940 Hitler wanted Spain in the war. Serrano Suñer met with Hitler Nov. 18 in Berchstesgaden, Hitler's Bavarian mountain retreat. At first Serrano Suñer said that Spain could not get into the war until the Spanish people were fed and Hitler agreed to Spanish territorial demands. But when Hitler stated "I have decided to attack Gibraltar," Serrano Suñer retreated and, it was reported, left Hitler with the impression that Spain would enter the war. According to German documents, the Germans were convinced that Spain would soon join them in the war even though no exact date was given. German Amb.-to-Spain Eberhardt von Stohrer telegraphed Hitler Nov. 28 that Franco had begun preparations to enter the war.

The U.S. State Department, however, was convinced, according to many authorities, that the Spanish could be kept neutral by supplying them with food. The U.S. authorized the first shipment of Red Cross wheat to Spain Jan. 7, 1941. Feis asserted in *The Spanish Story* that Serrano Suñer tried to "frighten us [the U.S.] into doing something more." But the State Department, according to Feis, was not frightened.

Meanwhile, the war had shifted to the Mediterranean area with the German occupation of Yugoslavia and Greece in Apr. 1941. The Germans increased their pressure on Spain to enter the war, while at the same time the U.S. decreased its sales of oil to Spain. Franco told the Germans that Spain could not fight; at the same time he instructed Spanish Amb.-to-Washington Juan Cardenas to get more oil.

By early 1941, according to Brian Crozier in *Franco*, Hitler began thinking of invading Spain. Because of the Balkan campaign and the invasion of the USSR June 22, 1941, Hitler abandoned the Spanish plan for the time. Hitler's invasion of the USSR was popular with the Spanish government. Franco July 17 delivered a major speech praising Hitler and Germany and condemning the Bolsheviks and their allies. Spain agreed Aug. 25 to allow Spanish workers to go to Germany. (40,000 Spaniards ultimately worked in Germany.) Franco also permitted the Spanish Blue Division (18,000 troops under the command of Gen. Agustín Muñoz Grandes) to fight on the Russian front.

Meanwhile the U.S. adopted a "hard line" toward Spain. Spanish Amb.-to-Washington Juan Cardenas was informed Nov. 29 that the U.S. would continue to sell oil to Spain only if the Spanish permitted U.S. inspectors to make sure that none of the oil was transshipped to the Axis and if Spain would sell its raw materials to the U.S. According to Feis (in *The Spanish Story*), the Spaniards were no longer transshipping the oil to the Axis but needed it themselves. The attack on Pearl Harbor Dec. 7, 1941, according to observers, confused the Spanish government and it did not respond to the State Department message.

Observers assert that by Jan. 1942, Spain was caught in a difficult position. Japanese Pacific victories convinced Serrano Suñer that the Axis would eventually win the war, but in the meantime Spain needed oil. In Feb. 1942 Spain had to close the oil refinery at Tenerife for lack of crude oil. The Spanish asked Germany for oil and showed the Germans the U.S. demand of Nov. 29. But Germany itself was short of oil and could not meet Spanish needs. The Germans said that while they objected to the presence of U.S. agents in Spain, they understood the Spanish position. The Germans, however, objected to the 2d U.S. demand—that Spain sell its raw material to the U.S.—because Germany needed everything Spain had to sell. Spain agreed in Mar. 1942 to permit U.S. agents to inspect all shipments of oil but said that Spain's raw material would be sold to the highest bidder. (One of Spain's most important exports was wolfram, an item of crucial importance in the manufacture of steel. The price per ton had jumped from $1,300 in Jan. 1941 to $20,000 in Nov. 1941. Germany, however, was still buying wolfram at a little above 1939's low price in partial repayment of money Spain owed Germany from 1936-9.)

Hitler ordered the German General Staff May 29, 1942 to prepare plans to invade Spain; orders were issued to the General Staff July 15 to prepare plans to defend Spain from a possible Anglo-U.S. invasion.

The Allies invaded French North Africa Nov. 8 and both the Allies and the Axis awaited Franco's reaction. The Allies feared that Germany might invade Spain or that Spain might join the Axis and use its troops in Morocco to attack the Allied armies racing toward Tunis. Hitler and Adm. Eric Raeder concluded Nov. 19 that the Allies would invade Spain. Raeder warned Hitler Dec. 22 that Spain was vital to Germany's war effort because of its wolfram and zinc. The official German summary of the Hitler-Raeder meeting stated that the 2 conferees agreed that Spain and Portugal had to be invaded if the raw materials were denied Germany.

The U.S. and Great Britain, meanwhile, were willing to buy whatever Spain was willing to sell, and at whatever price the Spanish charged. Between Jan. 1, 1942 and July 1, 1943 the Allies purchased

$75 million worth of Spanish goods to prevent them from reaching the Axis.

By Apr. 1943, with more and more Spanish raw material entering Allied storehouses, the German General Staff called for an invasion of Spain. But Brian Crozier wrote in *Franco* that Hitler refused to sanction the invasion. Hitler ordered the General Staff May 14 to cancel all plans to invade Spain. Adm. Karl Doenitz objected and said that it was essential to invade Spain. Doenitz May 31 again asked Hitler to order the invasion, but again Hitler refused.

Meanwhile both the Allies and the Axis increased exports to Spain in order to secure Spanish raw material. When the Spanish sold Germany 125 tons of wolfram at a bargain price in June 1943, the U.S. protested. The Spanish replied that this was part of a deal for arms that the Allies refused to furnish.

The Spanish government, capitalizing on the international demand for wolfram, placed a $10,000-a-ton tax on its export, and the Allies paid it. The U.S. had set aside $22 million in June 1962 to buy Spanish and Portuguese wolfram. Spanish exports of wolfram increased from 800 tons in 1941 to 4,000 tons in 1943, but the value of the export rose from $700,000 in 1941 to almost $60 million in 1943. The U.S. and Britain bought $116 million worth of Spanish wolfram in 1942-4, paying prices 20 times as high as the price then being charged for Bolivian wolfram.

Italy surrendered and the Allies had invaded France by June 1944, and Spain's ability to command high prices declined. The Allies informed Spain that, unless Spain limited its shipments to Germany, the Allies would embargo all goods to Spain. The Spanish agreed to the Allied demand. Observers reported, however, that while the Allies permitted Spain to sell Germany no more than 200 tons of wolfram, 3 times that amount was smuggled into Germany.

The end of the war in Europe May 7, 1945 ended the need for Spain's raw materials. Spanish unemployment, which had almost disappeared during 1942-4, reached 163, 759 by mid-1945.

The Allied powers, meeting in Potsdam, Germany July 17-Aug. 2, 1945 made final plans for the establishment of the UN and stated that "they would not favor any application for membership by the present Spanish government."

Spain was almost isolated after the war (Spain maintained friendly relations only with neighboring Portugal, Argentine dictator Juan Perón and a few Arab states). There also was talk in Allied circles of a possible Allied invasion of Spain. France called a conference of the Western powers Dec. 14 to discuss such a plan. The U.S. and Great Britain, however, would not agree to such drastic action.

France (where Communists were members of the cabinet) permitted various anti-Franco groups to use French soil as a base to overthrow the Franco government. French frontier guards ignored Spanish infiltrators who crossed the Pyrenees. The Spanish government Feb. 2 and 20, 1946 executed 14 such infiltrators. One of those executed, Cristino García, had been a leading member of the French underground. France closed its frontier with Spain Feb. 28, and in reaction to the executions, the U.S., France and Britain announced Mar. 4 that Spain could not join the family of nations "so long as Gen. Franco continues in control."

In response to the external threats, the Spanish government increased military appropriations to 38% of the total budget, and this was a further blow to the economy. By the end of 1945 conditions in Spain were worse than in 1940. Using 1940 as the base, food prices reached 174.5 by the end of 1945 and 243 by the end of 1947. By the end of 1946 the construction, shipbuilding, metallurgical and chemical industries were below their 1940 levels. Authorities agree that by 1946 most of the economic gains made in 1942–4 had been wiped out by Spain's isolation.

Law & Government

The basis of the Spanish legal system is the Roman Law. To this is added customary law traced to Visigothic and Arabic traditions, compilations by the feudal kings, edicts of Hapsburg and Bourbon kings, legislation of the Cortes and decrees of Franco. Unless a Spanish law is specifically changed or voided, it remains valid.

In assuming power, Franco did not wipe out 1,500 years of legal history. In some cases he reverted to laws declared void by the Republic. In other cases he introduced by fiat socio-political concepts of the Falange (e.g., wage and price controls). In most instances, however, the Spanish legal system was unchanged from the pre-Civil War situation.

In overthrowing the Republic, Franco reverted to the national governmental system operating in Spain under the Bourbon monarchs. Franco had both executive and legislative (but not judicial) power. In framing new legistation, Franco had to consider the established laws and customs and, therefore, was not absolute. According to many authorities, the only major innovation in contemporary Spain is the politico-economic syndical organization. The syndical group represents both management and labor. In theory, this group makes all social and economic decisions with the advice of the government. Because both labor and management are within one group, both strikes and lock-outs are illegal. Beside the social and economic functions, the syndical organization elects representatives to the provincial councils and the national Cortes.

During the period 1939–45, according to historians, Franco ruled Spain by playing the various groups within the government against each other. The 2 dominant political groups were the antagonistic Carlists and Falangists. In an attempt to improve his control of the Falange Española Tradicionalista (FET), Franco Aug. 9, 1939 had appointed his old friend Gen. Agustín Muñoz Grandes as FET secretary general. (Ex-Sec. Gen. Raimundo Fernández Cuesta was sent to Brazil as ambassador.) Muñoz Grandes failed to unite the 2 groups and resigned Mar. 15, 1940. No successor was named until May 19, 1941, when Franco appointed José Luis de Arrese as FET secretary general. Franco also appointed Falangist leader José Antonio Girón as labor minister and Miguel Primo de Rivera, brother of Falange founder José Antonio Primo de Rivera, as agriculture minister. The Joseantonioistas (members of the original Falange party founded by José Antonio), who were anti-monarchist and anti-clerical, refused to cooperate with the Carlists, who were monarchist and clerical. The 2 groups came to blows in Bilbao in Aug. 1942. During a clash a Falangist named Dominguez allegedly threw a bomb at Carlist leader Gen. José Enrique Varela, who was war minister. Varela was unhurt, but dozens of people were injured. Dominguez was arrested, tried and executed. But the Carlists were not satisfied, and 10 Carlist leaders resigned from the FET National Council. According to observers, Franco had to choose between the Carlists and the Falange; Gen. Varela was replaced Sept. 3 as war minister by the Falangist Carlos Asensio Cabanillas, 46.

During 1942–3 there was growing support for the restoration of Bourbon monarchy under Don Juan. In Feb. 1941, a month before his death, Alfonso XIII had proclaimed his son Don Juan as heir to the throne. (Prince Alfonso, the eldest son, had abdicated in 1933 in order to marry a Cuban. He died in 1938 in Miami in an auto accident. Prince Gonzalo, the youngest son, had bled to death as a result of an auto accident in Austria in 1934. The 2d son, Prince Jaime, had renounced the throne because of deafness, but he later retracted his abdication.) The anti-monarchist Falange, noting that there was dissatisfaction with the Carlist pretender, Francis-Xavier, because he was French, and with Don Juan, because he was alleged to be liberal, announced support for the candidacy of Prince Carlos, the son of Princess Blanca, eldest sister of Carlist "King Jaime." This claim was invalid under the Salic Law, but it divided the Carlists and confused the Bourbonists.

The reestablishment of the Cortes was decreed by Franco in July 1942. The Cortes had 438 *procuratores* (deputies), most of whom were appointed by either Franco or the FET National Council. Additional *procuratores* were to be elected by the syndical organization in stages: local syndics elect representatives to provincial syndics, who elect representatives to national syndics, who then elect the *procuratores*. The first stage of this election, however, did not take place until mid-1943. Under the decree that established the Cortes, its only power was to approve legislation given to it by the cabinet.

A municipal reorganization law, in the summer of 1945, established elected municipal councils. Each municipal council was to be divided into 3 equal groups. One group was to be elected by heads of families, the 2d group was to be elected by the syndical organization, and the 3d group was to be elected by the first 2. Although there usually was more than one candidate for each office, all candidates were selected by either the FET or Franco.

Franco July 16, 1945 issued the *Fuero* (law or constitution) of the Spanish People, sometimes called the Spanish Bill of Rights. But, many authorities state, the rights were all conditional. Among these were the right: (1) "to freely express . . . ideas so long as these do not prejudice the fundamental principles of the state," (2) "liberty of correspondence within the national territory," (3) to "assemble and associate freely for lawful purposes and in accordance with the law." Article 34 of the *Fuero* stated that the Cortes would "vote the necessary laws for the exercise of the rights."

Franco revised the cabinet July 20-25, 1945. Observers said this was done to broaden the base of support within Spain and to make Spain more acceptable to the Allies. Among the changes were the removal of Falangist leaders José Luis de Arrese as FET secretary general (the office was left vacant) and Gen. Carlos Asensio Cabanillas as war minister. (Fidel Dávila Arrondo, 67, the new war minister had no political affiliations.) Falangist José Antonio Giron remained as labor minister, while ex-FET Secy. Gen. Raimundo Fernández Cuesta became justice minister. Alberto Martín Artajo, leader of the clandestine Christian Democratic Party, became foreign minister. Martín Artajo was both a supporter of Bourbon pretender Don Juan and an ally of Bishop Angel Herrera y Oria of Málaga, leader of the social reformers among Spanish prelates. Martín Artajo also had close contacts with exiled Christian Democratic Party leader José María Gil Robles and with many of the Christian Democrats in Western Europe.

Franco announced Feb. 20, 1946 that he was a monarchist but did not indicate whether he was a Bourbonist or Carlist. The monarchy would be restored but there would be no monarch, Franco declared

Mar. 31, 1947. He said he opposed the introduction of capitalism into Spain because capitalism was "antiquated and unjust." Franco June 7 published his new constitution (called the Law of Succession), which changed the Spanish state into the "kingdom of Spain." The constitution was submitted to the Spanish people July 6, and it was approved by a vote of 14,145,163 to 722,565; there were 335,592 blank ballots.

Spain thus became a monarchy without a monarch. The "office of chief of state is held by the *caudillo* [leader] of Spain and of the Crusade, generalissimo of the Spanish Armies, Don Francisco Franco y Bahamonde," the constitution said. Franco was named chief of state for life and head of the National Movement, the new name for the Falange organization. The constitution also provided that: (a) Franco would appoint and preside over the cabinet. (b) Franco would appoint the Council of the Realm, a body created to establish the rules for the transition to a monarch (the council was to meet once a year). (c) The cabinet, at the discretion of the chief of state, may submit proposals to the Cortes, but the Cortes may only modify, the proposals—with cabinet approval. The Cortes had no initiative powers, and the chief of state had an absolute veto.

Subsequent legislation defined the Cortes as "neither a consultative body nor a parliament but . . . the highest organ of participation of the Spanish people in the work of the state." Subsequent legistaltion also defined the organization of the Cortes and other government organs. There were 595 *procuratores* (deputies) in the Cortes. 50 *procuratores* were appointed by the chief of state. The others were either appointed or elected by corporate bodies such a provincial and municipal officials, members of professional associations, members of the National Movement, heads of families, etc. The *procuratores* were elected for 3 years and may be reelected. They may also be removed at the pleasure of the chief of state.

On the local level, Spain was divided into 50 provinces. Each province had a governor appointed by the chief of state and a provincial assembly elected by corporate groups. Provinces were divided into municipalities. Each municipality had a mayor appointed by either the chief of state or the provincial governor. Municipal councils were also appointed. Beside their function in the municipal or provincial administration, each local official was an elector in the election for members to the Cortes.

Political Theory of the Franco State

Franco refers to the Spanish Civil War as a "constructive revolution" that created a state neither "Marxist nor capitalist" but, rather, a "state of law." The Civil War, according to Franco, ended all divisions within Spain. Political, economic, linguistic disputes no longer exist, Franco said. "Spain is a unity."

Under the Constitution of 1947 and subsequent legislation, Franco, as chief of state has absolute power. (In practice, observers note, his authority is limited by local customs, traditions and the existing political structure.) The 2d edition (1963) of the official *El Nuevo Estado Español* said: "The *caudillo* has full personal power responsible only before God and History."

In 1964 the Spanish Information Service published a collection of Franco's political thoughts (*Pensamiento politico de Franco*). The work contained not only Franco's beliefs but also a defense of his government. Among assertions Franco stressed:

● Spain is a Catholic country, and "the inspiration of Catholic ideals guides all the activities of the state." "Our laws are impregnated with the same Catholic spirit that animates Spain on its great role in history." "The most important aid that the Catholic Church has given Spaniards in the last few years is that of offering a social doctrine as outlined by the new Pope [John XXIII]. The Movement [the Falange] has taken these ideas as the basis of its programs for the betterment of the people."

● "The principles that have inspired our national revolution are based on the notion of the human individual." "The first of our labors is to elevate man as the carrier of eternal values."

● "It is a grave error . . . to consider our government a dictatorship . . . because the people . . . are subject to laws . . . which are administered by judges who have had long experience in serving the monarchy and republic . . . , and the judiciary is completely independent of the executive, and all Spaniards have an open road to the tribunals to obtain just satisfaction of their rights." "For the unity that we have achieved between man and the Spanish land, for this political organization, different from all others, we have been charged with being a dictatorship, as if Spain could live for 25 years under a full dictatorship and as if the Spaniard were not brave enough not to sustain dictation and arbitrariness."

● Liberalism and liberal democracy were rejected by Franco. "And what does the West have to offer? An aged political system, injustice inherent in the system of liberal capitalism; an inorganic democracy that divides and debilitates and a freedom that is reduced by reality to misery; the rich and opulant side by side with poverty; rich and powerful nations that live off the labors of the unfortunate colonial world." Liberalism is responsible "for the planting of hate and rancor." "The Spanish state is not a liberal state, and it is not a liberal state because it does not permit the liberty to exploit the weak."

● "The new [Spanish] state [created by the Civil War] is a social state" that "seeks to amplify the role of the syndicates, the family and the municipalities." "The new Spanish state will be a true democracy in which all citizens participate in the government through the professional activity and specific functions." "Spain today is a nation with an open constitution in which the guarantees of other normal constitutions are established." "The institution of referendum enables us to consult directly the people and not be taken in by the fiction and falsity of political parties." "Neither liberalism . . . nor socialism can solve the modern world's problems . . . but there exists a 3d solution: the modern state that Spain has developed in which the free initiative is stimulated and the freedom and dignity of the human being is defended." Spain has rejected liberalism, socialism, communism and fascism. Spain is "not a false democracy . . . but an organic democracy." We do not need "those artificial divisions into Left and Right born in the heat of the liberal regime. . . . We live with the ideal of all working for the communal good."

The Opposition

Observers of contemporary Spanish politics report great difficulty is defining the opposition in Spain. The problem, many say, is caused by the fact that the most powerful oppositional forces are not so much opposed to Franco as they are to each other. Authorities assert that during 1940-59 the Socialists, Communists, Anarcho-Syndicalists and Republicans—the so-called Left Opposition—were active but had little effect. Most members of the Left Opposition were reported to be either in jail, in Mexico, in France or behind the Iron Curtain.

The most forceful opposition to the Franco government, according to many observers, comes from groups supporting Franco. Many authorities report that a majority of the members of the Falange, the Church, the army, the pro-monarchist organizations and the upper class in general support the *caudillo*. But these bodies are not monolithic; within each are groups of individuals with specific programs, and these groups, observers say, support Franco only as long as he supports their policies.

The "opposition," then, includes these groups:

The Falange—The National Movement is the only legal political organization in Spain. The National Movement is the name given to the Falange Espñola Tradicionalista y de las Juntas de Ofensiva Nacional-Sindicalista group that Franco created when he forced the old Falange and Carlists to unite. After 1945 most Carlists left active participation in the organization to form clandestine groups; the Carlists, however, maintained membership in the National Movement. The National Movement was dominated by individuals who called themselves Falangists. There were 2 groups of Falangists: Those who joined before 1936 and those who joined afterwards. The first group was called either the Old Guard, the Old Shirts (*camisas viejas*), or Joseantonioists. The 2d group was called Francoists. The Joseantonioist group maintained the anti-monarchist, anti-capitalist and anti-clerical attitudes of the original Falange; the Francoists did not.

José Luis de Arrese, the last Falange secretary general, asserted that Joseantonioists were discriminated against and forced from all areas of power. Arrese wrote in 1947 that "the worst opponent of Falangism had always been the Right." According to Stanley Payne in *Falange*, "by 1947 the old guard Falangists were something of a laughing stock." The only Joseantonioist in power was Labor Min. José Antonio Girón, with his old Falangist distrust of capitalism. As the National Movement became dominated by Francoists, Joseantonioists became opponents of the Franco government.

Among the more out-spoken critics of the Franco regime was Dionisio Ridruejo, former Falange propaganda chief and author of the Falange hymn *Cara al Sol* (*Face to the Sun*). Ridruejo, becoming disillusioned with Franco after the Civil War, joined the Spanish Blue Division on the Russian front. Returning from Russia in 1942, he began to openly criticize the rightist aspects of the Franco regime. Franco, recognizing his contributions to the Nationalist victory, isolated him by exiling him to remote hamlets in the mountains of Andalucía and then Catalunya. For 6 years Ridruejo wrote anti-Franco poetry. Ridruejo told Sergio Vilar, who reported the conversation in *Protagonistas de la España Democratica*, that during his banishment from Madrid he was able to make "clandestine trips to Madrid." In 1948 Franco permitted Ridruejo to leave Spain for Rome.

The split between the Joseantonioists and the government widened during the debate on the 1950 budget. Over Joseantonioist objections, the Cortes Dec. 21, 1949 approved a budget of 18 billion pesetas (about $720 million), of which 31.8% was for defense. The Joseantonioists claimed that too much was being spent for defense and not enough for social services. The Falangist newspaper *Si*, claiming that funds could and should be used to solve the critical housing shortage, challenged a government report released Apr. 13, 1950 that the country lacked only 500,000 homes; *Si* insisted Apr. 19 that the country needed 2½ million homes and that the shortage was increasing by 70,000 a year.

Christian Democrats & Monarchists—Under the Republic, the pro-monarchist Christian Democrats had dominated the Center. Their party, La Confederaction Española de Derechas Autonomas (CEDA), held 115 of 435 seats in the Cortes of 1933 and 88 of 441 seats in 1936.

Although the party had the financial and political support of the Catholic Church, it was outlawed by the Franco government. In post-Civil War years the clandestine organization lost all influence despite the fact that several of its members were members of the Franco government.

There was also an exiled Christian Democrat organization under the leadership of ex-Republican War Min. José Maria Gil Robles. The exiles maintained close contact with both the clandestine Spanish Christian Democrats and the Monarchists.

According to historians, in 1939-43 there was little difference in the political positions taken by the rival Carlist and Boubonist factions. During 1943-5, however, while the Carlist pretender Francis-Xavier maintained the views of the Carlist organization of the early 19th century (*i.e.*, strong royal government with a limited power granted to the Cortes), Bourbonist Pretender Don Juan had become more liberal. In 1945 Don Juan, in Lausanne, Switzerland, issued a manifesto that called for the establishment of a constitutional monarchy in Spain.

Various Bourbonists, Christian Democrats and Catalan nationalists, under the vague leadership of Gil Robles, united in 1946 to form the Confederation of Monarchical Forces (Confederación de Fuerzas Monárquicas). This group attempted to reach an understanding with the underground remnant of the Left-of-Center Republican forces that had formed the National Alliance of Democratic Forces (Alianza Nacional de Fuerza Democraticas). The monarchists had a double purpose. First they wanted to form a united anti-Franco, anti-Carlist Center, and 2d, they wished to undercut the so-called Republican government in exile, which was based in Paris and had the unofficial support of the French government.

Claude Martin reported in *Franco Soldado y Estadista* that British Foreign Secy. Ernest Bevin not only supported the Christian Democrats' idea but tried to persuade the Spanish Left to join the alliance. While the leaders of the Anarcho-Syndicalists agreed, the Socialists at first refused.

Gil Robles and exiled Socialist leader Indalecio Prieto attempted during 1946-7 to reach some sort of agreement. Bourbonist pretender Don Juan, in an interview with the London *Observer* Apr. 7, 1947, indicated that he could accept some of the Socialist goals. During June the monarchists, Christian Democrats and Socialists united in an attempt to defeat the new Spanish constitution in the July 6 referendum. In Oct. 1948, according to ex-Republican diplomat Elena de La Souchere in *An Explanation of Spain*, Gil Robles and Prieto reached an understanding to work for the replacement of the Franco regime by a democratic, decentralized monarchy. But ex-Republican diplomat Salvador de Madariaga asserted in *Spain* that, having unified opposition to Franco, the monarchists "ran away from their success." The reason, according to Madariaga, was a deal between Franco and Bourbon Pretender Don Juan: Don Juan, who was living in Estoril, Portugal, went sailing on his yacht *Saltillo*; and Franco took a trip on his yacht *Azor*. The 2 met Aug. 25, 1948 off the coast of San Sebastián. According to private informants, Franco expressed his dislike of Don Juan's liberal tendencies. The conversation soon turned from Don Juan to the pretender's son Juan Carlos, born in 1938. Franco requested that the pretender send his son to Spain to be educated, and Juan Carlos, 10, arrived in Spain in Nov. 1948. Juan Carlos then had a minimum of 20 years (until 1968) to become eligible for the throne because the constitution approved in the July 6 referendum stipulated that the king would have to be at least 30.

The arrival of Juan Carlos, informants reported, split the Bourbonists and Christian Democrats into 2 groups: the supporters of Don Juan and the supporters of Juan Carlos. It also ended the Christian Democrat-Socialist alliance.

Basque & Catalan Nationalists—2 groups within Spain are not as much anti-Franco as they are anti-Castilian: the Basques and the Catalans. Both groups, who oppose almost all Spanish governments, contain a wide spectrum of political opinion—from feudal monarchist to Socialist and anarchist. Among the Basques, for example, one found the millionaire militant monarchist Joaquín Satrústegui, Bishop Antonio Pildain and José Dominguez de Arana, an anti-clerical monarchist (something of a novel position in Spain). Some Basques support the Carlists, others support the exiled Basque Nationalist Party, which was pro-Republican.

The Catalans are equally divided. The major center of Catalan nationalism was the great Monastery of Montserrat, where the Shrine of the Black Virgin acted as a magnet. Dom Aurelio María Escarre, abbot of Montserrat, became the outspoken leader of the nationalist movement. In tribute to the abbot's role in Catalan nationalistic affairs, Pablo Picasso, a member of the French Communist Party who was born in Spain, dedicated lithographs to Escarre. Like the Basques, the Catalans were too divided politically—although united culturally—to be an effective opposition.

The Church—Church leaders distrusted the Falange (privately many of them called Falangists "Bolsheviks"), and Franco made important concessions to the Church for clerical support: Compulsory religious education was introduced into the universities in 1944, and clerics had a veto power on all text books. A celebration in honor of Miguel de Unamuno, one of Spain's best known intellectuals, was canceled when Archbishop Enrique Cardinal Plá y Deniel of Toledo declared Unamuno a heretic.

Church leadership was said to be divided into 3 groups: (1) On the Right was a small group of extreme traditionalists led by Archbishop Pedro Cardinal Segura y Sáenz of Sevilla; Segura never recognized the legitimacy of the Franco government and criticized its policies as too "liberal." (2) In the Center was a group of prelates led by Bishop Leopoldo Eijo y Garay of Madrid who defended all government action. (3) On the Left were prelates who objected to the restrictive nature of the government and the government's social policies; this group was divided between passive opponents and activists; the passive opponents, led by Plá y Deniel, limited their opposition to pastoral letters condemning specific government action or inaction. The activists, led by Angel Herrera y Oria, bishop of Málaga, organized both clerical and lay opposition to government policy.

The chief legal vehicles for Church social action were Hermandades Obreras de Acción Católica (HOAC) and Juventud Obrera Católica (JOC). Both organizations were under the personal protection of Plá y Deniel, but, according to observers, the driving force behind them was Herrera y Oria. (Herrera, before taking holy orders in 1940, had been an active member of the Christian Democratic Party and editor of *El Debate*, the party's organ.) Under Herrera's direction, HOAC and JOC became the Church's political arm for social action. In conjunction with the Christian Democrats, HOAC was used to challenge Falange control of the syndical organization. The government permitted HOAC to exist, but members of the organization, both lay and clerical, were frequently jailed.

With the exception of *Ecclesia*, the Church journal under the personal control of Plá y Deniel, all Church publications were subject to government censorship. Church officials objected and frequently violated censorship rules. In 1950 *Tu* and *Razon y Fe*, 2 leading Catholic publications, were suspended temporarily because of anti-government statements.

Opus Dei–The Sociedad Sacerdotal de la Santa Cruz y del Opus Dei is a secret lay-religious order founded Oct. 2, 1928 by the Abbe José María Escriva de Balaguer y Albas, an Aragonese lawyer who had entered the clergy. Members of Opus Dei take vows of personal poverty, chastity and obedience in spiritual matters but may renounce the vows at will. Most known members are unmarried laymen, but there are also married men, priests and even women members. During the 1940s the organization became something of a power in Spain; in 1957 several members and suspected members entered the cabinet.

Father Escriva has said several times that Opus Dei has no political affiliation but that the organization has no objections to its members having and expressing political opinions. Escriva, according to informants, was on friendly terms with both Juan Carlos and Carlist Hugo Carlos. Rafael Calvo Serer, one of the more prominent and out-spoken members of the organization, is a close personal friend of Don Juan, a companion of Juan Carlos and a critic of the Falange. Calvo Serer's political opinions have forced him to take long vacations to avoid arrest or formal banishment. During vacations in Paris, Calvo Serer wrote anti-Falange articles for various newspapers.

Both the Falange and the Left view Opus Dei as a political organization and concentrate their attacks on it rather than on individual members.

The relationship between the Spanish branch of Opus Dei and the Vatican is uncertain. Escriva, in Rome since 1950, has had little influence over the organization he established. Arthur P. Whitaker reported in *Spain and Defense of the West* that Escriva opposed the entry of Opus Dei members into the cabinet in 1957.

Spanish Foreign Policy 1945-8

During most of 1945-8 Spain was isolated from the world community. Spain had friendly relation only with Portugal and Argentina. The friendship with Argentina was crucial because in Oct. 1945 Argentina lent Spain 350 million Argentine pesos to buy food. (Brian Crozier asserted in *Franco* that this loan "ensured the survival of Franco's regime.") Eva Perón, wife of Argentine dictator Juan Perón, visited Spain in 1947 and was treated with honor.

Other countries opposed the Franco regime. A UN resolution Feb. 6, 1946 called on all states to break diplomatic relations with Spain. The UN Security Council Apr. 6 approved a Polish resolution condemning the Franco government. Spain Dec. 12 was denied membership in the various UN subsidiary bodies that the UN had inherited from the defunct League of Nations. Spaniards, however, did serve the UN. Pablo de Azcarte was appointed by the UN as the head of its organization in Jerusalem. He arrived Jan. 1948, was not permitted to exercise authority by the British government but was called on May 28 to oversee the surrender of the Jews in the Old City of Jerusalem.

Growing fears of Soviet imperialism (sparked by Communist takeovers in Bulgaria, Rumania, Hungary and Poland and Soviet territorial demands against Turkey) led to the Truman Doctrine and caused a change in Western opinion about Franco. The U.S. House of Representatives Mar. 30, 1948 adopted, by 149-52 vote, a resolution calling on the U.S. to extend Marshall Plan aid to Spain. Pres. Harry S. Truman vetoed the resolution. The USSR began the Berlin blockade in July 1948; shortly thereafter the Communists seized control of Czechoslovakia and the USSR began its campaign against Pres. Tito of Yugoslavia.

Winston Churchill defended Franco during a debate in the House of Commons Dec. 10.   France, meanwhile, reopened its frontier with Spain, and several countries, including the U.S., reestablished full diplomatic relations with Spain.   In 1948 Franco sent José Felix Lequerica (who had been foreign minister 1944–5) to Washington as the Spanish ambassador, but the U.S. government refused to accept him because of his past dealing with Vichy France and Germany.   Franco ordered Lequerica to remain in Washington as "inspector of embassies and legations."   The U.S. recognized Lequerica as the Spanish ambassador Dec. 27, 1950.

FROM PARIAH TO INTERNATIONAL ACCEPTANCE (1949-50)

Spain's isolation from the world community began to end during 1949-50. Although Franco was still widely denounced as a dictator, and his government as a fascist regime, many nations that had previously shunned Spain became less unfriendly to the anti-Communist Spaniards as Cold War lines hardened. This acceptance abroad came fortuitously at a time when the Spanish economy was in serious difficulties and Spain, therefore, was in dire need of foreign aid.

Economic Woes

The Spanish economy had weakened seriously since the end of World War II. The number of registered unemployed industrial workers rose from 163,759 in 1945 to 175,827 by 1950. According to foreign economists, the figures for registered unemployed represented about 10% of actual unemployment. The standard of living declined by 17% between 1940 and 1950.

Spain's hopes for economic improvement were dashed in 1949-50 by severe drought. Even in normal years Spain suffered from a water shortage, but by the summer of 1950 Spain's too few reservoirs held only 10% of capacity. The lack of water brought the country to the brink of starvation and forced a reduction in the output of electricity. In Spain's most industrialized area, Catalunya (Cataluña, or Catalonia), the outdated hydroelectric plants (built between 1892 and 1929) and the inadequate thermoelectric stations (built between 1904 and 1934) provided insufficient power, forcing factories to close. The shuttering of textile and publishing houses created internal dislocations and reduced exports since cloth and publications were 2 of Spain's most lucrative export items.

By 1950 iron production was down to 84% of the output of 1931, while chemical production was 95%, textile production 98%, shipbuilding 71% and fertilizer production 78%.

Despite the plant closings, Franco insisted that all employers pay their workers. The result was a sharp rise in inflation. Prices increased by 6½% in 1949, another 18% in 1950 and almost 30% in 1951.

With the fall in production (the index for 1949 was below that of 1946) and the increase in prices (between 1940 and 1950 the price index climbed from 100 to 329.7), many Spaniards, it was said, found it impossible to satisfy basic needs. A dramatic result of the economic disaster was seen as the sudden rise in infant mortality, which had been declining steadily since the end of the Civil War. Infant mortality in

41

1949 rose from 6.43 per 100 live births to 6.89. In 1949 some 42,000 presumably dissatisfied Spaniards left the country, most of them for Venezuela.

The government attempted to alleviate some of the hardships. For example, when Aragon peasants refused to deliver their wheat to the Wheat Institute in Sept. 1949 because institute prices were unrealistically low, Franco ordered the institute to change its procedures. Instead of forcing the farmer to give all his wheat to the institute at prices established by the institute, he was required to turn over only part of the harvest while the balance could be sold on the open market. The result of Franco's action was a pacification of the farmers and an increase in production in 1950.

The government also resorted to direct financial aid. Franco Jan. 18, 1950 decreed a $230 gift to each working-class newlywed couple and tripled annual awards to large families.

Trifon Gómez, secretary of the exiled Spanish Socialist labor organization in Paris, predicted Apr. 7, 1949 that Spain's "catastrophic" economic troubles would bring about Franco's downfall in 1949 if he got no help from the Western powers.

A major problem facing Spain was the decline in agricultural production after the Civil War. In the Republican years, Spanish potato production had averaged 2.3 million tons annually, but between 1946 and 1950 potato output fell to less than 1.3 million tons a year. During the Republican era wheat production had averaged 2.2 million tons, but during 1946-50 it averaged only 1.7 million tons. Overall agricultural production in 1950 was only 86% of that of the Republican period. The result of the food shortages was social unrest and hunger demonstrations. (A demonstration by Madrid bank employes was broken up by the police Nov. 29, 1949.)

Government experts reported Dec. 10, 1949 that rains in late November had ended the drought and prevented a disasterous 1950 grain shortage. Actually, drought conditions did continue and the 1950 wheat crop was far from good. While the drought was the immediate cause of the agricultural disaster in 1949-50, experts agreed that the basic problem was the lack of funds to modernize agriculture.

The percentage of the national income invested annually in agriculture declined from 7.2% in 1942 to 4.6% in 1943. The percentage increased steadily during 1945-7 from 6.2% to 8.1% but dropped in 1948 to 6½%. The figure was 7.7% in 1949 and 8½% in 1950, but in 1951 it fell to 7.9%. The result was that Spanish agricultural production per acre was the lowest of any country in Western Europe, excluding Portugal. Furthermore, since money was tight, practically no new equipment was bought. In 1949, in all of Spain, there were 9,260 tractors, 4,500 of which dated from before the Civil War. Thus, in 1949 there was only one tractor for every 6,000 acres of farm land while in war-torn Germany at the same time there was one tractor for each 35 acres of farm land.

A 2d factor was the failure to modernize the fertilizer industry, which in 1947 produced only 50% of its 1935 quota. It was generally agreed that the industry's deficiency was caused by governmental policy, which favored industries that produced for export. (The textile and paper industries in 1947 had surpassed the production of the Republican period by 21% and 5%, respectively.)

According to the economists, another cause of Spain's economic ills was the fact that, although the Spanish population had recovered numerically from the decimation of the Civil War and the exodus of Republican supporters and again stood at 25.8 million, there was a large number of amputees who could not work and who had to be cared for by the state.

The Spanish government, avowedly anti-Communist, appeared to practice some of the paternalism of the Socialist countries. Franco complained in a Bilbao speech June 19, 1950 that some countries deliberately hindered Spain's industrial development for their own benefit. He had said in a June 3 speech that Spain must have a planned economy instead of uncontrolled free enterprise, and his cabinet June 5 announced plans for a new semi-state-owned steel industry to be operated by the National Institute of Industry (INI).

The shortage of goods plus government control of prices and foreign currency led to corruption and thriving black markets. Former Republican diplomat Elena de La Souchere said in *An Explanation of Spain* that "the black market is the most prosperous branch of the Spanish economy." She wrote that businessmen felt that they were forced to bribe officials to obtain the right to use foreign exchange or import raw materials. Some businessmen held that the only way they could make a profit was to permit part of their production to leak into the black market. 728 business firms in Sevillá and Orense Provinces were fined a total of $300,000 in Apr. 1950 for black-market activity. 18 firms were closed temporarily but ordered to pay their employes as usual.

Yet despite restrictions, some people became rich. Juan March, Spanish financier who had forced the $350 million Barcelona Traction, Light & Power Co. into bankruptcy, won control of the concern in liquidation proceedings in Barcelona Sept. 20, 1950 despite protests of U.S., British, Belgian, Canadian and French security holders. March and

18 other Spaniards were elected directors of the $200 million Compania Hispano-Americana de Electricidad (Chade) by Spanish stockholders in Madrid Sept. 27 although non-Spanish stockholders controlling 83% of the stock had voted in Luxembourg Nov. 18, 1948 to dissolve Chade and transfer its assets to the Luxembourg holding company Societé D'Electricité (Sodec). (Chade's holdings were in Latin America.)

Spain is not rich but has been a source of wealth in the past. The Romans, lacing the peninsula with roads and public works, had turned Iberia into one of the empire's richest provinces. The Muslims, who developed a massive irrigation system and brought industry to the peninsula, made Iberia the richest state in Europe. During the 10th century the Ummayyad kalifs had a greater income than the combined income of all Christian kings. Given modern technology, many experts agree, Spain could again blossom. Mid-20th century technology costs money, however, and Spain had very little gold or foreign currency. The gold reserve of the Spanish monarchy and Republic had been transferred to Moscow for safekeeping during the Civil War.

Without external stimuli, many experts held, Spain could not generate sufficient internal capital to develop its economy. The total Spanish investment made in industry and agriculture in 1949 was 15.8 billion pesetas, or approximately $600 million (depending upon which of various rates of exchange was used). This was a 1½% increase over the 1948 investment of 15.6 billion pesetas. In 1950 the annual investment was increased by 15% to 18.2 billion pesetas, but the value of the peseta had fallen so that the actual investment in terms of dollars was less than $500 million.

Opposition & Demands for Reforms

Economic conditions were considered so intolerable that some Bourbonist monarchists and Leftists united in an attempt to win either reforms or the overthrow of Franco. The government, however, rejected all political opposition. Several of those involved in the demand for reforms were sentenced Mar. 24, 1950 to prison terms ranging from 2 to 25 years on charges of illegal plotting against the government.

The demand for reform also came from various segments of the official establishment. A National Assembly of Farmers & Stock Raisers in Madrid Dec. 17, 1949 asked the government for such improvements as crop insurance, better distribution of farm machinery and higher farm prices.

Franco's response to various internal pressure appeared to involve 4 types of action; (1) Repression of all political opposition; (2) a series of social, political and economic reforms; (3) foreign credits to purchase needed food and manufactured items; (4) some minor saber rattling, apparently to divert attention from the internal misery.

Among developments in the government response to critics, reformers and opponents:

Repression—The last of the active revolutionists who had reentered Spain from France in order to start a revolution had been rounded up by 1947, and revolutionary activity had declined. The leader of the militant Communist Party, Enrique Lister, a former Republican general, admitted that Communist activity, which had increased steadily between 1944 and 1947, had fallen in 1948, was almost negligible in 1949 and was virtually non-existant in 1950.

The repressions had driven anti-Franco activists repeatedly across the frontier into France. When conditions appeared quieter in Spain, they had often returned to continue anti-government activity. In the summer and fall of 1950, however, the French government cracked down on Spanish activists in France, and it became less easy for Spanish activists to return to Spain to agitate against Franco. (By the summer of 1950 the Korean War had convinced the French government of the dangers of Communist conspiracy. Unable to move directly against the powerful French Communist Party, the French interior minister attacked foreign Communists exiled in France. The French Sept. 7 "detained" 160 members of the Spanish Communist Party, 30 of whom were deported to Eastern Europe. The balance of the group left Marseille Sept. 9 aboard a French cruiser for internment in the desert region of Oran, Algeria. The Spanish Communists in southwestern France had organized a group called Agrupación de Fuerzas Armadas Republicanas Españolas, which was put under the command of Lister. French Interior Min. Henri Queuille Sept. 7 declared the Spanish Communist Party and the Unified Socialist Party of Catalunya illegal. He suppressed the Spanish Communist newspaper *Mundo Obrero* and barred the legalization of "the Friends of *Mundo Obrero*," which, it was alleged, was a cover for Spanish Communist activity in France.)

The failure of overt revolutionary activity was presumably caused to some degree by the growing unwillingness of France to permit the guerrillas either to establish headquarters in southern France or to infiltrate Spain via purposely abandoned frontier posts. The main cause of the revolutionary failure, however, was said to be the growing efficiency of the Spainsh secret police. (An exception to the decline in revolutionary activity took place in Barcelona May 15, 1949 when the consulates of Bolivia, Brazil and Peru—sponsors of a resolution calling for Spain's admission to the UN—were damaged in bombings laid to anti-Franco agents.)

A military court in Ocaña Feb. 7, 1949 imposed the death sentence on Enrique Marcos Nadal, former French Resistance fighter, for anarchist activities in Spain since 1932. 3 other convicted anarchists received sentences of up to 30 years. 24 persons were sentenced to prison terms of one to 9 years in Ocaña Jan. 31 as leaders of a secret Spanish Socialist party.

In the first months of 1949 the secret police rounded up all members of the Anarchist-backed underground CNT (National Confederation of Labor). Once the Communist and Anarcho-Syndacalist threat to overt revolution was removed, the government turned to the more docile revolutionists, and some Left Center and Right oppositionists soon found themselves in jail.

18 persons were sentenced to prison by a military court in Ocaña Mar. 24, 1950 for trying to organize a rebellion in which Leftists and monarchists would have joined forces. Antonio Castanos Benavente received a 25-year sentence as leader of the plot, and Antonio Trigo Mairal, 52, ex-civil governor of Madrid, got a 2-year term as chief negotiator for the Socialists. Castanos admitted that he was secretary general of the outlawed National Confederation of Labor.

Prison terms up to 12 years were imposed on 12 men convicted by a military court in Ocaña Apr. 14 of spying on police for the anti-Franco Basque Nationalist organization.

The duchess of Valencia (Maria Luisa Narvaez), 35, monarchist leader, was acquitted in a Madrid military court June 15 of charges of conspiring to distribute subversive tracts. The lawyer and economist Bernardo Bernárdez, one of 4 other defendants, took responsibility for the tracts (seized by police in February) and received an 18-month sentence.

Liberalization & reforms—Franco apparently also attempted to still critics by releasing some of the political prisoners held in Spanish jails since the Civil War. 270,719 individuals had been in jail in 1940, but the number of prisoners had dropped to 74,095 by 1944. While these figures comprised all captives, most authorities agreed that the bulk of the inmates were jailed for political crimes. An amnesty for 13,000 prisoners was decreed Dec. 25, 1949 in honor of the Catholic Holy Year. Justice Min. Raimundo Fernández Cuesta reported Jan. 2, 1950 that there were 37,000 persons in Spanish prisons counting 5,000 still to be freed under the amnesty.

The Franco reforms included a crack-down on black marketers and actions to reduce the need of Spanish businessmen to resort to illegal activity to obtain needed foreign exchange.

In one area, however, Franco refused to budge: censorship remained rigid, although in this Franco appeared to face increased opposition. According to Gabriel Eloriaga, writing in *Working Paper No. 9, United Nations Conference on the Freedom of Information* (1964), the first open attack on censorship came in 1950 when Spanish primate, Enrique Cardinal Plá y Deniel, stated in a personal letter: "It is highly deplorable that it is not recognized that between the liberties of damnation . . . and the absolute state of control of the press exists a happy medium of responsible freedom of the press."

Saber rattling & territorial demands—Since Spain had little hope for its territorial demands, it was widely assumed that Franco used them to divert internal unrest.

Spain had 3 territorial demands: Gibraltar, parts of French Morocco and the area south of France (Roussillon) inhabited by Catalans. Franco had originally demanded these areas of Hitler as his price for entering World War II, but Hitler had refused until it became obvious that he was losing the war. By the time Hitler agreed, Franco seemed to have decided that it was wiser to remain neutral. After the war Franco abandoned claims to Roussillon but insisted on Gibraltar and parts of French Morocco. These claims contradicted other Spanish interests. The demand for territory in North Africa ran counter to Franco's policy of supporting Arab nationalism. (Franco had permitted various Moroccan nationalists to operate in Spanish Morocco.) The demand for Gibraltar angered Britain, Spain's best customer. (England's purchases from Spain exceeded by 153½ million pesetas British sales.) Nevertheless Franco told the Cortes (parliament) May 18, 1949 that Britain had reneged on a 1941 promise made by Winston Churchill to the duke of Alba, then Spanish ambassador to the United Kingdom, that Britain would persuade France "to satisfy just claims of Spain in North Africa" after the end of the war. And Franco said in an interview published Dec. 10 by *Arriba*, official Falange party newspaper in Madrid, that Britain must return Gibraltar to Spain. Gibraltar, however, "is not worth fighting a war for," Franco said. "It is a ripe fruit which will someday fall of itself." Franco contended that Britain had occupied Gibraltar in 1704 on behalf of Spanish allies and that its return was long overdue. (The rock fortress was taken from Spain by British and Dutch forces during the War of the Spanish Succession and was ceded to Britain under the Treaty of Utrecht in 1715.)

Devaluations & Quest for Foreign Aid

Franco tried 2 methods in 1949–50 to obtain gold and foreign currency needed for his country's economic development. He sought to borrow, and he also reduced even further the value of the peseta in hopes of attracting foreign investors and tourists to Spain.

Spain devalued the peseta Jan. 20, 1949. The new rates were 25 instead of 16.4 pesetas to the U.S. dollar for tourists and Spaniards repatriating capital from abroad; 16.4 instead of 10.95 pesetas to $1 for persons or corporations investing in Spanish firms.

A $25 million short-term private loan was granted to Spain by the Chase National Bank of New York Feb. 8, 1949.

Attempts to borrow money from the U.S. government, however, were frustrated initially by Pres. Harry S. Truman and State Secy. Dean G. Acheson. Truman told reporters June 2, 1949 that, although Washington did not object to Spanish negotiations with the Chase Bank, he did not favor a U.S. government loan to Spain.* Acheson said July 13 that he would not consider Spain a good risk for a loan from the Economic Cooperation Administration (ECA), which administered U.S. foreign aid operations. Truman July 14 voiced his unqualified opposition to making a loan to Spain while that country and the U.S. were not on friendly terms. But pro-Franco forces in the U.S. Senate, led by Sen. Pat McCarran (D., Nev.), attempted to attach to a foreign aid bill a rider earmarking $500 million of ECA funds to a loan to Spain outside the regular European Recovery Program (ERP). This plan failed when the Senate Aug. 4, by a 38–17 vote, upheld Vice Pres. Alben W. Barkley's ruling that the rider was out of order.

Failing to receive foreign aid, Spain again devalued the peseta. The decree Oct. 9, 1949 maintained the variable scale but changed the order of priorities. The Jan. 20 devaluation had aimed at attracting capital; the Oct. 9 devaluation was aimed at restricting Spanish foreign purchases. The official tourist rate remained at 25 pesetas to $1, but

---

*It had been disclosed in Washington May 16, 1949 that the U.S. Export-Import Bank had turned down, at least temporarily, Spanish requests for loans totaling $1,275,900,000. Spain's special financial emissary, Andrés Moreno, chairman of the Banco Hispano Americano, was said to have told several Southern and Midwestern Senators—before he met with Export-Import Bank officials—that if Spain got U.S. credits it would buy U.S. cotton, wheat and soy-bean oil. Spain's director general of economic affairs, Mariano Yeturalde, visited the State Department in Washington Dec. 22 and asked for U.S. financial aid to Spain. But the request was denied.

Spaniards had to pay 31% more for U.S. autos (old rate 23.99 pesetas to $1, new rate 34.67 pesetas to $1).

Economic conditions worsened in the winter of 1949–50: The Spanish Commerce & Industry Ministry appealed Jan. 14, 1950 to "any country whatsoever" to ship Spain 500,000 tons of grain to tide the country over to the year's wheat harvest. The day this appeal was made, the Argentine government, which also faced an economic crisis and had devalued the peso by 46%, announced the suspension of all credit sales to Spain. Argentina, up to that point, had advanced Spain credit totaling 202.9 million pesetas. At the same time internal problems forced Brazil, which had advanced Spain credits totaling 104.3 million pesetas, to suspend credits. The state of Spain's economy became evident later when sources in Madrid disclosed that $12 million in gold had been flown to New York Jan. 16 as collateral for a new $25 million loan from the Chase National Bank.

Mass starvation was averted by the purchase of potatoes from U.S. surplus stocks. Luis García Guijarro of the Spanish embassy in Washington said Feb. 15 that Spain had contracted to buy 1,120,000 pounds of potatoes from the U.S. government at 1¢ per 100-pound bag. (The bags alone were worth 30¢ each in Spain.) After obtaining a $20 million loan secured by gold from the National City Bank of New York Mar. 24, the Spanish government bought another 42,500 tons of surplus U.S. potatoes for 10¢ a thousand pounds—the price of one pound on the Spanish black market—and it ended potato rationing Mar. 28.

Spain signed favorable trade agreements with West Germany June 19, 1950, with Britain June 22 and with Colombia Aug. 9. The German treaty called for a yearly exchange of goods valued at $91 million; the British deal was for 18.2 million. The Colombian treaty covered a 3-year barter agreement. These treaties insured the export of Spanish iron and coal from the Basque provinces and cloth from Catalunya but did little to solve Spain's basic need for massive assistance.

The U.S. Senate had still refused financial aid to the Spanish government. During debate on a $3,372,450,000 foreign aid authorization bill, the U.S. Senate Apr. 27, 1950 rejected, by 42–35 vote, a $50 million Export-Import Bank loan to Spain proposed by Sen. McCarran. McCarran had the active support of Sens. Tom Connally (D., Tex.), Owen Brewster (R., Me.) and Dennis Chavez (D., N.M.).

But within days of the Communist invasion of South Korea, June 25, 1950, pro-Franco forces in the Senate, pointing to Franco's staunch anti-Communist position, asked the Senate to reconsider. The Senate agreed and voted 65–15 Aug. 1 to lend Spain $100 million for economic aid through the Export-Import Bank. The loan would be administered by ECA Administrator Paul G. Hoffman but would be outside the Marshall Plan.

Pres. Truman Aug. 3 condemned the inclusion of the Spanish loan in the ECA section of an omnibus foreign aid appropriations bill, but the Senate Aug. 3 tabled, by 65–15 vote, a motion to reconsider. Truman backed the views of State Secy. Acheson, who had told reporters Aug. 2 that such a loan should be made only through non-ECA channels. Acheson added that U.S. efforts to persuade the Spanish government to become more democratic had failed.

During August the U.S. Congress debated the loan to Spain as part of the omnibus aid appropriation, and a House version incorporating the $100 million Spanish loan was approved by 164–80 House vote Aug. 25. Rep. Alvin O'Konski (R., Wis.) led the House support for the loan to Spain. After considerable argument, during which time Congress cut $2.29 billion from the Truman Administration's total aid request, a $36,153,490,425 appropriation containing a $62½ million loan to Spain was passed by voice vote of both houses Aug. 28 and sent to the President. The Spanish loan, which Truman had denounced for a 2d time Aug. 24, had been cut by a joint conference committee from the $100 million originally approved.

Truman and the State Department, however, were unrelenting in their opposition to aiding Franco Spain. As late as Nov. 2, 1950 the President informed reporters that it would be a long, long time before the U.S. would send an ambassador to Spain. The ECA announced Nov. 15 that Spain would be given dollar loans through the Export-Import Bank from the $62½ million fund created by the aid bill. Loans were to be made for specific projects that Spain proved would benefit the economy.

Thus, 5 months after the start of the Korean War, the U.S. agreed to aid Spain's economic recovery. Spain, however, had to present a plan for the U.S. to approve, and this approval did not come until the beginning of 1951.

Meanwhile economic problems forced 2 further devaluations of the peseta. Spain Aug. 1 introduced a semi-free foreign exchange system that permitted tourists to exchange a U.S. dollar for 39.40 pesetas instead of 25 pesetas. Spain's tourist trade in 1950 was 40% heavier than in 1949, at least partly because of Holy Year travel to Rome. Because of the failure to secure immediate U.S. aid, the Spanish government Oct. 22 again devalued the peseta. Tourists still obtained the favorable rate of 39.40 pesetas to the dollar. Spaniards would have to pay only 16.425 to 19.71 pesetas for the dollar to import essential products, but non-essential importation was curtailed by the imposition of a rate of 39.86 pesetas to the dollar. On even some semi-essential items the government would supply only 60% of the dollars needed at the favorable rate; 40% had to be purchased at the 39.86 per dollar rate, and the average price of the dollar would be 27.77 pesetas.

Quest for Diplomatic Recognition

Forces that led the fight for economic assistance to Spain also attempted to make Franco acceptable to the Western powers. Before the end of 1950 these efforts resulted in a UN decision to admit Spain to the specialized UN agencies although not to grant membership to the Franco regime.

It was Portuguese Premier Antonio de Oliveira Salazar who first advocated Spain's inclusion in the North Atlantic Treaty. Salazar had told the UN Apr. 7, 1949 that the pact would be more effective if Spain were admitted.

Action to win diplomatic recognition for Spain was also gaining momentum at this time.

The UN General Assembly's Political & Security Committee voted 26–16 May 7, 1949 in Lake Success, N.Y. to approve a resolution that would let UN members resume full diplomatic relations with Spain. Bolivia, Brazil, Colombia and Peru sponsored the measure and were supported during the 4-day debate by most Latin American countries, the Arab states, South Africa, Pakistan and the Philippines. Poland led the anti-Spanish fight and offered a resolution on arms sanctions against Spain that lost by margins as much as 46–6 on a paragraph-by-paragraph vote May 7. Other countries voting against the Spanish-recognition move were the other Slav states, Australia, Costa Rica, Denmark, Guatemala, India, Mexico, New Zeland, Norway, Panama and Uruguay. The 16 abstainers were: the U.S., Britain, all other Atlantic Treaty states except Denmark and Norway; Afghanistan, Burma, Chile, Nationalist China, Ethiopia, Haiti, Iran and Sweden. Britain's Hector McNeil May 7 branded as "lies" a Soviet charge that Britain had been selling jet planes and other war-planes to Spain. Ray Atherton summed up the U.S. attitude May 6 as follows: The U.S. did not like Franco but did not think sanctions against him would help the Spanish people regain a place in "the community of democratic nations."

Attempts in the UN to change attitudes toward Spain continued to fail. For lack of a ⅔ majority, the UN General Assembly May 16 rejected a resolution to authorize UN member countries to renew full diplomatic relations with Spain if they wished. The resolution, sponsored by Bolivia, Brazil, Colombia and Peru, had been approved the previous week by the General Assembly's Political & Security Committee. The resolution would not have revoked that part of a 1946 resolution on Spain that censured the Franco regime as undemocratic and barred it from UN agencies. However, it would have repealed the 1946 recommendation that all UN countries withdraw top diplomatic representatives from Madrid. The vote: *For the resolution* (26)–Argentina, Bolivia, Brazil, Colombia, Dominican Rep., Ecuador, Egypt, El Salvador, Greece, Honduras, Iceland, Iraq, Lebanon, Liberia, Nicaragua, Pakistan, Paraguay, Peru, Philippines, Saudi Arabia, South Africa, Syria, Thailand (Siam), Turkey, Venezuela, Yemen. *Against* (15)–Australia, Czechoslovakia, Guatemala, India, Israel, Mexico, New Zealand, Norway, Panama, Poland, USSR, Ukraine, Uruguay, White Russia, Yugoslavia. *Abstaining* (16)–Afghanistan, Belgium, Britain, Burma, Canada, Chile, China, Denmark, Ethiopia, France, Haiti, Iran, Luxembourg, Netherlands, Sweden, U.S. *Absent* (2)–Costa Rica, Cuba.

The General Assembly May 16 then voted down a Polish resolution to bar UN members from (1) making treaties or other agreements with the Franco government, or (2) selling arms, ammunition or any kind of "warlike and strategic material" to Spain. This had only the Soviet bloc's support and lost by 40–6 vote (7 abstentions). The U.S. opposed it. The result was to leave the 1946 resolution in force. In debate on the Spanish question May 16: Poland's Julius Katz-Suchy and Britain's Hector McNeil traded accusations and denials that Poland and Britain had sold planes and other war goods to Spain. The U.S.' Ray Atherton denied Soviet-bloc charges that the U.S. was secretly pro-Franco. He also said the U.S. had no military affiliations with Spain nor any plans afoot to bring Spain into the UN, ERP (European Recovery Program) or Atlantic pact.

The U.S.'s ambivalent attitude toward Franco had been demonstrated May 3, 1949: the State Department disclosed that Spain had been authorized to negotiate with the Export-Import Bank for a loan, but it implied that Spain would have a hard time proving itself a good credit risk. The mixed feelings of the U.S. were further exemplified by the contrasting attitudes taken by State Secy. Dean G. Acheson and by some members of Congress. Acheson said at his news conference in Washington May 11 that the U.S. could not vote for restoring diplomatic relations with Spain because Franco's regime "was, and is, a fascist government and a dictatorship." He said the U.S. would abstain in the UN General Assembly on a Spanish-recognition measure that called for each country to decide on its own policy toward Franco. He said the U.S. hoped to see civil rights restored in Spain but had noted no progress in that direction by Franco's government. Acheson held that the return of a U.S. ambassador to Madrid would be "a symbol [that] we don't care much about these rights." Acheson's statement followed remarks in Congress May 10 by Sens. Tom Connally, Owen Brewster, Patrick McCarran and Styles Bridges (R., N.H.) and Rep. Dewey Short (R., Mo.), all favoring full U.S. relations with Spain. Sen. Arthur Vandenberg (R., Mich.) said May 12 that he favored sending an ambassador back to Spain, but both he and Connally opposed admitting Spain to the Atlantic pact.

Allied with liberals in opposition to Franco were many Protestants who opposed the Vatican. The Central Committee of the World Council of Churches, meeting in Chichester, England July 9-14, 1949, urged Christians to "stand firm against totalitarianism" and condemned "any church which seeks to use the power of the state to enforce religious conformity." The latter statement was directed against Spain.

During the summer of 1949, as a wave of anticommunism spread in the U.S., the Franco government became even more appealing to many members of the conservative community. A resumption of full U.S.-Spanish diplomatic relations was indorsed by 23 former U.S. ambassadors to various countries. This total was obtained in a poll announced Oct. 7 by James W. Gerard, pre-World War I ambassador to Germany. Several Americans who had recently paid friendly visits to Franco in Madrid included: (Sept. 30) Rep. James J. Murphy (D., N.Y.), who said he found Franco a "lovely and lovable character." (Oct. 5) James A. Farley. (Oct. 8) Sen. Owen Brewster (R., Me.) and Reps. James P. Richards (D., S.C.), Noble J. Gregory (D., Ky.), Eugene J. Keough (D., N.Y.) and W. R. Poage (D., Tex.).

Faced with growing demands for some understanding with Franco, Pres. Truman relaxed his opposition to all dealings with Spain. During the first official postwar visit by U.S. warships to Spain, Adm. Richard L. Conolly, U.S. Navy commander in the Mediterranean and Eastern Atlantic, met Franco in La Coruña Sept. 5. Franco, obviously pleased by the visit of the U.S. fleet, asserted in his New Year's Eve broadcast Dec. 31 that Spain and the U.S. were becoming "closer every day."

The U.S. actually had maintained ties with Madrid throughout Spain's period of isolation. A young assistant naval attaché, Lt. Comdr. John Fitzpatrick, had been stationed there since 1947. Fitzpatrick was the son-in-law of Adm. Forrest Sherman, and Mrs. Sherman paid frequent visits to Madrid. In 1948 the admiral had become commander of the U.S. 6th Fleet, and in 1949 he became chief of naval operations. Sherman was grateful to the Spanish government for its kindness to Mrs. Sherman during her visits to Madrid. It was Adms. Sherman and Robert

B. Carney, commander of U.S. Naval Forces in Northern Europe, who finally persuaded Pres. Truman in 1950 to change his anti-Franco policy.

Rep. John Kee (D., W. Va.), chairman of the House Foreign Affairs Committee, reflected a growing trend when he told the House in Washington Jan. 9, 1950 that it would be in the U.S.'s interests to renew full diplomatic relations with Spain.

State Secy. Acheson announced Jan. 19 that the U.S. would support a UN resolution to let member nations send their envoys back to Madrid. He had informed 4 Congressional leaders about this policy change Jan. 18 to ward off increasing criticism of his department's Spanish policy. Acheson added, however, that the restoration of full diplomatic relations would not mean that the U.S. approved of the Franco regime or its policies.

The indication that the U.S. was moving toward some sort of *modus vivendi* with Franco brought objections from the rather politically middle-of-the-road American Federation of Labor (AFL). At the AFL Executive Council meeting held in Miami Beach Jan. 30–Feb. 7, 1950, the federation assailed the State Department for its apparent moves toward the recognition of Spain.

While the U.S. still refused to treat with Franco, some states were reestablishing contact. Colombia resumed full diplomatic relations with Spain Feb. 25; pro-French Vietnam, Laos and Cambodia were recognized by Spain Mar. 4, and Korea also recognized Spain.

Despite the increased acceptability of the Franco government, however, Spain remained barred not only from the UN but also from UN subsidiary organizations. The International Union of Railways, for example, qualified for consultative status with the UN Economic & Social Council Apr. 20, 1950 after barring Spain from its General Assembly and executive board.

A major change in the situation took place after June 1950 when the Communist invasion of South Korea stilled most opposition to the Franco government. By mid-summer, further attempts to reinstate Spain among the family of nations were being made by several states. Peru and Bolivia proposed Aug. 24 that the UN General Assembly revoke (a) its ban on Spanish membership in UN specialized agencies and (b) the 1946 decision that UN countries should not maintain full diplomatic relations with Madrid.

U.S.-Spanish relations also became more cordial. The U.S. Congress voted Spain the $62½ million loan Aug. 28, and 4 Spanish generals were invited in Sept. 1950 to watch allied war games in Germany.

Under pressure from the military and from organizations such as the American Legion, which, at its 32d convention (held in Los Angeles

Oct. 9-12), insisted that the U.S. accord Spain full diplomatic recognition, the U.S. administration was divided as to what stance to take toward Franco. The Justice Department was revealed Oct. 19 to have barred Spanish Falangists from entering the U.S. a day after the State Department had decided they were admissible under the new Internal Security Act. As a result, the State Department Oct. 17 ordered its officials abroad to hold up all Falangists' visas.

While the U.S. acted undecided, some of America's staunchest supporters, presumably foreseeing U.S. recognition of Franco, changed their anti-Franco position. Philippines Foreign Min. Carlos P. Romulo, ex-UN General Assembly president, said in Rio de Janeiro Oct. 24 that the UN boycott of Spain served to sanction "the vengeance of the Politburo against the Spain it was unable to conquer in 1936." The Spanish embassy in London had said in July that 24 countries and the Vatican had either ambassadors or ministers in Madrid.

By the fall of 1950, with the U.S. in the lead, the UN began to reverse its policy on Spain. A U.S.-backed resolution (1) to indorse UN countries' reassignment of ambassadors and ministers to Madrid and (2) to let Spain join UN specialized agencies (open to non-UN members) was passed by the UN General Assembly by 38-10 vote Nov. 4 with 12 abstentions. The Assembly's Special Political Committee had approved it Oct. 31 by 37-10 vote. The measure repealed the diplomatic boycott of Spain voted by the Assembly in 1946, but it did not revoke the UN's disapproval of the Franco regime.

During the debate in the Special Political Committee Oct. 27, the resolution was supported by Sir Muhammad Zafrulla Khan of Pakistan, who said that "so far as we can judge, the government of Spain has the support of a large majority of the Spanish people." Noting that Spain had committed no aggression and that it seemed "more stable than it was in 1946," he said that the UN anti-Franco resolutions not only have "done no good" but contained "great possibilities of mischief." Furthermore, he continued, the resolutions were passed "under a mistaken conception of the functions of this organization [the UN] ." He concluded with a reminder of the inability of the UN to force members who recognized Spain to remove their envoys from Madrid. An opposite stand was taken by Prof. Enrique Fabregat of Uruguay, who contended that, since nothing had changed in Spain since 1946, there was no reason for the UN to reverse its position. Sir Frank Soskice of Britain, while agreeing with the Uruguayan view, announced that his delegation would abstain from voting on the resolution.

Sen. John J. Sparkman (D., Ala.), U.S. delegate on the Special Political Committee, said Oct. 31 that the U.S. wanted to do what it could

to help the Spanish people despite the continuation of Franco's dictatorship. He called the UN diplomatic boycott of Spain a failure.

The General Assembly vote *for the resolution*–Afghanistan, Argen-
tina, Belgium, Bolivia, Brazil, Canada, Chile, China, Colombia, Costa
Rica, Dominican Republic, Ecuador, Egypt, El Salvador, Greece, Haiti,
Honduras, Iceland, Iraq, Lebanon, Liberia, Luxemburg, Netherlands,
Nicaragua, Pakistan, Panama, Paraguay, Persia, Peru, Philippines, Saudi
Arabia, Syria, Thailand, Turkey, South Africa, United States, Venezuela,
Yemen. *Against the resolution*–Byelorussia, Czechoslovakia, Guatemala,
Israel, Mexico, Poland, Soviet Union, Ukraine, Uruguay, Yugoslavia.
Abstentions–Australia, Burma, Cuba, Denmark, Ethiopia, France, Great
Britain, India, Indonesia, New Zeland, Norway, Sweden.

Many reasons were given for the division of world opinion on the
resolution. Among many anti-Communist states there existed a feeling
that Spain was still a fascist dictatorship. In *Spain: The Gentle Anarchy*,
Benjamin Welles quoted Truman as saying to Adm. Sherman, "I don't
like Franco and I never will, but I won't let my personal feelings over-
ride the convictions of you military men." Mexico, which in 1950 still
considered the Spanish Republic as the legal government of Spain, could
could not be persuaded to accept Franco in the UN.

Israel's negative vote was reported to have disturbed Franco deeply.
The Israeli delegate made clear his feelings that the UN had no right to
examine the internal affairs of an applying state but that his government
was obliged to vote "no" because of Franco's support of Hitler during
World War II.

Franco, according to George Hills in *Franco*, took the Israeli attitude as a personal insult. Franco had done more than most European
leaders to save the lives of Europe's Jews. Acting on an old law that
gave Spanish citizenship to all Sephardic Jews (Jews of Iberian ancestry),
Franco had permitted all Jews free entry into Spain during the war,
had given Spanish Jewry in Morocco local self-government and also had
interceeded with Hitler and had persuaded the Nazi leader to free some
members of the Jewish community in Salonika, Greece. Not only did
the Jews arrive safely in Spain but Franco persuaded Hitler to permit
them to leave with some of their savings. There were many Jews alive
in 1950 who owed their lives to Franco. Even in Spain, Jews were permitted comparative freedom. Franco let Jews erect 2 synagogues; although there could be no outward sign that the building was a temple,
within its walls there were no restrictions. In many ways the lot of the
Spanish Jews was better than that of Spanish Protestants. (The Spanish
government June 17, 1950 had reaffirmed policies prohibiting non-
Catholics from holding public demonstrations, establishing schools or

recreational centers or making collections for churches. This action was its answer to Protestants who had asked Franco for protection.)

In contrast with the disappointing vote of Israel, the positive votes of the Arab states could have been accepted by Franco as a confirmation of the correctness of his policy toward the Muslim world. Many Arab states had condemned Franco and Spain for the Spanish colonies in North Africa. Furthermore, the Arab states, annoyed by U.S. support of Israel, had begun to court the USSR and could have been expected to support the Soviet position. Franco, however, had been working hard for Arab backing. Franco had permitted anti-French Moroccans to operate from Spanish Morocco, and when Arab statesmen such as King Abdullah of Jordan had visited the country, he had them taken on a grand tour of what had once been Muslim Spain to show Spain as a bridge between the Arab and Christian worlds.

Turkey, the first nation to act under the UN resolution, sent a minister to Madrid Nov. 5. Although the U.S. voted for the pro-Spanish resolution, which it had originally sponsored, Pres. Truman reiterated at his news conference Nov. 2 that it would be a long, long time before the U.S. sent an ambassador to Spain.

Once the resolution was passed, Spain gained membership in various subsidiary UN organizations. Spain was admitted to the Food & Agriculture Organization by the FAO Conference in Washington Nov. 10, 1950 and was restored Nov. 24 to membership in the International Civil Aviation Organization, from which it had been suspended in 1947.

There were voices of opposition, however. A resolution urging that the diplomatic boycott of Spain be maintained was passed in Brussels Nov. 3 by the new European regional organization of the International Confederation of Free Trade Unions, and the Spanish Republican government-in-exile in Paris protested in a manifesto Nov. 9 against the lifting of the UN boycott of the Franco regime.

As 1950 was drawing to a close Sir John Balfour was named Dec. 19 as the first British ambassador to Spain since 1946, and Spain and Chile resumed diplomatic relations Dec. 26 after a 4-year lapse.

Important improvements in the Spanish economy were noticable by 1951 although serious problems still existed. A wave of strikes started in Barcelona in March and quickly spread to other parts of the country. Spain embarked on a program to build up a modern military force. It made continued progress in gaining diplomatic recognition. Many U.S. leaders were urging steps for the U.S. to acquire military bases in Spain or to enlist Spain in the growing Western alliance.

Economic Health Still Shaky

Various indicators suggested that the Spanish economy had improved by 1951. While the recovery was uneven, and there were serious soft spots, the economy had not only overcome the 1949–50 depression but in some cases had surpassed 1948 and even 1936 production levels. It was reported, however, that most people did not benefit from the healthier economy until late 1951 or early 1952, and the economic distress resulted in serious unrest, strikes and riots lasting from February to June, 1951.

Inflation continued unabated. The price level, increased 29%: using 1949 as a base, it rose from 329 at the end of 1950 to 423.5 at the end of 1951. During the same period, however, per capita income increased by only 16%. The result was a further reduction in the standard of living. In 1951 only 1% of the population had an income of over $5,000 while more than 50% of the population had an income of less than $500. The pay of government employees was raised 20% Jan. 1, 1951. Many private workers had previously been granted cost-of-living increases, but official figures indicated that the average Spaniard had less than half the purchasing power of a Spaniard in pre-Civil War 1936.

While overall industrial production increased 13% over 1950, textile manufacturing, one of Spain's most important industries (employing some 125,000 workers), remained below the 1948 level. Production in cotton textile plants, which employ $1/3$ of all textile workers, fell during 1951. Steel output also fell, from 818,000 tons in 1950 to 812,000 tons in 1951, although 1951 production was still above the 1949 figure of 720,000 tons.

The overall picture, however, was good. Unfortunately, much of the improvement appeared only in the 2d half of 1951, while the rioting took place during the first half.

Despite a reduction in annual government investment in agriculture from 8.5% of the total national investment to 7.9%, by the end of 1951 potato production had doubled, tomato output was up 12% and dried fruit and olive production had trebeled. Cotton production increased 40%, tobacco production 20%. Part of the reason for the increased agricultural yield was the ending of the drought. The rains watered the soil and also increased the use of hydroelectric power on farms that had electricity. Other reasons for the improved yield were: an increase in the acreage of irrigated farms; the increased number of tractors available (12,000 in 1951), and the greater availability of chemical fertilizers.

Conditions in the extractive industries also improved. Wolfram output trebeled. Mercury production was reduced 50%, but the price of mercury had sky-rocketed so that the half-production of 1951 brought in 40% more money than the full production of 1950.

The government investment in the economy went up from 18.2 billion pesetas in 1950 to 22.4 billion, of which 92.1% went to industry or transportation. Cement industry output increased 10%; shipbuilding rose from 23 million tons to 39 million; nitrate production increased from 20 million tons to 40 million; motorcycle production rose from 5,000 units to 9,000, truck output from 178 to 369, bicycle production from 114,000 to 120,000. Shoe, book and salt production increased, as did the production of electricity and the consumption of butane gas, the latter by 30%. The government organized the Sociedad Española de Automoviles de Turismo (SEAT) to produce Fiat-type cars. An Atomic Energy Commission was formed; the government announced Oct. 24 that the new agency would be headed by the chief of the General Staff, Gen. Juan Vigon; but it added that Spanish nuclear research would be devoted to peaceful uses.

Government sources indicated that the quality of life was improving. The government built 30,985 apartments. Infant mortality dropped from 6.89 to 6.26 per 100 live births. Yet many of the people of Spain apparently were unaware of the improvement. In 1951, 56,907 people left the country, while only 8,937 immigrated to Spain.

At the end of Oct. 1951, with economic conditions still improving only slowly, Spain devalued the peseta again. Dropping the system of variable exchange rates for exports, the commerce minister Oct. 31 announced a new rate of 21.9 pesetas to the dollar for all exports. A government directive, however, allotted to 5 groups of exports varying percentages of foreign currency that exporters were permitted to sell (for higher rates) on the Madrid free market. The devaluation, at least temporarily, had the desired effect of stimulating exports and curtailing imports. But since the system sanctioned a quasi-legal (free market) rate of 39.89 pesetas to the dollar, the 21.9 rate was not stable. The net long term result was increased inflation and later devaluation.

Foreign Loans, Credits & Trade

In 1951, for the first time since 1945, Spain sold more than it bought. The surplus of 237 million gold pesetas was the greatest single shift in the balance of payments since 1915. (The gold peseta is a fictitious unit used for international bookkeeping. It allows banks and economists to calculate and compare events regardless of the actual fluctuations in the international value of the currency. Spain used the gold peseta for all economic information during the years 1922-59. When first introduced, the gold peseta was worth about $4\frac{1}{2}$ paper pesetas. By 1960, however, the gold peseta was worth about 85 paper pesetas, *i.e.*, in 1960 the paper peseta had declined to about 1/20 its 1922 value.)

The government had negotiated important treaties that either increased Spanish trade or made available foreign exchange that permitted Spain to buy much needed capital goods.

U.S. Export-Import Bank credits to Spain totaling $12.2 million for purchases of cotton, fertilizer, tractors and the equipment for a fertilizer plant were announced Feb. 13. They were the first grants under a $62\frac{1}{2}$ million loan authorization. Paul A. Porter, acting U.S. Mutual Security Administrator for Europe, announced in Madrid Dec. 31 that Spain would be given U.S. financial aid under a bilaterial agreement. He disclosed no amount but said a U.S. mission would be established in Spain "soon" to finance mining, power, agriculture and transportation projects. He said there would be no U.S. pressure on Franco to "liberalize" his regime.

The satisfactory conclusion of Spanish-British trade negotiations had been announced by the British Treasury Feb. 24. Commenting on the resulting pact, British Board of Trade Pres. Harold Wilson predicted in the British House of Commons that Spain would not only maintain the 1950 level of raw material exports, but would actually increase the volume.

Other countries' wars had generally meant profit to Spain through the sale of Spain's wolfram, which warring nations needed for steel production. Germany and the Allies had competed in buying Spanish wolfram during World War II and had forced up prices and production. The demand for—and prices of—wolfram collapsed after World War II. With the beginning of the Cold War, demand prices and production went back up. Spain had produced 4,038 tons in 1943 at the height of

World War II but only 293 tons in 1945. In 1947–8 production doubled under Cold War demand. Spain produced 819 tons in 1949. Then the Korean War started and Spain produced 1,864 tons in 1951. The demand for Spanish mercury also increased, and Franco raised the price of the liquid metal. Although Spanish production of mercury in 1951 was less than half of the production in 1950, the income in terms of gold pesetas almost doubled.

The *N.Y. Times* reported Mar. 5, 1951 that the shipment of Spanish wolfram to the U.S. had been suspended because of high prices growing out of the Spanish desire "to cash in" on U.S. rearmament. The price of Spanish wolfram rose from $2,300 a short ton in late 1950 to $4,740 delivered in the U.S. But the Spanish government had set a new minimum price of $4,970 before shipment from Spain. It also barred payment in cash, demanding compensating shipments of other strategic metals. Spain had also raised its price for mercury (in which it dominated world output) from $55 a "standard flask" (34½ kilograms) to $200.

Despite the U.S. anger at Franco's increase in the price of wolfram and mercury, the shipments were resumed, the U.S. continued to buy the metals, and the U.S. continued to grant credits to Spain. The U.S. Export-Import Bank Mar. 16 announced a $5 million credit to Spain for the purchase of U.S. wheat. The Export-Import Bank July 9 announced a $5¾ million credit to Spain for the purchase of U.S. coal for Spain's steel and coking plants and for additional purchases of U.S. wheat. A 3d Export-Import Bank credit to Spain, announced July 20, provided $7½ million for the improvement of the Spanish railway system. The Export-Import Bank lent Spain $5.6 million Aug. 7 for the development of hydroelectric power and mineral production.

The U.S. Economic Cooperation Administration (ECA) disclosed Nov. 7, in its 39th report, that the ECA had approved loans to Spain totaling $45,832,000 during the period Sept. 6, 1950 to Aug. 31, 1951. The $16,668,000 balance of the loan voted by Congress in Aug. 1950 was still available for use as the ECA approved Spanish programs. Among approved loans itemized in the report: $7½ million for the Spanish National Railways (RENFE), $6.7 million for steel and fertilizer plants, $4,101,000 for electric power stations, $4,831,000 for mineral production, $5 million for cotton, $3½ million for fertilizers, $3,450,000 for tractors and spare parts, $7¼ million for wheat, $3½ million for coal. The U.S. Congress voted Spain an additional $100 million Oct. 20.

Since Britain was Spain's best customer, Spain sought an understanding with the English-dominated sterling bloc. Negotiations in Madrid ended with an announcement Dec. 21 of a 2-year sterling payments agreement detailing the method of balancing accounts in sterling and pesetas. It was expected that as a result of the agreement the volume of trade and payments would exceed $112 million in each direction. The announcement noted that both sides recognized the importance of maintaining supplies of raw materials and other essential goods. It indicated that there had been some strain in economic relations: the Spanish representative had complained of British restrictions on the import of Spanish fruit, mainly oranges, and manufactured items, mainly cloths, while the British delegate had indicated dissatisfaction at the decline of British exports to Spain. The announcement said Spain had promised to buy more sterling-area goods provided that Spain maintained a high level of sterling earnings.

The pattern of Spanish trade, according to economic authorities, showed Spain to be an underdeveloped country. Its major income-producing exports were fruit (oranges, lemons, limes), minerals (iron, mercury) and food (tomatoes, wheat, rice). The only manufactured items of importance were cloth (cotton, wool, silk) and books. Also of importance were processed foods such as olive oil, wine and canned or dried seafood. Spanish shotguns had an excellent reputation among hunters, but the Spanish arms and ammunition industry had never played a significant role in Spain's foreign trade. Starting in 1950 Spanish arms salesmen attempted to secure foreign outlets for Spanish arms. The first large scale order came Aug. 2, 1951, when the West German government announced in Bonn the purchase of Spanish-made automatic rifles and ammunition to equip 1,500 West German policemen.

Strikes & Government Response

Fresh signs of unrest began to appear in Barcelona after Feb. 3, 1951, when the government increased the streetcar fares. Several underground groups began to organize. Pamphlets calling for a Mar. 1 boycott of the streetcars began to appear Feb. 8 along the Ramblas (main street in Barcelona). Posters calling for a boycott appeared throughout the city by Feb. 26. Dr. Eduardo Baeza Alegria, the civil governor of the city, asked Gen. Juan Bautista Sánchez González, the captain general of Barcelona, whether the military was ready to maintain law and order, but Sánchez González categorically refused to use troops to enforce peace.

The boycott started at dawn Mar. 1. By Mar. 3, according to Max

Gallo in *Histoire de l'Espagne Franquiste,* Baeza Alegria was ready to capitulate but waited for approval from Madrid. The fare increase was suspended Mar. 6.

The Congress of Falangist Unions convened in Madrid Mar. 6 in an atmosphere of tension. Some members apparently wanted to remove Franco from power. Pope Pius XII Mar. 11, the last day of the congress, broadcast to the unionists a message reminding them of the Church's position on the rights of workers. To some it almost seemed as though the pope had joined in supporting a revolution against Franco. (The international labor movement had protested for years against repressive measures the Spanish government employed to prevent the establishment of free labor unions.)

The day after the pope spoke to the Falangist unionists, a general strike started in Barcelona and adjacent industrial communities. The walkout, beginning Mar. 12, involved about 300,000 workers, who marched down the Paseo de Gracia to the Plaza de Catalunya (one of the city's largest squares). The police clashed several times with workers and students who had joined the demonstration. The incidents included an attack by dock workers on a train, an attempt to set fire to the City Hall, the burning of an ambulance, the overturning of streetcars and autos and the ambushing of the mayor. 3 persons were killed, 21 injured (including the mayor) and about 400 arrested. Most factories and textile mills in and around Barcelona were forced to close for a day, as were shops, offices and banks. Streetcars were stopped almost completely, but taxis and other forms of transportation were not bothered.

Civil Gov. Baeza Alegria the evening of Mar. 12 issued a statement attributing the strike to members of the outlawed CNT (Anarchist-backed Confederación Nacional del Trabajo), POUM (Trotskyist-leaning Partido Obrero Unificado Marxista) and PSUC (Partido Socialista Unificado de Catalunya). Similar statements were made by the Falange party newspaper *Arriba* and the Falange labor paper *Pueblo.* The Falange syndical (labor union) organization appealed to the workers to return to their jobs. The authorities stated that strike orders, purporting to have originated from syndical headquarters, were false.

By Tuesday morning Mar. 13 the Guardia Civil had full control of the streets of Barcelona and about half the workers were back at work. Meanwhile, a government spokesman in Madrid announced that the government intended to use all power available to supress lawlessness: striking workers would be dismissed immediately, and drastic measures would be taken against any employer who paid strikers for the time lost. The spokesman said that the government sympathized with the workers but that life in Spain was "less stringent than . . . in other states at the present time" and that, since the government was doing all it could to improve working conditions, there was little reason for the disturbances.

Barcelona was back to normal Mar. 14. To insure stability, the government had ordered 800 troops from 5 warships, including the cruiser *Mendez Nuñez*, to enter the city Mar. 13, and it had rushed 3,000 *Policia Armada* (special riot police) to Barcelona from Madrid and Zaragoza. The police arrived early Mar. 14. Workers in Tarrasa, Badalona, Pueblo Nuovo and Mataro stayed out until Mar. 15, while textile workers in Manresa refused to return under any conditions. The government closed the Manresa plants Apr. 28 and ordered a full investigation of conditions.

In response to government charges that the strike had been Communist-inspired, a spokesman for the Spanish Republican exile government in Paris insisted that the worker's actions were a "popular protest against the regime." Sergio Vilar reported in *Protagonistas de la España Democratica*, however, that Spanish Communist Party leader Gregorio López Raimundo was arrested during the demonstrations.

Why did the strike end so quickly? Former Republican diplomat Elena de La Souchere answered in *An Explanation of Spain* that "one more step and there would . . . [have been] open rebellion, [and] no one cared to begin a contest of strength." Impartial observers of the event, however, said that the workers returned because they felt they had the support of both the Falange and the Church in their struggle for better conditions. The workers, according to these observers, saw the refusal of Barcelona Capt. Gen. Juan Bautista Sánchez González to employ regular troops, the freeing of 40 workers who had organized the Mar. 1 streetcar boycott and the rescinding of the fare hike as signs that they could achieve their goals without violence.

Dr. Gregorio Modrego Casaus, archbishop of Barcelona, and Capt. Gen. Sánchez González, who, according to Stanley Payne in *Politics and the Military in Modern Spain*, "openly enjoyed the discomfiture of the regime's political appointees," appealed to the Madrid government Mar. 16 to permit all strikers, except arrested ringleaders, to receive pay for the time lost because they had been deceived by professional agitators and Communist agents. Madrid officials declared Mar. 17 that, despite earlier rulings, workers would be permitted to work overtime to make up the lost pay. It was also announced that all those arrested, save suspected ringleaders, would be released immediately. Madrid radio announced Mar. 18 that Dr. Eduardo Baeza

Alegria had been relieved of his post as civil governor Mar. 16 and had been replaced by Gen. Felipe Acedo Colunga, judicial counsel at the Air Ministry. Other government changes included the appointment of Sanz Catalan as syndical head of Barcelona and the shifting of Hierro Martinez from civil governor of La Coruña to police inspector-general in Barcelona. Foreign reporters stated that the workers felt that they had won a major victory.

Raimundo Fernández Cuesta, secretary-general of the Falange, asserted Mar. 20 that the disturbances had been caused by "immoral speculation and the desire of enrichment." Franco, in a speech Mar. 28, blamed profiteers and speculators for high food prices. He ordered a crackdown on black marketers Apr. 7.

The outcome in Barcelona apparently encouraged workers in other parts of Spain. In Spain's Basque country (the provinces of Alava, Guipúzcoa, Navarra and Vizcaya) a strange alliance was being formed. The Paris-based Basque Republican Nationalist Party, the clandestine *Solidaridad* (Basque Christian Union organization), the Church-backed HOAC (Brotherhood of Workers of Catholic Action), local priests, various Basque nationalists and even some disgruntled Carlists began to plan a strike.

Strikes first started in the Basque port cities of Bilbao and San Sebastián as well as in some interior industrial centers of Vizcaya and Guipúzcoa provinces Apr. 23 and then spread to the less industrialized Basque provinces of Álava and Navarra. Clandestine Basque organizations had circulated leaflets calling for a 48-hour work stoppage starting Apr. 23 in demands for a 50% wage increase, price controls and measures to improve the "chaotic economic situation." The strikes started Apr. 23 in the large steel, iron, cement, paper and armament plants as well as naval dockyards. While government sources assert that only 50,000 workers went on strike, the Paris-based Basque government-in-exile and several foreign correspondents claim that more than 250,000 workers were on strike. The workers rejected a demand by Vizcaya civil governor Riestra Díaz to return to work or face dismissal and other penalties.

The industrial workers were joined Apr. 24 by railroad workers and by workers in shops and offices; bank officials adopted a "go-slow" movement. Few disorders were reported even though some 500 workers were arrested.

As planned, the workers returned to their jobs Apr. 25, but when the government refused to release workers arrested Apr. 24, the strike began again Apr. 26. When the strikers refused to return to work, the government Apr. 28 ordered the dismissal of all strikers and ordered troops from the cruiser *Almirante Cervera* to restore order. Government sources claimed Apr. 29 that various "agitators" had urged a general strike on May Day in protest against penalties imposed on workers who had taken part in demonstrations. By Apr. 30 order had been restored in Vizcaya and Guipúzcoa provinces, and no general strike took place May Day.

The wave of strikes, however, moved inland to Álava and Navarra provinces. Unlike the coastal provinces of Vizcaya and Guipúzcoa and the province of Barcelona, always considered volatile and radical, Álava was conservative and Navarra traditionalist. The appearance of red-bereted *Requetes* (conservative troops loyal to the Carlist monarchist faction) among strikers in traditionalist Pamplona was said to indicate the depth of dissatisfaction with the government.

In protest against the rising cost of living and the black market, 30,000 workers in Pamplona (capital of Navarra) and an unstated number in Vitoria (capital of Alava) went on strike May 7. The number of strikers in Pamplona rose May 8 to 35,000, almost the entire male work force; all factories were closed, and almost all public services were shut down. The strikers clashed with police May 8, 9 and 10. 56 people were reported injured and 300 arrested. The strike ended May 12 after the authorities yielded to demands for increased rations and a "serious effort" to lower prices. The government also promised that strikers would suffer no penalties and that all those arrested would be released.

Franco responded to the unrest in several ways. He instituted some reforms; he tried to convince the workers that they were better off than most other workers in the world, and he used the police.

In a speech to peasant delegates in Madrid May 12 Franco condemned the strikes as "crimes against the motherland," as harmful to Spanish interests and as aiding foreign elements seeking to undermine Spanish prosperity. Franco singled out the British Broadcasting Co., which he claimed was in the "hands of Freemasonry," as a special enemy of Spain. He held that the machinery for settling industrial disputes was more advanced in Spain than in other countries. He added that the government had done its best to improve the conditions of the workers and the peasants. Admitting that much remained to be done, Franco insisted that "we cannot perform miracles" and that Spain could achieve prosperity only through hard work and discipline. In a statement released May 13, Franco promised that his government would take all possible measures to reduce unemployment and improve living conditions.

Meanwhile the police had been arresting suspected strike leaders in

Catalunya and the Basque provinces. Police authorities announced May 15 that 2 of those arrested were "Marxist agents" who carried papers proving that the strikes had been planned by Spanish Communists in France and Basque nationalists in the Basque provinces. The police announced May 16 the arrest of 15 men alleged to be members of the underground Confederación Nacional del Trabajo (CNT), the pre-Civil War Anarchist-supported labor union, who were accused of attempting to organize a May Day demonstration in Barcelona. Officials reported May 17 that 10 members of the illegal Spanish Communist Party, who had recently entered Spain from France, had been apprehended. The government announced May 19 that at least 50 individuals would be tried on charges of illegal revolutionary activity. Interior Min. Blas Pérez González disclosed May 19 that 9 "agents" and "ringleaders" responsible for the Vitoria demonstrations had been jailed, and that the government had "concrete evidence" that Bayonne-(France)-based Basque-government-in-exile funds as well as funds from the Spanish Communist Party in Toulouse had been used to support the disturbances.

Monarchists in Madrid attacked the alleged corruption of the Falange-controlled labor unions and called for a "white strike," *i.e.*, not a positive strike (illegal), but a boycott of transportation facilities since no law required people to use public transportation. As one underground newspaper put it, "the white strike will demonstrate that the government governs badly."

The "white strike" was preceeded by the clandestine circulation of handbills calling for the "supression of the existing syndical organization and the abolition of abuses in food distribution." 300,000 Madrileños then took part in a boycott of public transportation May 22. Since the handbills had declared that "no Spaniard with dignity should go to a café, bar, movie-house or theater," the city's places of entertainment were emptied. Foreign reporters noted that even habitués of the 6 sidewalk cafés took their drinks at home. Reports on the effectiveness of the demonstration varied: many authorities agreed that few members of the middle class walked to work; the government admitted that 75% of the working class supported the strike; but former Republican diplomat Elena de La Souchere said in *An Explanation of Spain* that 95% of the workers joined. The arrests reported were those of 22 "ringleaders" apprehended May 21.

Franco began a tour of poor sections of southern Spain June 6 and promised that his government would solve the economic problems soon.

U.S. Adm. Forrest Sherman arrived in Madrid July 16 to open

direct U.S.-Spanish negotiations. The prospect of unlimited American aid bolstered the Franco government. Elena de La Souchere reported that once the middle and upper classes realized that the continuation of the Franco dictatorship would not prevent U.S. aid to Spain, they "drifted back toward the established regime."

In mid-summer it started to rain. The drought that had plagued Spain since 1949 was over. By fall the reservoirs were ⅔ filled, and a bumper crop was harvested. The rains and Adm. Sherman's mission were said to have brought Spain at least temporary relief from the economic plight that had sent rioters into the streets.

Political Opposition

Impartial observers agreed that there was no effective Leftist opposition in Spain during 1951 despite government charges that a secret Leftist conspiracy had organized the riots. While some Communists and Anarchists had slipped into the country from France, their effectiveness had been curtailed by the French crack-down on anti-Franco organizations.

The Spanish Communist underground called through a Cominform publication June 8 for a "national-front" merger of anti-Franco elements in and outside Spain to overthrow the Franco regime. But chances of such a united opposition were ended when the liberal monarchists deserted the National Alliance of Democratic Forces, an underground organization established by the remnant of the pre-Civil War political parties that favored the Republic. The liberal monarchists had agreed to join the alliance on a platform of first removing Franco, then worrying about the type of government to be established. Elena de La Souchere asserted in *An Explanation of Spain* that the liberal monarchists had withdrawn from overt opposition to the Franco regime after Franco promised to make government changes that would favor a quick restoration of the monarchy. According to de La Souchere, Adm. Forrest Sherman's visit and the prospect of U.S. Aid permitted Franco to renege on the promise with impunity.

There was little effective monarchist activity during 1951. Duke Gabriel de Maura wrote clandestine pamphlets. When *ABC*, the leading monarchist newspaper (and one of the world's great newspapers) acted too independently (by printing articles supporting the monarchists), the government forced the owner, the Marquis Torcuato Luca de Tena, to hire a government official as editor. The frustration of the monarchists led to a worsening of relations between Franco and Don Juan, pretender to the throne, who demanded in a letter to Franco July 10 that he (Juan) be made king and that all restrictions on personal liberty in Spain be abolished.

The Falange criticized the government in March and supported the Barcelona strike and boycott, but it avoided open opposition in the spring and summer. Franco promoted several veteran Falangists in government administrative shifts announced Sept. 19. In a major change, José Solís Ruís replaced Fermin Sanz Orrio as head of the government's national labor organization.

The only strong voice of opposition came from the Church. A collective pastoral letter circulated June 3 condemned "modern totalitarianism which bestows absorbing and unlimited powers on the government authority." Led by Enrique Cardinal Plá y Deniel, archbishop of Toledo, Dr. Marcelino Olaechea, archbishop of Valencia, Angel Herrera y Oria, bishop of Málaga, Pablo Gurpide, bishop of Bilbao, and Dom Aurelio María Escarre, abbot of Montserrat, the Church demanded social and economic reforms ranging from establishing free Catholic trade unions to replacing the Falangist unions and to legalizing the Basque and Catalan languages. Archbishop Olaechea published the results of an investigation of working conditions in his archdiocese: the workers, he claimed, lived in slums, faced constant hunger and were paid subsistence wages. In Málaga, Valencia and Sevilla, clerics attempted to train priests to go into the countryside to organize workers. While most opposition prelates spoke in terms of the need to defend Catholic liberties and discounted talk of direct political action, the bishop of Málaga, who had been a leader of CEDA (Confederación Española de Derechas Autonomas) and editor of *El Debate* (the Christian Democrat newspaper), prepared for direct political confrontation with the Falange syndicals by openly supporting HOAC (Hermandades Obreras de Acción Católica), the Church-supported labor organization founded by Plá y Deniel.

Many authorities agree that only the army could have presented the *caudillo* with serious opposition but that, as Stanley Payne indicates in *Politics and the Military in Modern Spain*, most military men were so pleased by the prospect of new equipment from the U.S. that they feared to upset the apple cart. Franco had maintained the loyalty of the 25,000 officers by allowing them to receive full pay even though many were well above the retirement age. "Franco's elderly cronies," Benjamin Welles reported in *Spain: The Gentle Anarchy*, "enjoy dignities and prestige, soldier-chauffeured cars and free homes" and are elected "to the boards of banks and industrial empires, where their monthly emoluments may range between $2,000 and $3,000." Some army officers, Payne indicated, were permitted to dabble in politics.

Gen. Juan Bautista Sánchez González, who had defied the civil authorities during the Barcelona strike, was permitted to make contact with liberal monarchists and assume the role of defender of civil liberties. Gen. Rafael García Valiño, who, some authorities claim, was involved in various political deals, was removed from Spain Mar. 30 when he was appointed high commissioner of Spanish Morocco to replace Lt. Gen. José Enrique Varela, who died in Tetuan Mar. 24. Some observers said that the appointment was made to remove the general from Spanish politics.

Military Build-Up

Franco's supporters had claimed that Spain could put an army of 2½ million men into the field. Military observers commented that, except for a few Spanish-produced arms, most army equipment was obsolescent. Vice Adm. Luis Carrero Blanco, in *El Nuevo Estado Español*, described the Spanish fleet as "antiquated and useless." (The largest warship in the navy was the 10,000-ton cruiser *Canarias*, built in 1912.) The Spanish air force, with a proud tradition (Juan de la Cierva had fathered the autogiro; Franco's brother Ramón was the first pilot to solo across the south Atlantic), had no modern planes.

Furthermore, the Spanish army was one of the most underpaid in the world. A pay scale introduced Jan. 1, 1949 and in effect until 1956 provided the following annual salaries (given in dollars at a rate of 25 pesetas to the dollar):

Rank	Salary	Rank	Salary
Captain general	$2,400	Brigadier general	1,112
Lieutenant general	1,640	Colonel	840
Major general	1,400	2d lieutenant	364

With salaries so low, many Spanish officers took civilian jobs on the side, became involved in black market operations—or did both.

Despite Spain's limited resources, Franco expressed his determination to create an effective army. His cabinet announced July 21, 1951 that it intended to build up Spain's armed strength "within the means which foreign collaboration permits."

The Cortes Dec. 18 approved a record budget of 22,762,147,700 pesetas ($1.1 billion at the official rate of exchange). 9 billion pesetas were earmarked for the armed forces. Of the total budget, the army received approximately 19%, the air force 8% and the navy 6%.

While most Spanish military and naval officers appeared pleased with the determination to build up the forces, there was at least one "Young Turk" who was not. A 3000-word report criticizing waste and

inefficiency in the Spanish government and armed forces had been
submitted to the Cortes Nov. 1 by Lt. Col. Luis Serrano de Pablo an
air force commander in the Canary Islands and member of the Falange's
National Council. (Serrano later continued his objections on the floor
of the Cortes, but after an early 1952 speech objecting to the wasting
of Spain's slender resources on the military, Serrano was removed from
the Cortes.)

Cabinet Changes

Franco July 20, 1951 announced the first major shake-up in his
cabinet since 1945. Franco remained as chief of state and president of
the government. His cabinet ministers were: *Alberto Martin Artajo,
Foreign Affairs; *Blas Pérez González, *Interior;* *José Antonio Girón,
Labor; *Gen. Eduardo González Gallarza, *Air;* Gen. Agustín Muñoz
Grandes, *Army;* Adm. Salvador Moreno Fernández, *Navy;* Antonio
Iturmendi Bañales, *Justice;* Francisco Gómez y de Llano, *Finance;*
Joaquín Planell Riera, *Industry;* Manuel Arburúa de lo Miyar, Com-
merce; Rafael Cavestany y de Anduaga, *Agriculture;* Joaquín Ruiz
Jiménez, *Education;* Count Fernando de Vallellano, *Public Works;*
Gabriel Arias Salgado, *Information and Tourism;* Adm. Luis Carrero
Blanco, *Undersecretary to the President of the government;* †Raimundo
Fernández Cuesta, *minister without portfolio in charge of Falangist
party affairs.*

According to observers most of the members of the new cabinet
did not speak to one another outside of the cabinet and held divergent
views of Spain's future. It was also noted that, by increasing the size
of the cabinet from 12 to 16 (the commerce and industry portfolio was
divided into 2 positions; Franco added a minister without portfolio in
charge of the Falange and a minister of information and tourism, and
the undersecretary to the president of the government was raised to
cabinet rank), Franco could enlarge the scope of opinion.

The incumbent foreign minister, Alberto Martin Artajo, was a
member of the outlawed Christian Democratic Party and an ally
of Bishop Angel Herrera of Málaga, a leading supporter of HOAC
(Hermandades Obreras de Acción Catolica). The incumbent labor
minister, José Antonio Girón, was a leader of the Falange's Joseantonioist faction and opposed to both HOAC and the monarchy. Of the new
ministers, Army Min. Agustín Muñoz Grandes was a Falangist, ex-
commander of the "Blue Division" (which had aided Hitler on the

---

*Incumbent   †Former justice minister

Russian front) and, according to Stanley Payne in *Politics and the Military in Modern Spain*, one of the few officers "not involved in black market operations or other forms of financial corruption." Count Fernando de Vallellano, public works minister, an active monarchist, had been mayor of Madrid. Antonio Iturmendi Bañelas, minister of justice, was a Carlist opposed to Vallellano's attempts to restore the Bourbonist monarchy; he also opposed the liberal attitudes of HOAC and the Christian Democratic Party. Education Min. Joaquín Ruiz Jiménez, the youngest member of the cabinet (38), was a leader of the Left-Christian Democrats and a supporter of HOAC. Information & Tourism Min. Gabriel Arias Salgado was a conservative Falangist opposed to the policies of Labor Min. Girón and Foreign Min. Martin Artajo. Adm. Luis Carrero Blanco, also a conservative Falangist, was reported to have had connections with Opus Dei. The air, navy, commerce, industry, agriculture and finance ministers were specialists and professionals apparently not involved in politics.

In a final appointment July 22, José Ibañez Martín, education minister in the former cabinet (he had led the fight to reach an understanding with the Church on education) was appointed president of the Council of the Realm, which advises the government of legislation.

José María Gil Robles, exiled monarchist leader and adviser to Spanish pretender Don Juan, said in Lisbon July 21: The cabinet was "more Nazi and anti-democratic than ever. Franco has once again defied the Western democracies."

Diplomatic Recognition & UN Relations

Turkey and Spain agreed Jan. 1, 1951 to exchange ambassadors instead of ministers. Spain completed arrangements for the exchange of ambassadors with France and Britain Feb. 7 and with Denmark Jan. 15.

The U.S. established full diplomatic relations with Spain Mar. 1 when Amb. Stanton Griffis presented his credentials to Franco. Spain recognized the military government of Bolivia May 19. South Africa and Spain agreed May 25 to exchange diplomatic representatives for the first time. Spain established diplomatic relations with Pakistan Sept. 2 and Iraq Sept. 3. The pope welcomed the new Spanish ambassador Nov. 13 and urged the readmission of Spain to the family of nations, a goal that, for practical purposes, was already a fact.

Spain slowly took its place on various UN subsidiary organizations although it was not yet a member of the UN. The UN Economic & Social Council (ECOSOC) at its meeting in Santiago, Chile Mar. 21 had lifted the ban on granting ECOSOC consultative status to non-governmental organizations that have Spanish members. The vote was 11–5 (Soviet bloc, Mexico and Uruguay opposed; India and France abstaining). The Food & Agriculture Organization, which moved from Washington to Rome Apr. 12, accepted Spain as a member, and Spain was admitted to membership in the World Health Organization (WHO) at the opening of WHO's 4th session in Geneva. (Mexico was the only state to object to Spain's membership). The International Civil Aviation Organization (ICAO) assembly in Montreal elected Spain to the ICAO council June 18.

The U.S. & NATO

U.S. relations with Spain were generally presumed to be predicated on the American belief that the U.S. needed Spanish bases to protect Western Europe and the U.S.

Most U.S. military men had agreed at this time that should there be war with the USSR, the U.S. could not bring sufficient force to block a Red advance to Normandy. According to this view: The allies might make a desperate stand on the Rhine, but the Red Army could cross the river with little difficulty. Even if Tito of Yugoslavia, with his 50 divisions, joined the allies, the Red Army could not be stopped before the English Channel. Only the Alps and the Pyrenees could afford the U.S. sufficient time to launch a counter-strike. While U.S. bases in Germany and France could be overrun quickly, bases in southern Italy, Libya, French Morocco and the wild mountains of southeastern Turkey could be held because of their inaccessibility; the bases in Italy and Turkey, however, could be neutralized by Soviet air power. This would leave the U.S. with only African sites. But if Spain joined the allies, the U.S. could maintain a base in Europe. Furthermore, in 1951 the USSR did not have the power to attack Spanish bases.

The U.S. Navy also sought a base in Spain. Spain controlled the 32-mile Strait of Gibraltar and had excellent ports from which the U.S. 6th Fleet could operate. Naval bases in Spain would be relatively safe from the Red Air Force, according to U.S. Navy planners. When questioned as to why Spain was preferable to Morocco, where the U.S. had been given the right to build an air base (the U.S. opened its Nouaceur Air Force Base near Casablanca July 14), military and naval experts cited 2 problems: (1) the growing anticolonial movement in Morocco might force France to abandon the protectorate, and it was doubtful whether the U.S. could remain without French support; (2) Morocco offered no servicable port for U.S. naval operations.

Gen. Dwight D. Eisenhower, who had been selected to command

NATO forces, was urged by Premier António Salazar of Portugal Jan. 16, at Lisbon's Portela airport, to include Spain in the NATO forces. Salazar said Spain could raise a 2½-million man army in the event of war.

Franco, however, said in an interview with Karl von Wiegand of the Hearst newspaper chain Feb. 13 that "a direct accord of collaboration with the U.S. would be less complicated than Spanish inclusion in the Atlantic Pact." Franco had impressed U.S. authorities with Spanish hospitality Jan. 9 when parts of the U.S. 6th Fleet stopped at Barcelona. Vice Adm. John J. Ballentine was given a warm reception by Spanish civil and military authorities.

Members of the U.S. Senate appeared to be more interested in Spain's joining NATO than in a politically unpopular direct U.S.-Spanish agreement. The Senate recommended Apr. 4 that Spanish troops be used for European defense. Spanish military authorities, however, indicated more interest in direct U.S.-Spanish negotiations than in joining NATO, and they began to pressure Franco to reach some sort of understanding with Washington. It was reported in Washington Mar. 25 that Franco had offered the U.S. a Spanish military alliance in exchange for modern weapons. The Spanish army paraded only pre-World War II weapons when the 12th anniversary of Franco's Civil War victory was celebrated in Madrid Apr. 2.

Pres. Truman, said to have misgivings about Franco still, continued to block Marshall Plan aid to Spain. (The President could do little by use of Presidential powers since U.S. funds were granted to the European Community, and the European states distributed the grant.) Despite Truman's purported feelings, there was steady pressure from the Pentagon. Gen. Omar N. Bradley, U.S. Joint Chiefs of Staff chairman, said June 2, for example, that the Atlantic bloc "would be better off" with Spain in the alliance.

8 members of the U.S. Senate Foreign Relations Committee, led by Sen. Theodore F. Green (D., R.I.), visited Spain July 12–13 on a 2-day fact-finding mission. The members of Green's committee were Sens. Owen Brewster (R., Me.), Guy M. Gillette (D., Ia.), Bourke B. Hickenlooper (R., Ia.), Brien McMahon (D. Conn.), John J. Sparkmen (D., Ala.), H. Alexander Smith (R., N.J.) and Alexander Wiley (R. Wis.). They conferred with Franco, Spanish Foreign Min. Martín Artajo, various Spanish civil and military officials and U.S. Amb. Stanton Griffis. At a press conference in Madrid July 12, Green said that since the West faced "a common threat that demands coordinated action," some people in the U.S. believed that Spain could make a "substantial contribution to this common defense."

Having agreed to a change in U.S. policy toward Spain, Truman permitted Adm. Forrest Sherman, U.S. chief of naval operations, to go to Madrid to open negotiations with Franco. Sherman, accompanied by his wife and his son-in-law, Lt. Comdr. John Fitzpatrick, arrived in Madrid July 16, met with Franco and saw Adm. Ramón Estrada (chief of the Spanish naval staff) July 17. Sherman went July 19 to Paris, where he visited Eisenhower's headquarters, flew to Naples to meet Adm. R. B. Carney and then died of a heart attack July 22. Sherman's visit to Spain gave rise to fresh reports that the U.S. government wanted Spain to join NATO or was seeking bases in Spain.

Even though both Amb. Griffis and Comdr. Fitzpatrick were present July 16 at the Prado Palace and July 18 at La Granja Palace, where Franco gave a garden party for his visitors, the U.S. government received no details of the conversation between Sherman and Franco. In *Spain: The Gentle Anarchy*, Benjamin Welles quoted Fitzpatrick as saying that Franco and Sherman had agreed to leave the "question of bases and military or economic aid to later negotiations."

U.S. State Secy. Dean G. Acheson asserted during a press conference July 18 that U.S. military experts agreed Spain "is of strategic importance to the general defense of Western Europe." Acheson added that "tentative and exploratory" conversations with the Spanish government had "the sole purpose of ascertaining what Spain might be willing and able to do which would contribute to the strengthening of the common defense against possible aggression." He emphasized that the possibility of a Spanish connection with NATO was not currently being discussed.

Truman conceeded at his press conference July 19 that U.S. policy towards Spain had changed "to some extent" but that "we haven't decided yet" to what extent. "These are preliminary conversations to find out just what our necessity is and what Spain is willing to do," Truman said. He disclosed that the change was on the advice of the Defense Department, not of the policy-making National Security Council.

An indication of the extent of the U.S.-Spanish discussions was given in the announcement July 22 that Spanish military students would be trained in U.S. military schools as a result of recent U.S.-Spanish defense talks.

The new U.S. positions was supported by various U.S. Congress members. Members of Sen. Theodore F. Green's Senate Foreign Relations Committee delegation, after touring Europe, returned to Washington July 23 and reported Franco's assurances to them that Spain could supply 2 million troops if the U.S. would arm them. They indorsed a

U.S.-Spanish defense agreement but warned the U.S. not to anger other Atlantic Pact members by trying to get Spain into NATO. Green and Sen. H. Alexander Smith proposed Aug. 5 that the U.S. sponsor a Mediterranean pact similar to the Atlantic pact to get Spain, Greece and Turkey (all facing some opposition for Atlantic Pact membership) into the Western defense system.

The basic opposition to the inclusion of Spain came from Britain and France. It was thought that the European powers feared that the U.S. commitment to Spain and Morocco would divert U.S. energy from the defense of West Germany and the Rhine. At his July 18 press conference, State Secy. Acheson attempted to remove that fear when he promised that Atlantic Pact countries would still have top priority for U.S. arms aid. He said that the U.S. intended to see that all of West Europe was "defended," not "liberated" after it was overrun.

The British and French governments had announced their opposition to a Spanish-NATO link July 16 while Adm. Sherman was in Madrid. The British spokesman asserted that "these views have from time to time been conveyed to the U.S. government, which is well aware that we still hold them." The French spokesman said in Paris that France would have "strong objections" to any U.S.-Spanish military agreement because such an agreement would indicate that the U.S. supported a regime whose totalitarian philosophy was contrary to NATO concepts. Such a pact, the official continued, could only embarass America's NATO allies.

The U.S.-Spanish talks touched off a debate in the British House of Commons July 25. Foreign Affairs Undersecy. Ernest Davies said: "It is the view of his majesty's government that the strategic advantages of establishing any closer association between Spain and the West are outweighed by the effects which such an association would have on the morale of the other members of the Western community. These views have been made known to the U.S. government who, however, take the contrary view. There is no question at present of Spain's admission to the North Atlantic Treaty. . . . [The U.S.'] present objective is to conclude a bilateral arrangement to secure facilities in ports and airfields for the defense of the West, but they are not pressing for the inclusion of Spain in the North Atlantic Treaty."

Davies was told by members of the Conservative opposition that "in these dangerous times strategic considerations should take precedence over political considerations." He was asked whether it would not be "more statesmanlike to create a new defensive association than to perpetuate an old ideological feud." Davies replied: "This is not a political question. It is a question of which is the best way of defending the West. We have taken our view because of the bad effect on morale of bringing Spain in and because we do not consider that strategically there would be advantages in bringing Spain in, certainly not until the West itself is fully armed." Davies was also asked why it was "good for morale to help a Communist dictatorship in Yugoslavia and to refuse to have anything to do with a non-Communist dictatorship in Spain." Davies said: "There is a very considerable difference between [the 2 governments] . . . . The Communist government in Yugoslavia under Marshal Tito was an ally of ours during the war, which Franco was not."

The position of the Left wing of Britain's Labor Party had been established by Aneurin Bevan, who had said July 22 that the British government should continue efforts to discourage the U.S. from making a defense alliance with Franco. He said Britain did not need to "accept the spiritual and moral leadership of the U.S."

The pressure by NATO members on the U.S. aroused Spanish anger. The Spanish government announced July 29 that it had protested to the British and French governments against "these new attempts at interference in a matter which concerns Spain's sovereign right to entertain direct relations with another power." The Spanish statement warned that the British and French governments "must be held responsible for this unfriendly attitude, which might prejudice the peaceful relations between our peoples."

Spanish newspapers, especially the Falange organ *Arriba*, began a press campaign against Britain and France; Spanish claims to Gibraltar and parts of French Morocco and Algeria were reasserted.

Dutch Defense Min. Cornelis Staf asserted Aug. 2 that while his government saw no room for Spanish association with NATO it could not object to independent U.S. approaches to Spain in the interest of U.S. security.

British opposition to U.S.-Spanish negotiations ended as a result of the Oct. 25 British elections, in which the Conservatives defeated the Labor Party. Sir Winston Churchill was returned as prime minister and Anthony Eden as foreign secretary. Churchill did not hide his dislike for Franco, but he uttered no objections to Spain's joining NATO. Churchill took the same attitude toward Franco that he had taken toward Stalin in 1941: to save the British Empire he would ally his country with either. (As early as Dec. 10, 1948, in a speech in the House of Commons, Churchill had cautioned those who opposed Franco that the Spanish "are proud people and rather than be spurned and dictated to by the outside world, [they will give their] allegiance to him [Franco] which he had never won before." Churchill's willingness to include Franco in the Western system did not mean, however, that Britain would sacrifice Gibraltar.)

In the fall of 1951 the Pentagon sent Maj. Gen. James Spry to Spain on an indefinite fact-finding mission. Before he left the U.S., the various services decided that they too needed information about Spain. The result was that instead of a small group of U.S. Army officers going quietly to Spain, about 100 members of the U.S. Army, Navy, Air Force and Marines flew to Madrid. Franco apparently assumed that the mission had come to discuss terms of a defense treaty. But Spry informed the Spanish that he and his fellow officers were just gathering data. For 6 weeks the U.S. officers and their Spanish counterparts traveled around the country. Then the Americans left, and no result of their travels was ever made public.

Improvements in the Spanish economy were recorded throughout 1952-3, but there were disappointments as well. A new Concordat with the Vatican, concluded in Aug. 1953, pledged state cooperation with the Church in Spain. During the complicated struggle involving Spain and France in Morocco, France deposed the Sultan Muhammad V and, despite Spanish objections, allowed his replacement with Mulay Muhammad bin Arafa. The U.S. concluded negotiations for military bases in Spain.

Lopsided Economic Recovery

Despite an increase in the annual national investment from a total of 25.8 billion pesetas in 1952 to 29.2 billion in 1953, industrial production, while generally improved, remained uneven.

Textile production increased from 111% of the 1929-31 average in 1952 to 137% in 1953 whereas the production of shoes decreased from 22.4 million pair in 1952 to 20.1 million pair in 1953. Cement production rose about 10% from 2.5 million tons to 2.8 million. Book production increased sharply after a decline in 1951; in 1952 some 3,455 different titles were produced, while the following year the number rose to 5,662. Shipbuilding had also declined from its high in 1951, but by 1953 it not only recovered but exceeded the 1951 mark. Truck production increased from 278 units in 1952 to 418 in 1953 and motorcycle output from 20,342 to 33,584, but bicycle production fell during the period from 119,379 to 116,956. Spain produced 47 tractors in 1953.

The government established an iron and steel company, Empresa Nacional Siderurgica S.A. (ENSIDESA), in 1953, with a capitalization of 1.4 billion pesetas ($35 million at the free rate of exchange). The National Institute of Industry (INI) put up 400 million pesetas and the rest came from 4 British concerns acting through various banks.

Electrical output increased from 319% of the 1929-31 average in 1951, to 362% in 1952 and 380% in 1953. Actual consumption increased from 6.26 billion kilowatt hours in 1951 to 7.16 billion in 1952 and 7.28 billion in 1953.

Perhaps the most significant economic improvement was in tourism. 1,485,000 visitors came to Spain in 1952, 1,710,000 in 1953. The profit on tourism in 1953 was $94 million. The tourist industry required new hotels, increased road facilities and more personnel. Eventually it became Spain's most lucrative industry. To attract U.S.

tourists, Spain agreed Jan. 21, 1952 to eliminate visa requirements for visiting Americans, effective Feb. 21, and the number of American tourists increased from 31,000 in 1950 and 45,000 in 1951 to 91,807 in 1952.

To increase its income from tourism and fully utilize the U.S. grants for industrial production, Spain had to improve its internal transportation system. The Spanish railway network, operated by the Red Nacional de los Ferrocarriles Españoles (RENFE), was obsolete. The tracks inadequate and under poor repair, and the rolling stock was old and in dangerous condition. While there were small steam engine repair shops scattered throughout Spain, only Orense, Madrid and Sevilla had shops capable of repairing diesel engines. There were no shops equipped for electrical engines. The net result was an increasing deficit in railroad operations—from 363 million pesetas in 1952 to 394 millions in 1953. Roads were in no better condition. Many roads, even those constructed after the Civil War, were so winding (there was a constant complaint from motorists that they could not see the road because of the turns), bumpy and narrow that speedy auto transportation was impossible. Because of the nature of Spanish topography, numerous bridges were necessary, but many were so rickety that truck transportation was impossible. In 1950 the government had announced a new highway development program, but as of Dec. 1953 there were no new highways.

The rugged topography made air transportation imperative. Even though Iberia Airlines showed a profit every year, except in 1950, Spanish facilities and equipment were substandard.

The fish catch rose. The catch of bacalao (an important item in the Spanish diet that usually has to be imported) was up from 30.7 million kilograms in 1952 to 32.1 million in 1953. 25.2 million kilos were imported in 1952, but in 1953, because of tight money, only 17.2 million kilos entered Spain. Thus, despite an increase in the catch, the per capita consumption declined from 1.97 kilos to 1.72.

Mine production largely improved. The net output of alum, nickel, cooper, coal, lead, potasium salt, superphosphates and wolfram increased, while zinc, mercury, and phosphate output declined. In some instances the net change was slight. Wolfram output rose from 2,736 tons in 1952 to 2,964 in 1953; mercury production declined from 1,525 tons to 1,505, potasium salts from 1,215 tons to 1,248 tons; superphosphate output rose from 1.2 million tons to 1.3 million while phosphate production dropped from 23.3 tons to 21.8.

Farm production declined despite an increase in the percentage of public expenditures invested in agriculture (11.6% in 1952 and 12.6%

in 1953). Production fell from 108.45% of the 1931–5 average in 1952 to 97.27% in 1953; wheat, potato and tomato production declined steadily from their 1951 highs. In 1953 only tobacco production and cotton output (which increased 150% over 1951 and 15% over 1952) defied the general trend.

Poor harvests in 1952 and 1953 notwithstanding, 1951's bumper crops and purchases of U.S. surplus wheat gave the government some flexibility in controlling food. Spain ended bread rationing and relaxed controls on meat and fats Apr. 1, 1952.

Franco had tried to stimulate exports and retard imports by manipulating the peseta's value during 1951. The devaluation of the peseta stimulated exports but did not inhibit imports. During 1952 and 1953 Spain imported 26% more than it exported. There was no great drain on the Spanish gold reserve only because of the foreign exchange received from tourism and the millions of dollars that Spaniards living abroad remitted to relatives in Spain.

It was widely agreed that Spain's economic ills were compounded by decisions based on political rather than economic considerations. For example, in what was considered an attempt to please the U.S., the Spanish government Jan. 12, 1952 terminated all trade in strategic materials with the Soviet bloc, and at the same time the government authorized an increase in the import of U.S.-produced motion pictures.

Another cause of the unfavorable balance of trade was Spain's rearmament program. The British government announced July 4, 1952 that it had lifted its embargo on the export of military equipment to Spain to allow the sale of surplus war material for civilian and military use. Laborites in Parliament objected July 7 to this action. This was the first change in British policy toward the Franco government since World War II. State Min. Selwyn Lloyd told Parliament that the continuation of the embargo would "deprive British firms of important commercial advantages" and that the export of obsolescent materials not needed by Britain and its associates was "desirable on economic grounds." Spain's military equipment was so antiquated, however, that what was considered obsolete by Western governments was up to date in Spain. But the British Foreign Office announced Dec. 15, 1953 it had also lifted a ban on the export of some modern military equipment to Spain. This action made it possible for Spain to buy older models of British jet fighter planes.

Despite its difficult economic position Spain fulfilled its international financial obligations in order to maintain its credit rating. The International Telephone & Telegraph Co. revealed in New York Sept. 10, 1952 that Spain had paid the balance of a $50 million 4% bond issue 8½ years ahead of schedule. Final payment on the bonds, given to IT&T in 1945 as payment for the nationalization of its Spanish installations, was made June 30.

The Spanish government made various efforts to help the average citizen. 34,497 government financed apartments were built in 1952 and 36,502 in 1953. Spanish medical service was improved; the infant mortality rate dropped from 6.26 to 5.47 per 100 live births in 1952 and to 5.28 in 1953. The government even helped establish cooperatives, but the cooperative movement was not very popular. In 1951 there were 4,585 coops with 924,783 associated families. In 1952 there were 4,858 coops with 1,074,422 families; by 1953 the number of coops had risen slightly to 4,968 with 1,115,839 families. The Instituto Nacional de Colonización brought irrigation to 15,992 acres of farm land in 1952 and to an additional 22,202 acres in 1953. To undo the plundering of Spain's once extensive forests, a massive program of reforestation had been contemplated after the Civil War. Although funds were lacking for the full plan, the government did begin a modest program. 181,963 acres were reforested in 1952 and another 279,745 acres in 1953.

One result of the various government expenditures was a jump in the public debt from 2 billion pesetas in 1951 to 6 billion in 1952. The debt was reduced to 5 billion in 1953.

Despite these efforts, living conditions were worse for many Spaniards. The inflation, which seemed to be halting in 1952, when the price level increased only 1% to 427.1, increased during 1953, when the price level rose to 457.5. Using the 1953 peseta as a standard of value, per capita wages decreased from 8,363 pesetas in 1952, to 8,000 in 1953, *i.e.*, about $200 a year using the free rate of the peseta which was 40 to the dollar. The European Economic Commission reported in 1953 that Spain's standard of living was still 10% to 30% below the Civil War level. Emigration, therefore, continued. 56,648 Spaniards left the country while only 13,964 immigrants entered in 1952, and 44,572 emigrated and only 15,299 immigrated in 1953.

Opposition

Following the 1951 riots Franco had cracked down on any positive open opposition. Harmless opposition, however, was tolerated.

Major strikes took place in Barcelona in Mar. 1952 and in Bilbao in Dec. 1953, but neither the domestic nor the foreign press reported any concrete facts about them. 30 Catalan Anarchists were brought before the military court in Barcelona in Feb. 1952 on charges of committing various types of anti-government acts. Death sentences were pronounced Feb. 7 on 11 "extremists" and Feb. 12 on 9 "leaders" among the 30. The other Anarchists received sentences of from 2 to 30 years in prison. The 11 Anarchists sentenced Feb. 7 were convicted of murder and robbery. 5 of them were executed by firing squad Mar. 14; the sentences of the 6 others were commuted to life imprisonment. The 9 "leaders" sentenced Feb. 12 were not executed, but no public disclosure of their fate was made. The Spanish Republican government-in-exile, in Paris, denounced the executions Mar. 15 and said that the deed showed "once more what the internal situation in Spain is like."

50 members of the illegal PSOE (Partido Socialista Obrera Español) were arrested in Feb. 1953, but no information as to their fate was made public.

Sometime in 1953 an architect's draftsman named Tomás Centeño, 40, was arrested by the *Brigada Social y Política*—the secret police. Benjamin Welles asserted in *Spain: The Gentle Anarchy* that Centeño died as a result of "the 3d degree." During the interrogation, Centeño admitted that he was general secretary of the illegal Socialist labor union UGT (Unión General del Trabajadores). The secret police was considered very effective against conspirators. Many secret organizations had been penetrated by the police, just as many open groups such as the army, the Church and the Falange had been penetrated by Socialists, anarchists and, above all, by Communists. As a result of police activity, many opposition leaders disappeared. Many deaths, like Centeño's, were attributed officially to suicide.

The Spanish Communist Party (PCE), led in exile by Dolores Ibarruri, widely known as La Pasionaria, did nothing overt during the period 1952–3 in the hope, according to observers, that "Spanish pride" would prevent the conclusion of the agreement with the U.S. The PCE, these observers said, held the view that should Franco insist on the treaty, he would be toppled by the obscurantist wing of the army and the Church led by Pedro Cardinal Segura y Sáenz, archbishop of Sevilla; if he failed to sign the treaty then, the PCE held, the misery of the people would force his overthrow. This PCE position was challenged by PCE leader Fernando Claudin, who claimed that, in the light of U.S. aid to Franco, the policy of the "Socialists, anarchists, Republicans and others," based on the hope of "liberation by the intervention of democratic nations," was bankrupt and that only an active PCE campaign would end Franco's dictatorship.

Among leaders and former leaders of the Falange, only ex-Falangist intellectual Dionisio Ridruejo, who had returned to Spain in 1951, openly spoke against the government in this period. Ridruejo received permission from Education Min. Joaquín Ruíz Gimenez in 1952 to establish a magazine *Revista* (Ruíz even granted *Revista* a small subsidy). Various intellectual Falangists such as Pedro Lain Entralgo and Antonio Tovar contributed articles, but Ridruejo told Sergio Vilar in *Protagonistas de la España Democratica* that "the censor made my life impossible, and the project had to be abandoned" after a few issues.

After vainly attempting to defeat the U.S.-Spanish agreement and a new Concordat ultimately signed with the Vatican Aug. 27, 1953, the Falange met Oct. 29, 1953 in what was called the First National Congress of the Movement (some observers interpreted the change in name as an attempt by Franco to reduce Falangist influence in the country). The Falange leadership repeated old proposals for more nationalization, a better distribution of the national wealth and other objectives.

In what some observers called a "placebo" for the Joseantonioist wing (anti-monarchist and anti-capitalist group) of the Falange, Franco ordered José Antonio Girón, the Joseantonioist Falangist labor minister, to implement a new labor law Nov. 1, 1953. The legislation had been authorized in 1947 but had remained dormant because the regime had considered inadvisable to institute "prematurely a delicate instrument of such political novelty." (Elizabeth Wiskemann insisted in *Fascism in Italy* that Franco constantly vetoed Falangist plans because he disliked fascism.) The legislation decreed the establishment of Mussolini-style councils of employers and employes (*jurado de empresa*) in commercial establishments employing more than 50 workers at any one place. Since the idea was so experimental and unusual, it was decided that the law would be enforced only at businesses that had 1,000 or more employes as of Jan. 1, 1953. Deviating from the Italain model, each *jurado* would consist of the owner, or manager, who was to act as chairman, and from 4 to 12 elected representatives of the workers; the number of workers depended on the size of the shop or factory (in the Italian system the council was tripartite, with the government being the 3d section). Each *jurado* was to meet at least once a month and was empowered to make recommendations to the management on matters such as production, efficiency, labor conditions, the prevention of accidents and the observance of social legislation. Even though the *jurado* was strictly advisory, the management was required to give it an annual account of the establishment's financial position and prospects. Strikes being illegal, the individual *jurado* could not enforce any suggestion.

The monarchist faction was disunited. The Bourbonists were reported to be courting Franco during this period, and even Don Juan retreated from his anti-Franco position. Diplomatic sources in Madrid reported Jan. 14, 1953 that Don Juan had sent Franco a conciliatory letter saying that the restoration of the Spanish monarchy would be feasible only "with Franco." Duke Jaime of Segovia, 43, oldest son of the late King Alfonso XIII, announced in Paris Mar. 1, 1953 that he was renewing his claim to the throne. He had surrendered his claim to his brother Don Juan in 1932 because he was a deaf mute and suffered from hemophilia. Since this renunciation, however, he had been taught to speak by his wife, Austrian opera singer Charlotte Tideman, whom he had married morganatically in 1949.

The only public voice of discord in the military during 1952-3 was that of Col. Luis Serrano de Pablo. It was disclosed May 12, 1952 that Serrano, Nationalist hero who had criticized Franco's financial policy in 1951, had been dropped from the National Council of Falange Party and consequently had lost his seat in the Cortes.

Various steps were taken by the regime to improve the army or at least to keep it quiet. In a move to make possible the advancement of ambitious younger officers, blocked by a top-heavy echelon of aging (and allegedly incompetent) senior officers, the government announced July 13, 1953 that army officers could retire on full pay. Only a few of the older officers took advantage of this offer. An army reorganization order announced by Franco July 17 reduced by 2 years the age limits for field officers and non-commissioned officers. It also provided for the transfer of many officers to army administration or civilian jobs. Franco said large numbers of officers no longer were needed in military posts. It was announced July 18 that all reserve officers could take full-time civilian jobs. As a result of these actions, some 2,000 officers above the rank of captain resigned from the army, while an unstated number moved from the active to the reserve list.

By the fall of 1953, according to observers, Franco had a better army with fewer officers. There was considerable consolidation, and the number of divisions was reduced from 24 to 18, made up of about 250,000 men. Meanwhile, Spanish equipment was being produced to accomodate American shells. The trimmed-down army held maneuvers in northern Spain Sept. 11-14 to test its ability to halt an aggressor crossing the Pyrenees from France.

Until Enrique Cardinal Plá y Deniel's attack on censorship in his 1950 pastoral letter, there had been no effective opposition to the rigid press controls. The National Council of the Catholic Press in 1952 submitted a list of demands for the relaxation of state control, but the government ignored it. The National Congress of the Spanish Press met in Madrid in 1953 and, for the first time, openly challenged governmental policy. The congress objected to the "extension of censorship to nonpolitical news," and, according to the International Press Institute publication *The Press in Authoritarian Countries*, demanded "the elimination of controls." The government at first did nothing. But faced with the deluge of tourists so needed by the Spanish economy, the government reconsidered its position. Americans, Englishmen, Frenchmen and Germans complained about not being able to buy the *N.Y. Times*, the London *Times*, *Le Figaro* or similar papers in Spain. Tourists held that living in Madrid was as bad as living in Moscow. To the government, the problem was that if foreigners could buy uncensored newspapers, Spaniards would soon pick them up. Franco, for the time, did not yield.

Amnesty

While the government either jailed members of the active opposition or removed them in other ways, Franco also freed former opponents no longer considered dangerous.

The government Feb. 2, 1952 announced an amnesty for crippled soldiers of the old Republican army living in exile. The Foreign Ministry Feb. 17 offered to repatriate veterans of the former Republican army living in France since the end of the Civil War. (It was estimated that there were 2,000.) The announcement specifically excluded from the offer those accused of "blood crimes." The statement promised that there would be no discrimination against repatriated men in eligibility for such social benefits as public assistance and medical treatment.

Franco paroled 45 political prisoners Feb. 18, 1952 and granted amnesty May 2, a day after a Eucharistic Congress convened in Barcelona, to all the estimated 30,000 prisoners in Spain except those deemed politically dangerous. Those serving terms of 2 years or less were freed, others had their terms reduced.

Church-State Conflict

With the exception of a small group of clerics led by Dr. Leopoldo Eijo y Garay, bishop of Madrid-Alcalá, Spanish clerics were held to be generally at odds with government policy.

A group considered reactionary, led by Pedro Cardinal Segura y Sáenz and personified by the ancient village priest in his 16th century garb, was interested largely in the preservation of the ancient forms; it opposed 20th century technology, the voice of the Vatican, the Falange and the Yankee dollar. William Ebenstein asserted in *Church and State in Franco Spain* that Segura's "ideal ... [was] the theocratic monarchy of the 16th century." Conservatives led by Enrique Cardinal Plá y Deniel worried about defending ancient morality but supported change led by the Church. Another group, led by Marcelino Olaechea, archbishop of Valencia, Dr. Casimiro Morcillo, bishop of Bilbao, and Dom Aurelio María Escarre, abbot of Montserrat, held that the immorality was a result of the political and social malaise. The workers "think themselves slaves, they seek for pleasure to lighten their yoke," Olaechea wrote in *Ecclesia* in Dec. 1951. "Once upon a time," he continued, "slaves were bought, today they are rented." Another group of priests and monks, considered radicals, followed the teachings of Dr. Angel Herrera y Oria, bishop of Málaga. They helped organize the Hermandades Obreras de Acción Católica (HOAC) as a counterweight to the Falange unions and went into the countryside to "stir up" the masses. Younger clerics, like some of the old ones, spoke of social justice and condemned the inaction of the establishment.

The most persistent voice in opposition to Franco policies, according to observers, was that of Pedro Cardinal Segura y Sáenz. Segura, originally appointed archbishop of Toledo by King Alfonso XIII, was an active defender of the *status quo* until the overthrow of the monarchy. His opposition to the Spanish Republic was so great that the papal legate had persuaded Pope Pius XI to remove Segura from Spain and "accept his resignation" as archbishop of Toledo. When the Civil War started, Segura was in Rome, and he refused to sign the July 1, 1937 letter (which was signed by 41 other Spanish prelates) praising the Franco revolution. During the Civil War Segura was appointed archbishop of Sevilla. He returned to Spain and began criticizing the Franco government.

Segura in Feb. 1952 issued a pastoral letter urging a renunciation of any American aid that required Spaniards to tolerate heretical concepts. Segura Mar. 9 issued a pastoral letter deploring the spread of Protestantism in Spain. He called it a "heresy" threatening the Church, and he criticized Pres. Truman for his "dislike of the Spanish people." *Arriba*, official organ of the Falange, which had announced its support of U.S.-Spanish collaboration Mar. 4, said Mar. 12, the day State Secy. Dean Acheson formally announced the start of aid negotiations, that the archbishop's fears were exaggerated and that the government was not favoring Protestants. Segura May 1 issued a new pastoral letter blacklisting *Arriba* for its editorial against Catholic demands for curbing Protestantism in Spain. The archbishop halted the circulation of the letter May 6 after he learned that Franco had written the *Arriba* editorial. Segura July 11 defended his atacks on the government's "benevolence" toward Protestants. He did so in the first in a series of "pastoral instructions" on controversial subjects. He said Catholics in Spain "must preserve [Catholic unity] . . . even if it means shedding our blood." But in a pastoral letter Aug. 15, Segura challenged the legal status of non-Catholic sects in Spain. He said he had no assurance that the Vatican approved (as the Franco government claimed) articles in the 1945 Spanish bill of rights allowing the private exercise of religions other than Roman Catholicism. This was followed Sept. 17 by another pastoral letter in which he denounced freedom of thought, religion and the press as "liberties of perdition" and blamed them for the "great evils of the world!" Segura Nov. 3 attacked the "neo-pagan cult of death" of the Falange, and Nov. 7 he warned Spanish youths studying priesthood that the custom of spending part of their vacations in Falange youth camps was "gravely harmful" to Church interests.

Throughout 1952-3 Franco attempted unsuccessfully to silence Segura. In 1953, when visiting the spring fair in Sevilla, Franco decided to hear Mass privately in his residential chapel. Not being on speaking terms with the archbishop, Franco did not bother to inform Segura. When the archbishop learned of the proposed private Mass, he decreed that the *caudillo* "would be deprived of Mass" as punishment for this affront to ecclesiastical dignity. When word reached Franco's entourage that Segura had ordered that no priest under his jurisdication perform Mass, the politicians sought a cleric not subject to the archbishop of Sevilla. They found one in Madrid, and Franco had his Mass. A few weeks later Segura suddenly "became ill" at a church gathering held in Zaragoza when he learned that Franco was present. As long as Franco remained at the conclave, the archbishop absented himself.

Enrique Cardinal Plá y Deniel, appointed archbishop of Toledo by Franco, was a supporter of Hermandades Obreras de Acción Católica (HOAC) and had been in the forefront in demanding respect for the Church's liberties. The cardinal, however, also used his publication, *Ecclesia*, to demand rigid governmental supervision of morality. He campaigned for the government to clean up the *barrio chino* (the red-light district in Barcelona, just off the Ramblas near the waterfront), to cut a scene from a movie because the kiss was too long, "to prevent mixed bathing on public beaches," to enforce a prohibition of women wearing sleeveless dresses and to take the works of Miguel de Unamuno off public library shelves. Bishop Antonio Pildain of the Canary Islands, in the Oct. 1953 issue of *Ecclesia*, called Unamuno "a major heretic" and agreed that his works should be prohibited. In Feb. 1952, after the government had permitted bars and dance-halls to remain open an extra half hour, *Ecclesia* condemned the government for "encouraging licentious amusements, incontinence and libertinage."

Father Florentino del Valle, writing in Mar. 1952 in the Jesuit publication *Razon y Fe*, complained that unless the Church did something to help the workers, the workers would abandon the Church. In Andalucia, the author stated, churches "are never filled." Following this article, *Razon y Fe* was shut down for a while.

With the exception of *Ecclesia*, which was under the personal control of Plá y Deniel, all clerical newspapers were under government supervision. But some young priests organized underground newspapers. The government then applied pressure on the upper clergy to discipline the dissidents. *Egiz*, an anti-Franco Basque nationalist periodical published clandestinely by Basque priests for 3 years, announced Oct. 18, 1952 that it would cease publication in conformity with an order issued by bishops of Bilbao, Vitoria and San Sebastián Mar. 20. The signing of the order by the highly independent Bishop Casimiro Morcillo of Bilbao was considered indicative of the pressure Franco presumably applied.

A major area of conflict between the Franco government and the Church was education. 76% of primary school children attended state-run schools in 1952–3, but only 16% of secondary school children attended state-run schools. While 60% of Church-operated primary schools were free, only 27% of the secondary schools did not charge. High-school education, therefore, was not available to the children of the poor. 95% of the population could not afford to educate their children in the state-run colleges and universities. Some 14.24% of the adult population over 10 years of age was illiterate in 1952–3, and a small, almost self-perpetuating group of college-educated upper-class individuals tended to dominate business, industry and the higher echelons of government.

Church and state were in conflict over the economics and supervision (or control) of education. The government denied tax exemption to Church schools. In many cases where the Church-run institutions charged only a registration fee, the government forced the school to surrender that fee.

As for supervision (control), both Church and state reject complete freedom of education, but each had its own ideas as to what should be restricted. The state, for example, took pride in the genius of Miguel de Unamuno, but both Archbishop Enrique Cardinal Plá y Deniel of Toledo and Bishop Antonio Pildain of the Canary Islands proscribed his works. The state, on the other hand, objected to the

study of Marx permitted in some Church-run high schools and opposed
the liberal position on social issues taken by Plá y Deniel and such
bishops as Angel Herrera y Oria of Málaga and Marcelino Olaechea of
Valencia. Subjects prohibited in one school system were permitted in
the other. Christian Democratic Education Min. Joaquín Ruíz Gimenez
proposed in 1952 that the Church schools be placed under state
supervision, and some Church liberals had no objections.

Archbishop Olaechea of Valencia announced in Madrid July 31,
1952 that the Vatican had approved a high-school-system reform
proposed by the Spanish government. He told Catholic opponents of
the program to stop fighting school reform legislation. But most
Catholics objected despite the Vatican's approval. The Spanish
National Board of Catholic Bishops complained Oct. 2 that the government had given the Church only "minimum rights" over high-school
education.

The Cortes passed the reform legislation Feb. 25, 1953. The law
was something of a revolution in the Spanish educational system.
While the number of hours a student would spend in school was
unchanged, the law substituted sports and physical education—subjects
almost completely absent from Spanish high-school curricula—for some
academic subjects. In order to obtain Church support for the innovation, 2 concessions were made. First, Church-operated schools would
not be subject to government inspection but would be inspected by
individuals appointed by ecclesiastical authorities. 2d, co-education
would be forbidden in the high schools as well as in elementary schools.
The new law, however, stipulated that all teachers, whether in public or
private schools, would be examined by panels appointed by the
Education Ministry.

New Concordat with Vatican

The new education bill was important to Franco because of the
protracted negotiations with the Vatican (since 1941) on a new
Concordat to replace the Concordat of 1851, which had been voided by
the Spanish Republic in 1931. It was held that the new law would
strengthen Franco's bargaining power with the pope and that the
Concordat could be used to silence Pedro Cardinal Segura and his supporters. In 1953 Franco entrusted the post of ambassador to the
Vatican to Fernando María Castiella y Maíz, former member of the
Spanish Blue Division; this was considered indicative of the importance
he placed on the treaty.

The Concordat, pledging state cooperation with the Catholic

Church in Spain, was concluded Aug. 27, 1953 and signed by Papal Pro-Secretary of State Domenico Tardini and Spanish Foreign Min. Alberto Martín Artajo in Vatican City.

While the text of the Concordat (36 articles and a protocol) was not published, spokesmen in Vatican City and Madrid and the papal newspaper *l'Osservatore Romano* released some of the provisions. According to the Vatican paper: "Spain reaffirms those principles which form the basis of the prosperity of the family and the nation: full recognition of religious marriage, the Christian education of youth and freedom for the Church to carry out her apostolate. The Holy See . . . confirms—with the adaptations required by the contingencies of the present day—the traditional privileges that have been conceded to Spain in the course of centuries." The paper commented that "the Concordat inaugurates no new order in relations between the Holy Office and Spain but, rather, sanctions and stabilizes an extant *de facto* situation."

Among provisions of the Concordat:

(1) Article I of the Concordat noted the Spanish government's reaffirmation that the "Catholic, Apostolic and Roman" religion was the sole religion of the Spanish people. The Holy See recognized the validity of Article 6 of the Spanish constitution—that "no person may be molested" for holding and practising "other beliefs." (The word used in the Spanish constitution describing "other beliefs" is best translated as "cults." Article 6 also prohibited all public manifestations of the cults.)

(2) Article VII stated that Spain would have the unique privilege of having 2 "representatives" instead of one in the Supreme Court of the Vatican Rota (*Tribunal de Rota*). In past centuries the kingdoms of Castile and Aragon each had a representative on the Rota, but when the 2 kingdoms were united to form Spain, the representation was reduced.

(3) Since Spanish was the mother-tongue of 40% of the world's Roman Catholic population, the Spanish language would be admitted as an official language, along with Latin, in cases of beatification and canonization.

(4) Articles XXVI–XXXI, dealing with educations, required that instruction in the Catholic religion be given in all Spanish schools, although non-Catholic children could be excused if their parents so desired. The instruction, except in primary schools, must be given by clerics.

(5) Article XXIX guaranteed the clergy the right to censor dangerous books.

(6) Church feasts would be Spanish national holidays.

(7) Police authorities could not enter Church property without ecclesiastical permission.

(8) Priests would be tried in Church courts except for civil offenses. Church authorities had to be informed of any action taken against a cleric.

(9) The method of appointing archbishops and bishops as established by the convention of July 1941 was reaffirmed. Under this system, the pope selects 3 names from a list of 6 submitted by the head of state (Franco); the latter then picks one of the 3 within a period of 30 days. (Since this article specifically

voided Article 329 of the Papal Canon Code and left the choice of prelates in Franco's hands, it was considered by observers to be a major victory for Franco.)

(10) The state would respect the "seal of confession."

(11) Only Catholic Church marriages were valid.

(12) Tolerance granted to non-Catholics in Spanish Africa (*i.e.*, Muslims and Jews who have mosques and synagogues) would remain in force.

(13) While clerics could not be drafted into the armed forces, an archbishop could require a priest to serve as an army chaplain for a term equal to that of conscription.

(14) All church property, including educational institutions, was exempt from taxation. (This was considered a major victory for the Vatican.)

(15) Article XXXIV permitted the church to engage in "Apostolic" activities via Catholic Action. (This was considered a major victory for the liberal prelates who sponsored HOAC [Hermandades Obreras de Acción Católica] labor unions.

The Concordat was considered a papal defeat by some observers. George Hills wrote in *Franco* that "the Vatican capitulated." The former Republican diplomat Elena de La Souchere asserted in *An Explanation of Spain* that "the Church shed her semi-reserve of 14 years and signed . . . an alliance with a regime at the risk of definitely alienating the working class." The Falange, on the other hand, called the Concordat a surrender to the Vatican and complained particularly over the tax, education and Catholic Action provisions.

Franco argued before the Cortes for 50 minutes and forced the Falangist organ *Arriba* to publish his entire speech. After 2 months of pressure, the Cortes ratified the Concordat Oct. 26, and Franco pledged that non-Catholics could practice their religion in Spain if they did not interfere with "Catholic unity." Franco Dec. 21 was awarded the Supreme Order of Christ, the highest secular decoration granted by the Pope.

Britain, Gibraltar & Protestants

According to differing estimates, there were 20,000 to 30,000 declared Protestants and a few thousand foreign Protestants in Spain. There were few Protestant chapels, but, according to Benjamin Welles in *Spain: The Gentle Anarchy*, some 90,000 Spaniards secretly attended these services regularly.

Pedro Cardinal Segura y Sáenz, the leading anti-Protestant in Spain, directed his attacks mainly against Spanish Protestants. George Hills, in *Franco*, quotes Segura as telling him that Anglicans were "very correct, sincere in their beliefs, however mistaken, and often model Christians whom we would do well to emulate in their virtues." In his pastoral letters, however, Segura did not distinguish between foreign and domestic Protestants. The anti-Protestant pastoral letters coincided with an anti-British campaign in the Falangist organ *Arriba* and renewed Spanish claims to Gibraltar.

During this anti-British, anti-Protestant agitation, the British-owned Protestant Chapel in Sevilla was burned Mar. 4, 1952.

Sir Douglas Savory, an Ulster Unionist, questioned British State Min. Selwyn Lloyd as to what actions the British government was taking. Lloyd replied Mar. 19 that the government had protested to Spain and reserved the right to demand compensation. Savory brought up the matter again Mar. 31. Lloyd replied that while the Spanish government had expressed regret and promised to punish the vandals, no offer of compensation had been received. Under continuing pressure from Protestant groups, Lloyd told the House of Commons May 7 that the British ambassador had been instructed to present Madrid with a bill for the damage.

Meanwhile the anti-Protestantism spread. Students from Badajoz college Apr. 6 broke into a Protestant chapel, which had been closed since 1949, and burned hymn and prayer books. Madrid authorities announced the arrest of 21 students Apr. 15. The Badajoz chapel was not British-owned, and its desecration brought protests from American Protestants.

The Spanish Foreign Affairs Ministry said Sept. 22, 1952 that "foreign intervention" on behalf of Spanish Protestants was viewed by Spain with the "greatest distaste" and would do more harm than good. The warning was issued in a reply to a request from the Rev. Paul E. Freed, Greensboro, N.C. Baptist minister, for a statement of the Spanish government's attitude on Protestantism.

Arriba, the most stridently anti-British voice in Spain, warned its readers that following British customs would lead to the degeneration of Spain. As Falangists marked the 1704 loss of Gibraltar with anti-British "Gibraltar Day" meetings Aug. 4, 1952, *Arriba* warned that "Spain has not given up" claims for the return of the base. When the British announced that Queen Elizabeth II would visit Gibraltar sometime in 1954, *Arriba's* anti-British campaign intensified. But Franco, who needed British trade and arms did not permit the Gibraltar dispute to interrupt normal Anglo-Spanish commercial relations.

Arabs & Morocco

Spain continued its campaign to win Arab goodwill. Spanish Foreign Min. Alberto Martín Artajo visited Lebanon, Syria, Jordan, Saudi Arabia, Iraq and Egypt in Apr. 1952 during a 3-week tour of Middle

Eastern countries. Martín Artajo was accompanied by Gen. Muhammad ben-Mizzian ben-Kazem (a senior Moroccan officer in the Spanish army and a long-time friend of Lt. Gen. Rafael García Valiño, Spanish high commissioner in Morocco), Prof. García Gómez (an eminent Arabist), Franco's daughter Carmencita and her husband, Cristóbal Martínez de Bordiu, Marquis de Villaverde.

Before the mission's departure the *caudillo* broadcast to the Islamic world a message stating that the purpose of the visit was to express Spain's gratitude to the rulers and statesmen of Islam for their "defense of Spain and justice" and to underscore the Hispano-Islamic solidarity in achieving "a peaceful life in a better world." Having mentioned that for centuries the 2 peoples "shared the same ground," Franco emphasized that the 20th century was witnessing "a parallel resurgence of the Arabic and Hispanic peoples, in contrast to the decrepitude of other countries." Describing Spain as "the crossroads of world communications," Franco concluded with the statement that, because of its historic role in the Western and Arabic worlds, Spain was the "link with those peoples who, with youthful impulses, are shaping a new life for themselves."

Martín Artajo and his entourage viewed the sights of Beirut, Damascus, Amman, Baghdad, Riyadh and Jidda, the port city of Mecca. While in Damascus Apr. 18, Martín Artajo signed a friendship and cultural pact with Syria. The welcome the Spanish group received in the Arab world was impressive. Claude Martin asserted in *Franco* that the U.S. was impressed by the reception because the U.S. needed a friend in the Arab world to counter its support of Israel. In fact, according to Martin, the ties between Spain and Islam made the conclusion of a U.S.-Spanish treaty all the more desirable from Washington's view. The climax of the trip was a visit to Cairo where the Spaniards were entertained by King Farouk, Egyptian Foreign Min. Ahmed Naguib al-Hilaili Pasha and Secy. Gen. Abdul Rahman Azzam Pasha of the Arab League.

At a Cairo press conference Apr. 26 Martín Artajo declared that his trip had "opened a new era of friendship and close relations based on mutual understanding and cooperation" between Spain and the Arab world. Martín Artajo and Azzam Apr. 27 held a joint press conference during which the Spanish diplomat stated that as a result of his discussions with Arab leaders an *entente cordiale* had been established. Calling the Mediterranean area "a determining factor in international politics today," Martín Artajo said: "We Spaniards believe in a Mediterranean policy which will take into consideration the renaissance of the Arab nations as well as the struggle against Communist aggression. Any system of collective security among the Mediterranean countries should recognize in principle these 2 fundamental facts if a positive result is to be reached." Azzam described the Spanish visit as "cementing relations between the Spanish and Arab peoples, whose bonds of friendship date back to the days of Carthage." Carthage had been colonized by Phoenician Tyre. Southern Spain was ruled between 800 BC and 200 BC by either Tyre or Carthage.

Martín Artajo, in an interview with Cairo's semi-official *Al Ahram*, was queried Apr. 28 about the possibility of Spain acting as mediator in the dispute Egypt had with France and Britain. Martín Artajo replied: "Spain has not offered to play such a role, but the fact that certain countries have spontaneously thought of it is perhaps due, on the one hand, to the fact that we are part of Europe, and on the other to the fact that our history and our blood links us equally with the Arab and Spanish-American worlds."

When asked about relations with NATO, he said: "Spain has never asked for admission to the NATO; neither has she asked for admission to the United Nations, or to participate in the Marshall Plan. Spain does not ask for charity, but she does not refuse to play her part in the defense of Europe or to evade her international responsibilities. Rather than enter into a pact linking a number of countries, which might prove embarrassing, we would prefer a direct pact which would reinforce our mutual and cordial Iberian pact with Portugal and which would assure coordination in the general plans for European defense."

Questioned as to Spain's attitude toward the actions of France's resident (high commissioner) in Morocco Gen. Augustin Guillaume, who was using Thami el-Glaoui, pasha of Marrakesh, as a tool to oust Sultan Muhammad V bin Yusef, Martín Artajo answered: "Franco-Spanish relations present numerous aspects and cannot be limited to a single factor. Neither France nor Britain have treated us with justice in recent times. Spaniards have many reasons to complain of those countries. But we are not going to let ourselves be influenced by a desire for reprisals, which would only profit our common enemy Soviet communism."

Within a few days of Martín Artajo's departure for the Middle East, Franco had apparently attempted to put pressure on the Western powers. Franco Apr. 7 had asked for Spanish control of the Tangier police forces. He did so in notes to countries besides Spain that shared control of the Tangier zone. (The U.S., Britain, France, Italy, Belgium and Portugal had representatives on the Tangier control commission. The USSR, which was entitled to a representative had not sent one.) The other powers did not reply.

A treaty of friendship between Spain and the kingdom of Yemen was signed May 19 at the Spanish embassy in Cairo. The treaty established diplomatic and cultural relations between the 2 states. It was announced Aug. 12 that Spain and 3 Arab nations—Jordan, Iraq and Lebanon—had agreed to promote their missions from legation to embassy level.

Meanwhile, Arab nationalist leaders in Spanish Morocco said Apr. 27 that Spain Mar. 12, 1952 had given them permission to revive political parties banned for many years and that they would campaign for independence of French and Spanish Morocco as a single country.

Gen. Augustin Guillaume, the French resident general (high commissioner) in Morocco, apparently attempted in Jan. 1953 to undercut the Spanish position by claiming that Istiqlal (the Moroccan Independence Party) was a Communist-front organization that had the direct support of Moscow and the Arab League. France then made a direct appeal to Franco to withdraw his support from Sultan Muhammad V and the Istiqlal, and Franco ordered his Moroccan officials to be more circumspect in the support of the nationalists.

A Spanish official in Tangiers was said to have assured France Feb. 8, 1953, that Spain would not permit anti-French activities by Arab nationalists living in Spanish Morocco. On the other hand, the Spanish high commissioner for Morocco's Spanish Zone, Lt. Gen. Rafael García Valiño, announced Feb. 8 that he had carried out a series of reforms that would permit the 1,000,000 Muslim residents of the Spanish Zone greater autonomy. (In *Politics and the Military in Modern Spain*, Stanley Payne described García Valiño as "one of the most competent, hard-driving men in the army . . . known for his ambition . . . political adroitress . . . and his financial dealings.")

During the summer of 1953 Guillaume began to organize pro-French Moroccans in what was called a plot to force Muhammad V's abdication. The French had the active support of Thami el-Glaoui, pasha of Marrakesh, Moulay Idris, leader of the Democratic Party of Free Men, Sherif Abdelhai el-Kittany, an old foe of the House of Alawite (the sultan's family), and about 75% of the Moroccan officials. Guillaume, following a policy originated by the former French resident, Gen. Alphonse Pierre Juin, sought to change the constitutional structure of the Moroccan kingdom so that the elected representatives would be 50% Muslims and 50% European. This would turn the kingdom into a state in which the Muslims and Europeans would be co-sovereign at the expense of the position of the sultan. Guillaume's plan, it was said, would have violated both the Treaty of Fez of 1912 (which had established the legal basis for the Moroccan protectorate) and the secret treaty of 1904 between France and Spain (which guaranteed the sovereignty of the sultan).

El-Glaoui, born in 1878 and one of the richest men in Morocco (his personal wealth was estimated at over $50 million), had financial interests in almost every Moroccan industry (including Marrakesh prostitutes) and a large personal army, but his wealth and power were said to depend on the presence of the French. It was reported that el-Glaoui ordered his subordinates to riot throughout French Morocco to force the sultan's abdication. El-Glaoui Aug. 13 began circulating a petition calling for the deposition of Muhammad V and the recognition of the sultan's cousin, Mulay Muhammad bin Arafa, as the new sultan. After a 5-hour conference Aug. 15, Guillaume, apparently considering that he had no alternative, agreed to permit el-Glaoui to proclaim bin Arafa as "Imam of the Faithful" and to seize the royal residence in Marrakesh. Muhammad V refused to be deposed, and for the next 2 days there was rioting throughout the French sector of Morocco.

Mark I. Cohen and Lorna Hahn reported in *Morocco: Old Land, New Nation* that the French "government in Paris tried to arrest the revolt." Guillaume flew to Paris Aug. 17 to discuss the matter with French Foreign Min. Georges Bidault. He returned to Casablanca Aug. 19 and attempted to reach a compromise, but el-Glaoui refused to compromise. Guillaume then demanded Muhammad V's formal abdication. The sultan refused, and the French cabinet ordered Guillaume to arrest him. Troops under French command entered the royal palace at Rabat Aug. 20 and placed Muhammad V (still in his pajamas), his 2 wives, 8 of his concubines and 5 children on a plane for Corsica; Muhammad V was eventually flown to Madagascar for safe-keeping. Mulay Muhammad bin Arafa was proclaimed sultan Aug. 21, 1953. During the following days the French imprisoned 1,023 of the ex-sultan's followers. M'Barek Ben Bekkai, pasha of Sefru and one of the leaders of the Democratic Party for Independence (PDI), went into voluntary exile.

Lt. Gen. Rafael García Valiño, Spanish high commissioner in Morocco, Aug. 25 welcomed Khalifa Hassan el-Mehdi of Tetuan, a supporter of deposed Sultan Muhammad V, to Tetuan, capital of the Spanish Protectorate. (By the Treaty of Fez and subsequent agreements the sultan appointed the khalifa as his representative in Spanish areas; all legislation had to have the khalifa's seal of validation. The khalifa had a cabinet, the *makhzen*, that had very little real authority. The chief legislator and chief executive actually was the Spanish high commissioner.) García Valiño informed the khalifa, who had come to Tetuan for the *Aid el-Kebir* festival, that Spain did not approve of the deposition of Muhammad V and that the Spanish government had no intention of recognizing the new sultan. In a note of warning to Paris he said that "nothing of a political nature can be done in Morocco without the consent of Spain" and that as long as France acted unilaterally it would be "difficult in the future for an atmosphere of confidence to exist." After the speech, prayers were offered in the name of the deposed sultan.

Meanwhile, despite Spanish objections, France secured the recognition of the new sultan in the international zone of Tangiers Aug. 23.

Franco sent to Paris a formal note of protest against the deposition of Muhammad V without the prior approval of the Spanish government. Calling the new sultan a "Quisling," Franco placed the Spanish-controlled Radio Tetuan at the disposal of Ahmed Balafrej, one of the leaders of the Istiqlal, and authorized the Spanish press to attack bin Arafa, el-Glaoui and the French imperialists. Meanwhile García Valiño opened secret negotiations with representatives of Abd el-Khalek Torres, founder of Islah (the National Reform Party), who had been exiled from Morocco's Spanish sector in 1948 for his activities. Torres was in Cairo, where he had joined forces with Allal al-Fassi, who had been active in Moroccan nationalist circles since 1926, and with Abd el-Krim. The 3, with the aid of Egyptian King Farouk, had organized the North African Liberation Committee. When García Valiño permitted the reestablishment of Islah, the way was paved for Torres to return to Tetuan. But because of strife within the North African Liberation Committee, caused by a boycott of the committee by Abd el-Krim, Torres remained in Egypt through the end of 1953.

Spain & the U.S.

Negotiations for U.S. military bases in Spain had been opened in Madrid in Apr. 1952.

Under agreements finally signed by U.S. Amb. James C. Dunn and Spanish Foreign Min. Alberto Martín Artajo Sept. 26, 1953 at Madrid's Santa Cruz Palace, Spain authorized the U.S. to "develop, maintain and use" military bases in Spain in return for at least $226 million worth of economic and military aid.

3 agreements signed provided for joint use of air and naval bases "in support of the policy of strengthening the defense of the West." Spain was to retain sovereignty over the bases and be given their installations intact if the U.S. stopped using them. Effective on signature, the agreements were to be in force for 10 years and continue automatically for 2 successive 5-year periods unless terminated by either government. They were executive agreements not requiring U.S. Senate approval. The specific location of the bases was left to "competent authorities" of both governments.

$226 million had been appropriated for Spain by the U.S. Congress to support the agreement on bases. $85 million was to be used for economic aid, $141 for military assistance. (The $226 million included $125 million carried over from 1951-2.) The cost of improving the Spanish bases was estimated at an additional $200 million.

The U.S. announcement said:

The governments of Spain and the United States today concluded 3 bilateral agreements designed to strengthen the capabilities of the West for the maintenance of international peace and security. The 3 agreements cover (1) the construction and use of military facilities in Spain by the U.S.A., (2) economic assistance and (3) military end-item assistance . . . . Under the terms of these agreements, Spain becomes eligible for U.S. economic, technical and military assistance under the Mutual Security Program, and the United States is authorized to develop, build and use jointly with Spanish forces certain military airfields and naval facilities in Spain . . . .

Of the $125 million carried over from previous appropriations for aid to Spain, $50 million is to be expended on military end-items which will provide training equipment and military material. The balance of $75 million will be used for defense support assistance to strengthen the economic foundation for the support of the program of military cooperation. This assistance will finance Spanish imports of raw materials, commodities, and equipment, and will provide such technical assistance as may be required in connection with the program. In addition to the $125 million Spain will receive $91 million for military end-item assistance and $10 million for defence support assistance from funds appropriated for the Mutual Security Program in the fiscal year 1954.

The United States will start construction to develop certain existing Spanish military airfields for joint use by the Spanish Air Force and the U.S. Air Force and will modernize certain naval facilities for use by the Spanish and U.S. navies. The agreements also provide for the subsequent development of additional military facilities as future conditions may require.

The Spanish government will make its contribution to the development and support of the jointly-used military facilities by devoting a portion of the peseta counterpart resulting from defense support assistance towards defraying construction costs which are payable in Spanish currency.

The military areas to be used jointly remain under Spanish sovereignty and command. The U.S. Command in each case is responsible for U.S. military and technical personnel and for the operational effectiveness of military facilities and equipment.

To facilitate carrying out the terms of the agreements, 2 groups will be immediately established in Spain, under the general direction of the U.S. ambassador, similar to those which are normally maintained in countries receiving economic, technical and military aid from the United States. In connection with the economic and technical assistance to Spain, a U.S. operations mission is being set up. Similarly, a military assistance advisory group is being established to coordinate the military assistance program with the Spanish authorities.

Today's signing marked the successful conclusion of negotiations which were opened with the Spanish government in Apr. 1952. Initial steps leading to these negotiations included an exploratory conversation which the late Adm. Forrest Sherman held with Gen. Franco in Madrid on July 16, 1951 to ascertain what Spain might be willing and able to contribute to the strengthening of the common defense against possible aggression. Following this visit, economic and military surveys were made in Spain prior to the opening of negotiations. The negotiations were brought to a conclusion by Amb. Dunn. A joint U.S. military group, headed by Maj. Gen. A. W. Issner (USAF), assisted the ambassador in the negotiations leading to the agreement on the construction and use of military facilities and on military end-item assistance; a Mutual Security Agency economic group, led by Mr. George F. Train, aided in the negotiations for the economic aid agreement.

Text of the agreement:

Preamble. Faced with the danger that threatens the Western world, the governments of the United States and Spain, desiring to contribute to the maintenance of international peace and security through foresighted measures which will increase their capability, and that of the other nations which dedicate their efforts to the same high purposes, to participate effectively in agreements for self-defense, have agreed as follows:

Article 1. In consonance with the principles agreed upon in the Mutual Defense Assistance Agreement, the governments of the U.S.A. and Spain consider that the contingencies with which both countries may be faced indicate the advisability of developing their relations upon a basis of continued friendship, in support of the policy of strengthening the defense of the West. This policy shall include:

(1) On the part of the United States, the support of Spanish defense efforts for agreed purposes by providing military end-item assistance to Spain during a period of several years to contribute to the effective air defense of Spain and to improve the equipment of its military and naval forces, to the extent to be agreed upon in technical discussions in the light of circumstances, and with the cooperation of the resources of Spanish industry to the extent possible. Such support will be conditioned, as in the case of other friendly nations, by the priorities and limitations due to the international commitments of the United States and the exigencies of the international situation and will be subject to Congressional appropriations.

(2) In consequence of the above-stated premises and for the same agreed purposes, the government of Spain authorizes the U.S. government, subject to terms and conditions to be agreed, to develop, maintain and utilize for military purposes, jointly with the government of Spain, such areas and facilities in territory under Spanish jurisdiction as may be agreed upon by the competent authorities of both governments as necessary for the purposes of this agreement.

(3) In granting assistance to Spain within the policy outlined above, as the preparation of the agreed areas and facilities progresses the U.S. government will satisfy, subject to the provisions of Paragraph 1, the minimum requirements for equipment necessary for the defense of Spanish territory, to the end that, should a moment requiring the wartime utilization of the areas and facilities arrive, from this moment the requirements are covered to the extent possible as regards the air defense of the territory and the equipment of the naval units, and that the armament and equipment of the army units be as far advanced as possible.

Article 2. For the purpose of this agreement and in accordance with technical arrangements to be agreed upon between the competent authorities of both governments, the U.S. government is authorized to improve and fit agreed areas and facilities for military use, as well as to undertake necessary construction in this connection in cooperation with the Spanish government, to station and house therein the necessary military and civilian personnel, and to provide for their security, discipline and welfare; to store and maintain custody of provisions, supplies, equipment and material; and to maintain and operate the facilities and equipment necessary in support of such areas and personnel.

Article 3. The areas which, by virtue of this agreement, are prepared for joint utilization will remain under Spanish flag and command, and Spain will assume the obligation of adopting the necessary measures for their external security. However, the United States may, in all cases, exercise the necessary supervision of U.S. personnel, facilities and equipment.

The time and manner of wartime utilization of said areas and facilities will be as mutually agreed upon.

Article 4. The Spanish government will acquire, free of all charge and servitude, the land which may be necessary for all military purposes and shall retain the ownership of the ground and of the permanent structures which may be constructed thereon. The U.S. government reserves the right to remove all other constructions and facilities established at its own expense when it is deemed convenient by it or upon the termination of this agreement; in obth cases the Spanish government may acquire them, after previous assessment, whenever they are not installations of a classified nature.

The Spanish state will be responsible for all claims made against the U.S. government by a 3d party in all cases referring to the ownership and utilization of the above-mentioned land.

Article 5. The present agreement will become effective upon signature and will be in force for a period of 10 years, automatically extended for 2 successive periods of 5 years each unless the termination procedure hereafter outlined is followed. At the termination of the first 10 years or of either of the 2 extensions of 5 years, either of the 2 governments may inform the other of its intention to cancel the agreement, thus initiating a consultation period of 6 months. In the event concurrence is not reached on extension, this agreement will terminate one year after the conclusion of the period of consultation.

(Under the agreement, the U.S. eventually was granted: air bases at Torrejon, near Madrid, at Zaragoza and at Morón de la Frontera; a naval and air base at Rota on the Bay of Cádiz; a major air supply depot at Sevilla; naval depots at El Ferrol de Caudillo and Cartagena; the use of Spanish airports at Sevilla and Palma de Mallorca; 7 radar sites and 20 other sites throughout Spain for military, naval and air installations plus the right to build a 500-mile-long jet fuel pipeline from Rota through La Mancha to Torrejon and Zaragoza.)

Franco summoned the Cortes Sept. 30 to approve the agreements. In a 20-minute speech, he asserted that the agreements were "the most important achievement of our contemporary foreign policy." Spain had been the only country to realize the nature of the Communist peril, Franco said, but nevertheless it had seemed that "Spain must cross alone the troubled waters of the postwar period" because of the "blindness with which our aims were received." Spain had tried unsuccessfully to improve relations with Britain but in the face of persistent hostility had shifted its efforts towards the U.S., whose "idealism and youthfulness" the Spanish people valued highly. "No one could believe that aggression against the West would halt of its own choice on our frontiers," Franco declared. "To believe this would be to disregard the objectives of Soviet communism. The defense of the West against Communist aggression is just as important, or even more so, for us as it is for the United States." Foreign aid was needed to help Spain build up its defenses, Franco declared, but "it is not our intention that others shall defend us."

After a 2-month delay, the Cortes Nov. 30 unanimously ratified the agreement. Before the vote, Foreign Min. Martín Artajo said that the Truman Administration had delayed the understanding but that "with the arrival in power of the Republican [Eisenhower] Administration, certain obstructions that threatened at one time to make negotiations interminable disappeared." Martín Artajo blamed Britain and France for the "diplomatic and economic blockade" of Spain in 1946 and for keeping Spain out of the Marshall Plan and the Atlantic Pact.

Some observers suggest that until Gen. Dwight D. Eisenhower was elected President of the U.S. in Nov. 1952, Franco had feared that the U.S. might not go through with the agreement and that, therefore, Franco tried to induce favorable opinion in the U.S. by demonstrating that Spain was progressive and a firm anti-Communist ally. According to the *N.Y. Times*, Franco Jan. 3, 1952 invited U.S. labor leaders "to visit Spain in order to study the nation's social evolution and the progress realized by workers . . . [in] a nation where strikes were archaic." Foreign Min. Alberto Martín Artajo stated Jan. 10 in *Ya*, Madrid's Catholic daily, that "Spain . . . considers [that] Russian Communist aggression demands retribution. As a consequence, the first object of Christendom's military strategy should be the deliverance and liberation of the [oppresed] peoples." *Pueblo*, the Falangist labor daily, reporting May 28 on riots in Paris in opposition to Gen. Mathew Ridgeway, ex-UN commander in Korea, who arrived in Paris to replace Eisenhower as NATO chief, asserted that the riots were part of a Communist plan to sabotage U.S. defense efforts in Europe. The Falangist organ *Arriba* June 9 and July 15 published long articles describing how the Spanish Blue Division (which had aided Nazi Germany on the Russian front) had fought "for the defense of Christian civilization."

With such exceptions as the open opposition of Pedro Cardinal Segura, Spaniards reacted favorably to the conclusion of the U.S.-Spanish agreement. (Arthur P. Whitaker asserted in *Spain and Defense of the West* that "the opposition in Spain cannot be documented or measured because of the absence of freedom of speech and press, but there can be no doubt that it was strong and widespread." Whitaker quoted Martín Artajo as saying that one of the reasons for the delay in reaching the agreement was the need to "allow the evolution of favorable opinion.") Enrique Cardinal Plá y Deniel, for example, indorsed the agreement but, in effect, warned Nov. 1 that the Church would condemn "external manifestations" of worship by non-Catholic Americans in Spain.

According to Stanley Payne in *Politics and the Military in Modern Spain*, some misgivings were felt by the Spanish military whose pride was hurt by the fact that "the Spanish were always on the receiving end." Gen. Emilio Herrera, one of the founders of the Spanish air force, who since 1939 had been a member of the Paris-based Republican government-in-exile, wrote several letters to Spanish officers Nov. 14, 1953. One letter, addressed to "his old comrade in arms, Gen. Don Eduardo González Gallarza, minister of air of the Franco government," stressed the dangers to Spanish pride, honor and independence that, he held, the treaty signified. González Gallarza did not respond, but Payne quoted another officer as saying: "We are not so vile as to tolerate the sale of our national sovereignty. The catastrophe that you foresee for Spain does not worry us at all; we are absolutely sure that, when the moment of danger arrives, the *caudillo*, with his brilliant ability, will take the necessary action to free Spain of any risk."

Franco Nov. 4 ruled out direct Spanish military ties with Britain, France or NATO. He said the U.S.-Spanish agreement "completely assured" the West of "efficient help" against Soviet aggression without the need of relationships opposed by "various public opinions."

(A report attributed to U.S. Air Force leaders that the U.S. planned to store atomic weapons in Spain was denied Nov. 3 by U.S. State Secy. John Foster Dulles and Defense Secy. Charles E. Wilson. USAF Secy. Harold E. Talbott and Gen. Nathan F. Twining were reported to have said in Madrid Nov. 2 that U.S. forces based in Spain "eventually" would be supplied with atomic weapons. Talbott denied the story Nov. 3, but it aroused alarm among Allied countries in Europe.)

The U.S.-Spanish agreements, coupled with the Vatican Concordat, were described generally as a major victory for Franco. Herbert L. Mathews, writing in the *N.Y. Times*, made this comment on the events of 1953: "It was the high spot of Franco's postwar career. He had defeated his enemies in and out of Spain, he has refused to yield one inch to liberalism; and now his efforts had gained the highest sanction from 2 of the highest powers in the world, religious and secular—the Vatican and the United States."

Other Foreign Relations

A presumably unforeseen consequence of the U.S.-Spanish agreement was what was described as the cooling of Spanish relations with Latin America.

Since the end of the Civil War Franco had attempted to revive the concept of *La Hispanidad*, a union of Spanish-speaking peoples, which had been a favorite idea of José Antonio Primo de Rivera. During World War II such a policy was considered impossible because most of Latin America had joined the Allies against Hitler. After the war, however, Falangists invited the Latin American states to join Spain in a social-economic union from which the English-speaking world would be excluded.

Because most British and Americans mistakenly, it was said, considered the Falange a Right-wing organization, the Left-wing anti-capitalist side of Falangist ideology was usually discounted. But it was reported that Latin Americans who had complained of Anglo-Saxon or German economic control responded favorably to the voice of Madrid.

The election of Juan Perón as president of Argentina in Mar. 1946 had given the Falangists an ally in their anti-capitalist—and primarily anti-American—policy. Argentine-Spanish discussions took place on the possibility of creating a Spanish-speaking customs union, with Cádiz as Latin America's free port to Europe. One benefit to Franco was loans to buy Argentine wheat and meat. Having received the loans, Franco began to procrastinate on a firm treaty of union, and Perón terminated the negotiations.

Spain, however, continued to talk of *La Hispanidad*. Poverty-stricken Spain offered scholarships to Latin Americans to study in Spain and even raised funds from its destitute population to aid Chileans and Peruvians when natural catastrophe struck. Spain offered its friendship to Left-wing nationalist groups while sending military and police instructors to help military dictatorships in Peru, Colombia, Venezuela and the Dominican Republic. But the U.S.-Spanish agreement was reported to have destroyed the trust Latin American nationalists had for the Falangists. Many of these Latin Americans held that Spain had sold out to the U.S.

Despite Spain's inability to join the UN, diplomatic relations with Spain were being accepted more readily by most of the non-Communist world during 1952-3. Among developments reported:

The Canadian government Feb. 21, 1952 announced the establishment of direct diplomatic relations with Spain at the embassy level. Canada had maintained a trade commissioner in Madrid and Spain a consul general in Montreal, but diplomatic relations between the 2 countries had previously been handled through Great Britain.

Spain agreed June 28 to establish diplomatic relations with Nationalist China and to send a diplomatic mission to Taiwan.

Liberian Pres. William Tubman visited Franco Aug. 19.

Iran and Spain signed a friendship and peace treaty Nov. 22.

Spain maintained its close ties with Portugal throughout the period. Franco and Portuguese Premier António Salazar, accompanied by diplomatic and defense officials, conferred in Ciudad Rodrigo, Spain Apr. 14-15 in a meeting that gave Spain its first links with a North Atlantic Treaty member and was regarded as a Portuguese move toward getting Spain into NATO. A communiqué issued after the meeting, said that Franco and Salazar had discussed "the common position which the 2 peoples and governments have for long taken in forming a solid front against the dangers menacing Christian civilization."

Spain's acceptance into UN subsidiary agencies continued throughout 1952-3 despite a special UN committee report June 23, 1952 that Spanish legislation indicated that forced labor "might" be practiced. Spain's admission to the UN Educational Scientific & Cultural Organization (UNESCO) was approved by 12-5 vote of the UN Economic & Social Council May 21, 1952. The USSR, Czechoslovakia, Poland, Mexico and Uruguay cast the opposing votes. UNESCO admitted Spain to membership Nov. 19 by vote of 44 to 4 (Burma, Mexico, Uruguay and Yugoslavia), with 7 abstentions (Denmark, India, Israel, Luxembourg, Norway, Netherlands and Sweden). (At a meeting in Milan, Italy, Oct. 17-21, 1952, the Socialist International had voted to protest the inclusion of Spain in UNESCO.)

At a meeting of the International Telecommunications Union in Buenos Aires, Argentina, Spain not only was readmitted to membership Dec. 4, 1952 but was elected to the governing council.

ERRATIC ADVANCE (1954-5)

The Spanish economy, benefiting by increasing government aid, continued to show progress in most areas during 1954-5 although there were some reverses, most notably in agriculture and foreign trade. Franco reiterated his opposition to freedom of the press, and a new press law reaffirmed the government's control of the press. The dispute with France over Morocco became more bitter as rebels allegedly aided by the Spanish attacked civilian as well as military targets in French Morocco. France ultimately agreed to the abdication of the recently installed Sultan Mulay bin Arafa and to the restoration of Muhammad V. But Franco still resisted early independence for Morocco. In a major triumph for Franco, diplomats at the UN worked out a compromise under which Spain was admitted to the world organization.

Economic Improvements & Reverses

Although major economic improvements were recorded in 1954-5, not all sectors of the economy benefited, and agricultural output actually declined between 1954 and 1955.

Industrial production, however, was largely good.

Using 1929 as a base, non-agricultural production reached 214 in 1954 and 240 in 1955.

The output of the extractive industry generally improved during the 2 years. Coal, aluminum, lead and zinc production increased. Sulfuric acid increased slightly from 800,000 tons in 1954 to 820,000 in 1955; potassium salt output rose from 1.22 million tons to 1.28 million tons, phosphate production from 22,200 tons to 23,200 tons. The output of some segments, however, dropped: wolfram production declined from 2,892 tons to 1,716 tons in 1955; mercury output fell from 1,500 tons with a value of 25.6 million gold pesetas to 1,111 tons with a value of 26½ million gold pesetas; potassium chloride production fell from 244,533 tons with a value of 20.6 million gold pesetas to 241,590 tons with a value of 19.3 million gold pesetas.

The Spanish government announced July 5, 1954 that preliminary agreements had been reached for nationalizing the Rio Tinto Co., which owned and operated copper and sulphur mines in Huelva province. The government and 6 Spanish banks planned to buy a ⅔ interest in the company, and the balance was to remain in private hands.

Industrial production was almost uniformly up. Cement output rose from 4 million tons in 1954 to 4.4 million tons a year later.

Tractor production increased from 60 units to 850, truck production from 420 units to 713, motorcycles from 45,790 to 69,150, bicycles from 144,888 to 166,627. The government began to produce vehicles in the SEAT plant in Barcelona (the Sociedad Española de Automoviles de Turismo was owned by the Spanish National Institute of Industry and the Italian FIAT organization). Spain produced 14,422 autos, 178 buses and 846 military trucks in 1955. The government began to produce rolling stock for its antiquated railroads: 48 locomotives and 1,641 freight and passenger cars were manufactured in 1955. Shoe production increased from 21.3 million pair in 1954 to 23.6 million pair in 1955. Book production, although below the 1953 mark, increased from 4,678 titles to 4,811 titles in 1955. Beer production, which amounted to 6 million liters in 1950, jumped to 16 million liters in 1955.

Iron production increased from 112% of the 1929-31 average to 135%, while the output of electricity surged from 395% to 471%. Electrical consumption increased from 7.29 billion kilowatt hours in 1954 to 9.28 billion in 1955. The consumption of butane gas increased from 7,784 units to 12,821 units during the same period.

The shipbuilding industry also improved markedly. Spain produced 60,000 tons of shipping in 1954 and 74,000 tons in 1955. Capacity increased from 225,000 tons to 255,000, while contracts for new shipping jumped from 263,000 tons to 326,000 tons.

Only in the important textile industry was there continued disappointment. Output rose from 96% of the 1929-31 average in 1954 to 101% in 1955, but as of 1955 the industry's output was still below that of 1953.

Tourism and its profits improved. In 1954 2 million tourists visited Spain, producing a net profit of $90 million. 2½ millions came in 1955, and the profit reached $96.7 million.

The railroads remained a drain on the treasury. The official *Memorias de Consejo de Administración de Red Nacional de Ferrocarriles* announced a deficit of 1.99 billion pesetas in 1954 (revenue 5.4 billion, expenses 6.3 billion, financial charges but not amortization .4 billion, depreciation .7 billion) and a deficit of 2.4 billion pesetas for 1955 (revenue 5.7 billion, expenses 6.7 billion, financial charges .5 billion, depreciation .8 billion).

The government announced in the fall of 1955 that the highway improvement program had been successful and that 35% of the projects had been completed. (But a UN report 5 years later said Spanish highways were obsolete and dangerous for modern transportation.)

Agricultural production remained erratic. Output declined from 111% of the 1931-5 average in 1954 to 105% in 1955.

In 1954 Spain produced 322,000 tons of sugar, imported 14,000 tons and exported 50,200 tons; the average Spanish consumption of sugar was 9.9 kilograms a year. The following year the native production fell to 284,000 tons, 29,000 tons was imported, none was exported, and the average Spanish consumption rose to 10.8 kilos a year.

Wheat production rose slightly in 1954 to 4.8 million tons, but the government announced Mar. 15 that it had to buy 300,000 tons of surplus U.S. wheat to prevent shortages. Wheat production fell in 1955 to only 4 million tons. Rice production decreased in 1954 but rose in 1955. Potato production rose in both years but was still below the bumper crop of 1951. Tomato production increased in both years, while onion production increased in 1954 and fell in 1955. Olive oil output declined both in 1954 and in 1955. Cotton continued a steady increase through the period. The tobacco harvest, which had reached an all-time high in 1954, fell sharply in 1955.

The fish catch improved in both 1954 and 1955.

Spanish livestock had not recovered in numbers from the Civil War devastation. The figures for 1933, 1948 and 1955:

	1933 (in millions)	1948 (in millions)	1955 (in millions)
Cows	3.6	3.3	2.7
Chickens	19.1	15.9	15.9
Pigs	5.4	2.7	2.8
Goats	4.5	4.2	3.1
Horses	.6	.5	.6
Mules	1.2	1.1	1.1

Fruit continued to be the mainstay of Spanish agricultural export. The fruit harvest remained almost constant during 1954-5, and Spain dominated much of the world's orange trade. In 1955 Spain produced one million tons of oranges—54% of all oranges grown in the Mediterranean area.

The government continued its efforts to improve conditions. 47,-467 housing units were built in 1954 with government assistance; the following year 57,898 units were built. (But Spain needed a minimum of 70,000 new units each year.)

The government sponsored a form of collectivization whereby small farms were combined into larger parcels so that modern machinery and techniques could be employed. 20 units of a total of over 200,000 acres were formed in 1954; 117 plots of a total of over 386,000 acres were formed in 1955. The result in improved production and the improved use of Spain's limited technological facilities proved beneficial in the long run, but initially it created some dislocation since some of the peasants abandoned their homesteads and moved into those provinces (Madrid, Barcelona and the 3 Basque provinces) where the expanding industrial or commercial activity offered the best chance for employment.

Through the Instituto Nacional de Colonización, the government continued its irrigation efforts. An additional 53,000 acres were irrigated in 1954; over 60,000 acres received water for the first time in 1955. According to government statistics, in normal years irrigated fields produced, on average, twice the amount of wheat per acre as unirrigated fields, while in semidrought periods, the amount of wheat per acre on an irrigated field was 3 times that of the unirrigated fields.

The government also continued its efforts at reforstation. More than 270,000 acres were planted in 1954, and 318,000 acres of new forests were started in 1955.

Inflation remained a serious problem. Using 1940 as the base, the price index increased slightly from 457.5 to 459.8 in 1954. In 1955, however, it jumped to 477.7. (Some authorities blamed the increase on a reduction in interest charged by the Banco de España. The bank July 1, 1954 lowered its rate to 3¾%; it had charged 4% since Mar. 23, 1949.) Using the 1953 peseta as a base, per capita income rose slightly to 8,943 pesetas in 1954 and 8,982 pesetas (about $225) in 1955.

With increased hospital services and a rise in the standard of living, infant mortality reached an all-time low of 4.92 per 100 live births in 1954; it rose slightly in 1955 to 5.09.

According to government reports, unemployment was decreasing steadily. There were 111,207 registered unemployed (out of a total estimated population of 29 million) in 1955. Foreign observers said, however, that registered unemployed did not include, among others, agricultural workers who worked in southern France part-time and, therefore, represented about $1/10$ the actual unemployed.

The agricultural laborer, was still low man in Spain, and his position was still below that of 1936; as of 1955 his standard of living was about 97.2% of that of 1935.

52,418 Spaniards left the country in 1954, while only 14,633 individuals entered; 62,237 left the next year, and 14,863 entered. The net loss was 85,154 in 2 years.

Foreign Trade

Spain's foreign trade suffered mounting deficits. Spain imported 1.9 billion gold pesetas and exported 1.44 billion gold pesetas in 1954; the net deficit was 460 million gold pesetas. The figures changed fractionally in 1955, and the deficit increased to 520 million gold pesetas.

The bulk of Spain's exports during 1954-5 were foodstuffs or raw material, while the bulk of the imports were manufactured products. Some manufactured items, however, were beginning to play an important role in Spanish exports—small arms, textiles, shoes, books and furniture. With the exception of the latter, Spanish manufactured products were shipped to other underdeveloped countries, primarily in Latin America, North Africa and the Middle East. (Spanish furniture, still a handicraft rather than an industrial item, was just starting to enter the U.S. market.) Spain's trade with the underdeveloped world, however, did not help provide needed hard currencies. Outside of tourism, Spain still lacked an industry capable of producing hard currencies.

In what some observers called a "propaganda move," Franco July 6, 1954 called for a complete economic boycott of Communist countries as a sure way to thwart Red aggression. But some sources questioned the honesty of his proposal. Experts suggested that Spain would trade with the Communist bloc if it could. Franco's position, they claimed, was based on Spanish fear of being excluded from such trade. In fact, Franco predicted that Germany and Japan would win the Communist markets anyway "once the channels for interchange are open."

Reports reaching the U.S. and Great Britain indicated that Spain did trade with Communist states. The *N.Y. Times* had reported June 19 that Spain had traded 300,000 metric tons of iron ore to Poland for 178,950 metric tons of coal in recent weeks. The *Times* said Spanish sources did not consider this in conflict with Franco's opposition to Communist trade because the ore technically was bought by Atlas Handel Co. of Munich, West Germany, and Spain took no responsibility for its destination. British MP George Jeger told Britain's House of Commons July 19 that Spain engaged in "extensive" trade with Communist countries while declaring itself opposed to such trade.

After British State Min. Selwyn Lloyd had announced in the House of Commons Dec. 14, 1953 that Britain would lift some of its restrictions on the sale of arms to Spain, some British MPs protested because of the increased anti-British propaganda in the Spanish press. The Conservative government not only went ahead with its plans but agreed to send a delegation to Madrid to discuss future trade arrangements. Despite the hostility of the Spanish government to the British presence on Gibraltar, Britain and Spain arrived at a trade and payments plan after discussions in Madrid Nov. 29–Dec. 22, 1954. Spain promised to increase its importation of British goods if the English would increase their purchases of Spanish raw materials. The Spanish also promised to pay some of the debts that they owed to British manufacturers.

Economic considerations both caused and led to the final resolution of a brief diplomatic dispute between Spain and the U.S. and Britain over the question of the sale of surplus Spanish war material. The inclusion of Spain in U.S. defense plans forced the Spanish government to increase Spain's ability to produce its own arms. But the increased Spanish production of weapons resulted in a surplus, and Spain sought markets for its unwanted war material. Since most Spanish arms manufacture was of light arms, Spanish customers were relatively underdeveloped states that could afford only cheap light weapons. Previously, the underdeveloped states had been able to buy military equipment only from the U.S. and its Western allies or the USSR. Few underdeveloped states then bought arms from the USSR, so the Spaniards became competitors of the U.S. and Western arms dealers.

The U.S. and Britain, the chief supplier of small arms to the underdeveloped states, were said to have used the sale of arms as a political tool to control some states. Egypt and several of the arms-buying nations, then involved in anti-imperialist campaigns, turned to Spain not only for arms but, it was reported, to free themselves from Anglo-Saxon domination. The Anglo-Saxon powers then put pressure on Franco. They objected specifically to Spanish arms sales to Egypt in the fear that the arms would be used by the revolutionary government of Egypt to seize the Suez Canal. (Pres. Muhammad Naguib of Egypt had already stated his intention to terminate the independence of the Anglo-Franch controlled Suez Canal Co.)

The U.S. State Department said July 19, 1954 that it had inquired in Madrid about Spanish exports of arms to Egypt and other countries. It expressed "concern" that such export might violate terms of the U.S.-Spanish military aid pact. Britain revealed the same day that it had asked Spain several times to stop sending arms to Egypt. The British Foreign Office confirmed that Spanish arms makers had contracted to sell to the Egyptians weapons that had been reported to be worth $3½ million and to include hundreds of mortars, more than 200,000 mortar shells and 900 machine guns. Franco apparently yielded to the pressure, and the British announced July 22 that Spain had agreed to sell no arms to Egypt. In order to prevent unfavorable sales of Spanish equipment, however, the U.S. agreed to buy the Spanish surplus. Lt. Gen. Orval Ray Cook, commander-in-chief of U.S.

forces in Europe, announced Oct. 4, 1954 that the U.S. had either bought or ordered $15,810,000 worth of Spanish armaments during 1953-4.

The Press & the Government

The Church continued to oppose state control of the press throughout this period.

Father Jesús Iribarren, editor of Enrique Cardinal Plá y Deniel's magazine *Ecclesia*, wrote in May 1954: "How can we consider our press regime as ideal when it obliges people to look elsewhere for the news that is the newspapers' *raison d'être?*" Unable to fine *Ecclesia* (being under the personal control of Plá y Deniel, it was the only publication in Spain not subject to government authority), the government, according to reliable first-hand underground sources, forced Plá y Deniel to fire Iribarren, who moved to Paris to continue the struggle.

Plá y Deniel, without mentioning the affair, indicated his displeasure, according to informants, in a pastoral letter in which he told Spanish Catholics July 1 that the church was "not tied to any regime" in Spain although it might "collaborate cordially" with the state. Franco responded that he did "not believe in freedom of the press." Newspapers were "mercantile enterprises," he declared, and press freedom meant freedom only for a few newspaper owners.

The government had been preparing a new press law. Information & Tourism Min. Gabriel Arias Salgado presented the measure to the cabinet Dec. 10, 1954. Although details of his proposal were not made public, Camille M. Cianfarra reported Dec. 16 in the *N.Y. Times* that the proposed law "would empower the government not only to control but actually to manage all Spain's privately owned newspapers." José María Areilza, Count Motrico, Spanish ambassador to the U.S., challenged Cianfarra's accuracy. The *Times* asserted Dec. 22 that Cianfarra's account must have been correct because, rather than deny the story, the Spanish government had prevented the sale of the Dec. 16 and Dec. 18 editions of the *Times* in Spain; it was those editions that contained the original and follow-up accounts.

Spanish press censorship was again sharply criticized Jan. 8, 1955 by *Ecclesia*. The magazine attacked a Dec. 13, 1954 speech in which Arias Salgado had said that the press should be at the service of the state. *Ecclesia* said that government pressure on newspapers, which should reflect public opinion, "obliges newspapers to publish as their opinions the views of the ruling circles." This, the article concluded, was an attack on human rights.

Ecclesia's position was defended, in an open letter, by the bishop of Málaga, Angel Herrera y Oria, who had been the pre-Civil War editor of *El Debate.* According to Henry F. Schulte in *The Spanish Press, 1470–1966*, the government backed down before Herrera's "needling."

An altered press law was proposed by Arias Salgado to the Cortes, and the revised proposal was enacted Apr. 28, 1955. The new press law called for the establishment of a Press Tribunal, which, according to Article 2 of the law, would try "dishonorable acts committed by those holding official press cards." Punishment under Article 5 would be "separation from the journalistic profession." The law did not change the government's power to punish newspapers by either closing the paper, removing the postal franchise or limiting the amount of newsprint available.

Opposition

The Church also opposed the government on other issues than press censorship. In several pastoral letters during the spring of 1954, Bishop Angel Herrera y Oria of Málaga and Archbishop Casimiro Morcillo of Zaragoza criticized the Franco government for failing to institute social reforms. Both prelates warned employers that they were evading their religious duty when they exploited the masses. Herrera indicated that he would like the government to force employers to make social reforms.

Many senior army officers, Stanley Payne wrote in *Politics and the Military in Modern Spain*, privately questioned the wisdom of Franco's Moroccan policy because it endangered not only their "honor" but their pockets. There were a number of fears, none of them stated publicly: Franco's support of Arab nationalists might result in the loss of African soil drenched in Iberian blood; Franco's policy might lead to the independence of Morocco, which would result in the loss of extra pay (those who served in Morocco received a bonus).

Of great threat to the *caudillo*, according to observers, was a growing Bourbonist tendency among the army officers. Conde de los Andes, who ex-Republican leader Salvador de Madariaga called "the recognized head of Spanish monarchists," visited Barcelona Feb. 17, 1954 and had an almost-public "private" interview with Lt. Gen. Juan Bautista Sánchez, military governor of the city.

During the late summer of 1954 a private poll was taken of the opinion of the Madrid garrison on the November municipal election. According to Stanley Payne, a large majority of the army favored the monarchist candidates.

Don Juan, pretender to the Spanish throne, met with Franco Dec. 29, 1954. According to Jean Creac'h in *Le Coeur et l'Épée*, he informed Franco that he had recently received the support of 4 additional lieutenant generals.

Monarchist opposition took several forms: (1), open pro-monarchist propaganda, (2), challenging Falangist candidates in municipal elections and (3) behind the scene alliances with various other dissident groups.

The government tried vainly to silence Madrid's leading monarchist paper, *ABC*. The Marques Torcuata Luca de Tena was removed in 1953 from his post as editor-in-chief of the paper even though he owned *ABC*. The paper, however, did not change its editorial policy and, according to Henry F. Schulte in *The Spanish Press, 1470-1966*, its tax exemptions on the purchase of newsprint was canceled by the government Dec. 15, 1954; in reality this action was a fine that cost the paper $400 a month. Despite the fine, *ABC* continued to back monarchist causes.

Luca de Tena, meanwhile, decided to challenge the Falange by seeking election to the Madrid city council. Several other monarchists also decided to run for office. Despite the fact that the Falange had used, what Benjamin Welles (in *Spain: The Gentle Anarchy*) called "goon-squads" to break up monarchist election rallies, the monarchists were able to poll 20% of the votes—only heads of families have the franchise—in the Nov. 21, 1954 nationwide municipal elections. In Madrid the Falange, the only legal party in Spain, received only 77.8% of the vote.

Various sources reported considerable clandestine monarchist activity. According to Benjamin Welles, Juan Claudio, Conde de Ruisenyada, "a Catalan industrialist, ... forged the link between the monarchists and Opus Dei," the Catholic lay organization, "by creating the Amigos de Maeztu," a private club where monarchists could meet secretly with other politicians. Rafael Calvo Serer (who, William Ebenstein reported in *Church and State in Franco Spain*, was considered by Opus Dei members to be their "most authoritative source"; Arthur P. Whitaker asserted in *Spain and Defense of the West* that he was known as "the philosopher of Opus Dei") was a close personal friend of the pretender Don Juan and since 1955 a confident of the latter's son Prince Juan Carlos. Observers asserted that the clandestine monarchist contacts with Opus Dei and the military led to a meeting between Franco and Don Juan.

Don Juan and Franco held their secret 9-hour meeting Dec. 29, 1954 at the Estremadura (southwest Spain) estate of the Conde de

Ruisenyada. The conclave had 2 other monarchists, the Conde de los Andes and the Conde de Frontenar. Observers said that the discussion revolved around the education of Don Juan's son Juan Carlos, 16, and the whole question of the future of the Spanish monarchy.

Juan Carlos, accompanied by his tutor, Carlos Martinez Campos, Duke de la Torre, arrived Jan. 18, 1955 in Madrid, where he was welcomed by several hundred monarchists. The members of the royal party announced that the prince would remain in Madrid for about 6 months and then enter the Military Academy at Zaragoza.

The appearance of the young prince set off a wave of protest from the Falange, which opposed the restoration of the monarchy. According to observers, Franco became so incensed at the Falangist attacks that he summoned the editor of *Arriba*, the leading Falangist newspaper, to the Pardo palace and demanded that the attacks stop. The interview, carefully worded by Franco, then appeared in the Jan. 23 edition of *Arriba:* Franco reminded the editor that the Succession Law of 1947 established Spain as a monarchy and promised the restoration of the monarch after his (Franco's) death or incapacity. He said: "Although I enjoy excellent health, the fact that I am 62 years of age suggests that everything possible should be done to ensure that the proposals in the Succession Law are implemented, and that there is no break in continuity." Franco indicated that the stay of Juan Carlos in Spain did not indicate that he would be the next sovereign, but, he said, it was "natural that we should be interested in seeing that the princes of the Spanish dynasty are prepared, although the time for formal recognition has not yet arrived." Apparently to calm the fears of the Falangists, Franco stated that "it is definitely the case" that the "principles of the Falangist Movement" would be the foundation of the monarchist government.

Observers agree that the interview did not pacify the Falange. The editor was again "summoned" to the palace, according to George Hills in *Franco*, and the new interview appeared in the Feb. 27 issue of *Arriba:* Franco called it an "indispensable premise" that the monarchy would be "completely identified with the National Movement, *i.e.*, the Falange." Franco said he could understand the apprehension among some elements of society. "We must remember," he said, "that more than half the nation knows very little about the monarchical system and that many people judge it by its last stages of decadence. This may justify the distrust felt for that institution by a great number of those who compose the younger generation. . . ." Franco said that when he spoke of the restoration of the monarchy, he implied the Bourbonist branch, not the Carlist. He indicated that he considered Don Juan the head of the Bourbón branch.

Franco insisted that the new monarchy would be on a different basis than the old: "We need to change the framework of the old monarchy for a new aristocracy of knowledge, military leadership, work, and service to the nation. We must do this to secure the social progress of the people, as the monarchy did in its best periods. We are all agreed that it is vital for us to preserve what we have forged for ourselves. The political and social essence of our national movement cannot be endangered."

Franco then announced that the next day he and all his ministers, the leaders of the armed forces, the Council of the Realm, members of the Cortes and the Diplomatic Corps would go to the Escorial to attend a solemn requium for the repose of the soul of Alfonso XIII. Anti-monarchist feelings were again demonstrated at a Falange celebration Nov. 55 in Madrid's Teatro de la Comedia when Falangists shouted: "We don't want idiot kings."

Observers reported that the Falangists were also angered at Franco's policy of permitting some books to be published in Basque and Catalan (Falangists, as nationalists, recognized only Castilian as the language of Spain and considered Basques and Catalans as traitors to Spain). Franco, without public announcement, permitted publishers in Bilbao and Barcelona in 1954 to print "some popular" works in the local languages; books were also published in the Galician dialect. Without public announcement, Franco permited the establishment of chairs of Catalan and Galician at Madrid University in 1954; a chair of Basque was quietly established at Salamanca in 1955.

According to some observers, Falangist anger with Franco exploded Nov. 20, 1955, when Franco appeared at the Escorial for a memorial mass for José Antonio Primo de Rivera, Falange founder, dressed in the uniform of a captain general instead of the blue shirt and white jacket uniform of the Falange. According to Claude Martin in *Franco*, *Soldado y Estadista*, the honor guard of Falangist Youth booed the *caudillo*. Brian Crozier reported in *Franco* that "Franco retaliated by dismissing the entire leadership of the Falangist Youth Front."

Don Juan, 42, despite his previously expressed liberal sentiments, said at a press conference at Estoril, Portugal (his home in exile) June 24, 1955 that the monarchy had always been in agreement with the ideals of the "nationalist movement" and that he considered himself the "repository of the rights inherited from" Alfonso XIII.

During 1954-5 the position of the Falange was considered increasingly difficult. Spain was drifting in paths of which the Falange did not approve, while Franco, in several public speeches, had begun to make a distinction between the National Movement, which was supposed to be based upon the ideas of the Falange, and the Falange. Even though the government July 5, 1954 had announced the first stage in the Falangist plan to nationalize the Rio Tinto Co., the British operator of various copper and sulpher mines, the Falange found itself unable to oppose the growing capitalism within the country.

Most Falange members were anti-monarchist but could do little to oppose the apparent eventual restoration of the monarchy. When the Falangist-dominated Sindicato Español Universitario (SEU) in Feb. 1955 distributed leaflets detailing a whole list of crimes committed by the last 6 Bourbón kings, Franco ordered a halt to the distribution. The *Boletín Oficial de Estado* announced Dec. 12 that José Antonio Elola Olaso had been removed Dec. 9 as national delegate of the Falangist youth "for reasons of health." (Elola Olaso had held the post since 1939.)

Both Max Gallo in *Histoire de l'Espagne Franquiste* and Sergio Vilar in *Protagonistas de la España Democratica* mentioned a student strike at Madrid University Jan. 25-7, 1954, but no further information seems to be available. The only student organization allowed on campus was the Falange-controlled Sindicato Español Universitario (SEU), but, according to observers, it had few regular members; all students had to be members, but few participated in the organization. Observers also noted that the students were disenchanted with government leaders. Herbert Matthews, in *The Yoke and the Arrows*, quoted a confidential poll taken in 1955 by Pedro Lain Entralgo, rector of Madrid University, which found that "75% of the students considered the government to be incompetent and 85% accused the ruling class of immorality. 90% thought the military hierarchy ignorant, bureaucratic, and worthless; 48% accused the military of being brutal libertines and heavy drinkers; 52% considered the ecclesiastical hierarchy to be immoral, ostentatious and ambitious."

Several Falangists led by Dionisio Ridruejo, who had become disenchanted with the capitalistic attitude of the government, formed a clandestine organization, Nuevo Tiempo, in 1955 to challenge SEU control of the campus. (Sergio Vilar, who interviewed several former Falangists, reported that the period 1954-6 was crucial in the minds of the intellectual Falangists, and it was during this period that many determined to move into open opposition of the government.)

Spanish philosopher José Ortega y Gasset died Oct. 18, 1955, and the intellectual Falangists decided to use his funeral as an excuse to demonstrate for university reforms. The chief speakers at the funeral, which was held in Madrid, were Dr. Pedro Lain Entralgo, rector of Madrid University, director of the Falangist Editora Nacional, member of the Council of the Realm and one of Spain's leading medical historians, and Joaquín Ruíz Giménez (also Jiménez), the leader of the Left-wing of the Christian Democratic Party and minister of Education. Both men called for the liberalization of political thought and a freer atmosphere on campus. After the service, more than 1,000 students followed the coffin through the streets of Madrid shouting reform slogans.

The 5th Congress of the Spanish Communist Party was held in Paris in Nov. 1954. The party called for a united anti-Franco alliance of all from the middle class to the proletariat, but none of the other Spanish opposition groups responded.

Spanish secret police rounded up various active opposition leaders in 1954-5, and the "revolutionists" received stiff sentences. Narcisio Julian, leader of the Spanish Communist Party and member of the Central Committee, was given 2 20-year sentences in Jan. 1954.

A court in Vitoria, capital of Basque-populated Álava Province, handed down sentences Mar. 30, 1954 in the trial of 17 Basque nationalists charged with organizing strikes during Apr. 1951 in the Basque provinces of Vizcaya and Guipúzcoa. The main defendants, Julian Aguirre and Pablo Olaverria, who the government claimed were, respectively, the president and general secretary of the Clandestine Basque Nationalist Party, and for whom the government had demanded prison sentences of 25 and 21 years, were freed. One other prisoner was also acquitted. The remaining 14 were given sentences ranging from 3 months to 14 years and 5 months and fined from 2,500 pesetas (about $64) to 32,500 pesetas (about $900).

The case, which had gone to trial Mar. 25, had received worldwide attention as a result of a protest sent to the Duke de Primo de Rivera, Spanish ambassador in London, by 13 members of the British Parliament, who, as their letter of Mar. 17 stated, were retaliating for Spanish objections to the visit of Queen Elizabeth II to Gibraltar. According to reliable informants, the 17 defendants had been apprehended after the Apr. 1951 strikes but released in a 1953 amnesty. Shortly after their release, they were rearrested on the same charges and held in jail. The verdict stipulated that all those whose sentence was less than 12 months were to be released because they had already spent more than a year in prison.

Prison terms of one to 15 years were imposed on 17 anarchists and a monarchist convicted in Madrid Feb. 5, 1954 of anti-government activities. Cipriano Damiano, 36, secretary general of the anarchist Confederación Nacional del Trabajo (CNT), received a 15-year sentence.

A Spanish court-martial in Ocaña convicted 34 men Mar. 30, 1954 of subversive attempts to reorganize the Communist Party in Spain. They received prison sentences of one to 20 years.

In honor of the Catholic Marian year, Franco decreed a political amnesty July 25, 1954 and freed an undisclosed number of political offenders.

The government announced Dec. 17, 1954 that Spaniards who had left the country during the Civil War could return to Spain for visits of up to 30 days and then depart without any special authorization. Specifically excluded from this offer were Spaniards guilty of crimes for which they had received neither pardon nor amnesty. Many exiles, including ex-members of the Catalan Republican Government, had already been returning to Spain for brief visits since 1950.

U.S. Relations

The 1953 U.S.-Spanish military agreement, frequently called "the Pact of Madrid," did not list U.S. installations to be built. During 1954 and 1955 these details were negotiated. U.S. military experts, concerned about growing turmoil in Morocco, where a wing of about 45 U.S. B-47 Stratojet bombers, capable of long-distance atomic strikes, was placed Jan. 29, 1954, were eager to get the Spanish bases completed before the U.S. had to evacuate the Moroccan positions.

According to information presented before the U.S. House Appropriations Committee in Jan. 1954, the U.S. at that time intended to build 4 air bases, one naval base and 6 naval fuel and ammunition dumps. According to the published report of the hearings (Jan. 31), the U.S. planned to enlarge the Torrejon airport near Madrid at a cost of $43 million and to expand Spanish facilities at the El Copero and Moron de la Frontera airfields near Sevilla and the Zaragoza airport at a cost of $57 million. Work on the 4 fields was scheduled to begin in May. The naval station was to be established at the small port of Rota on the Bay of Cádiz and was budgeted at a cost of $50 million. A 540-mile oil pipeline linking Rota with the 4 airbases was to be built at an estimated cost of $41 million. The locations of the various fuel and ammunition dumps were not revealed, but it was stated that the costs would be comparatively small.

Since the U.S.-Spanish agreement had not been cleared by the U.S. Congress, some members began to question the right of the U.S. to use the bases in wartime. U.S. Air Force Secy. Harold E. Talbott had said at a news conference Jan. 26 that Spanish bases would be used in war although existing agreements provided only for peacetime use. He explained later that the bases would not be used for war without Spain's consent.

The U.S. Senate, meanwhile, undertook a study of the matter. Sen. Dennis Chavez (D., N.M.) visited Spain and French Morocco. He then told the Senate Appropriations Committee Feb. 20 that Spain should be admitted to NATO and that the British-French opposition to its admission was "shortsighted." He reported that the U.S. planned to build a deepwater port and naval air station at Rota as one of its first projects in Spain and a 350-mile $9,700,000 aviation fuel pipeline from Cádiz to airfields at El Copero and Torrejon (The pipeline eventually reached Zaragoza, 100 miles northeast of Madrid.)

A U.S. House Armed Services subcommittee visited Spain and then Dec. 28 demanded an investigation of Navy "red tape" and "bureaucratic intermeddling" that allegedly was holding up construction of the Spanish bases.

Spain had received its first arms shipment under the U.S.-Spanish mutual defense pact when 1,800 tons of U.S. military equipment reached Cartagena Feb. 15, 1954.

The Spanish government Apr. 29, 1954 disclosed this planned distribution of $85 million the U.S. was providing in economic aid during the fiscal year ending June 30, 1954: cotton, coal and other raw material, $31 million; railways, $11 million; electric power, $12½ million; agricultural tools, $8½ million; steel industry, $8 million; technical assistance $1 million; roads and irrigation, $5 million; cement manufacturing, $4 million; civil aviation, defense industry and mining, $4 million.

Spain had announced Mar. 15 that it would buy 300,000 metric tons (10 million bushels) of surplus U.S. wheat to prevent a summer shortage in 1954. The U.S. was to apply the proceeds (in pesetas) toward expenses at the air and naval base construction projects in Spain. By paying for the wheat in paper pesetas, which the U.S. government would then use to pay the salaries of Spaniards working on U.S. installations, the Spanish government could buy needed commodities without increasing its balance-of-payment deficit. (Eventually, however, the process led to inflation and a further devaluation of the peseta because the U.S. began to accumulate pesetas faster than they could be spent. Since the U.S. had unneeded pesetas, and because U.S. personnel had to buy basic consumer goods on the open market at inflated prices, the U.S. and Spain agreed to let U.S. personnel buy their pesetas at the finance office at the black market rate instead of the legal rate.)

Antonio Jiménez Arnau, director of the Spanish Economic Corp., warned the American Chamber of Commerce in Barcelona Feb. 12, 1955 that inadequate U.S. aid might jeopardize Spanish-U.S. relations. Newspapers had reported Jan. 7 that 250,000 U.S. food packages had been distributed to needy families as part of $170 million in economic aid and surplus farm commodities granted by the U.S. Foreign Operations Administration. The Foreign Operations Administration reported Mar. 27 that Spain already had received $202,582,000 in U.S. economic aid. The Spanish Agriculture Ministry Feb. 2 had disclosed U.S.-aided plans to irrigate 1¼ million acres of arid land.

The U.S. Foreign Operations Administration announced Jan. 31, 1955 that Spain had been given $14.8 million worth of surplus raw cotton in return for a promise to manufacture an equivalent value of armaments for the Spanish army.

The U.S. announced May 3, 1955 that it had concluded an agreement to moderize about 20 Spanish destroyers, gunboats, corvettes, minesweepers and other vessels and to provide them with new armaments, radar and fire-control equipment. The U.S. was to supply some of the equipment. Spain and other European countries were to produce the rest.

U.S. Pres. Eisenhower announced June 11, 1955 that the U.S. and Spain had reached an agreement for Spain to receive U.S. atomic information for peaceful purposes.

U.S. Amb. John Davis Lodge had told the American Chamber of Commerce in Barcelona May 31 that the U.S. had allotted more than $500 million worth of military and economic aid to Spain since signing the agreement on U.S. bases in Sept. 1953. Despite the quantity of U.S. aid being committed to Spain, however, Franco had said in a speech to the Cortes May 16 that the effect of U.S. aid on the Spanish economy was not yet visible.

U.S. State Secy. Dulles flew to Madrid Nov. 1 for a 2-hour talk with Franco during a recess of Big 4 talks he was attending in Geneva. Dulles' trip was in response to Spanish suggestions for such a meeting for more than a year as strains appeared in U.S.-Spanish relations. He was the first U.S. State Secretary to visit Spain. A Spanish Foreign Ministry communiqué Nov. 1 said: Dulles and Franco had "examined the present international situation, reviewing the principal problems that affected the peace and security of free nations. They found themselves in mutual understanding [on] these questions." They also discussed "Spanish-American relations within the framework of agreements on mutual defense assistance, economic aid and defense support." They reaffirmed "the spirit of collaboration" that led to the agreements of 1953.

The *N.Y. Times* had reported from Madrid Dec. 25, 1954 that the Spanish General Staff and the U.S. Military Group in Spain had drafted an agreement requiring that the Catholic Church in Spain sanction marriages between Catholic and non-Catholics in Spain involving Americans. The Defense Department in Washington, responding to U.S. Protestant protests, said Dec. 17, after consultation with the State Department and U.S. Air Force, that the draft agreement was to be "reviewed in Washington." The proposed agreement was reported in Washington Mar. 10, 1955 to have been dropped by the U.S. State Department because of the U.S. protests. But the question of such marriages remained a ticklish problem. Franco finally intervened, to the annoyance of the Church. A civil case was instituted, and the state violated Church Law. The right of Spanish Catholics to enter into civil marriages with non-Catholics was upheld June 18, 1955 by the Madrid Court of Appeals. The court ruling abrogated existing administrative regulations based on Canon Law, which forbade such marriages except in grave circumstances and did not recognize a Catholic's personal renunciation of membership in the faith.

It was announced in Madrid Aug. 10, 1954 that José María de Areilza, Conde de Motrico, had been appointed Spanish ambassador to the U.S. to succeed José Felix de Lequerica. Areilza, 45, a leading industrialist with close contacts with Christian Democratic politicians, was an active supporter of the pretender Don Juan.

British Relations

When the British had announced that Queen Elizabeth II would visit Gibraltar at the end of a world tour in 1954, Franco, according to Benjamin Welles in *Spain: The Gentle Anarchy*, had "pulled out all stops" on anti-British propaganda. While Franco demanded that Britain return Gibraltar to Spain, some observers held that it was worth more to Spain in British hands. There were 9,000 to 10,000 Spaniards employed on Gibraltar. These workers, who returned home to Spain every night, earned about £6 ($16.80, or 750 pesetas) a week—or more than a Spanish civil servant earned in a month. Franco permitted the workers to keep $1/5$ of their salary in sterling, while the balance was converted to paper pesetas, at an unfavorable rate of exchange, at the La Linea frontier post. As a result of this transaction the Spanish government received £3 million in needed hard currency annually.

The Duke Primo de Rivera, Spanish ambassador in London, called on English Prime Min. Anthony Eden Jan. 12, 1954 requested that the English cancel the queen's visit to Gibraltar. The British Foreign Office said Jan. 17 that the Spanish ambassador had been informed that the visit would go as planned and that Queen Elizabeth's visits to any of her territories was the concern of no foreign power. The Spanish Foreign Ministry asserted Jan. 19 that the visit was not only "imprudent" and that it would adversely affect Anglo-Spanish relations but that it would also undoubtedly evoke a "national protest" from Spaniards. "Gibraltar is Spanish territory to which the people of Spain do not renounce their claim," the statement concluded.

Having issued a warning, Franco, it was reported, permitted the Falangist Youth Front to riot. Several thousand students carrying Spanish and Falangist flags broke windows at the British embassy and at the British Institute in Madrid Jan. 22. After the damage was done, the Spanish police disbursed the mob. An estimated 30,000 individuals Jan. 25 attacked a cordon of police thrown around the embassy. The police fired blanks in the air and charged the mob. 18 police and 30 demonstrators were injured; 4 of the injuries resulted from gun shot wounds. While the main action took place in front of the British embassy, other groups of individuals roamed through Madrid smashing the windows of the Madrid branch of the Bank of London and South America, ripping up magazine stands that carried foreign publications showing the queen's picture, stoning official cars and even attempting to enter the Madrid Radio station. Some reporters commented on the festive nature of the demonstration: the students sang Falangist and anti-British songs and shouted obscenities against the queen.

Other demonstrations took place in Barcelona, where windows of the British consulate were smashed; in Sevilla, where the British consulate was pelted by oranges; in Granada, where students managed to hoist the Spanish flag atop the vice-consulate building (the Spanish police eventually removed the banner), and in Córdova, where students paraded in a demand for the annexation of Gibraltar by Spain.

Some British Parliament members linked the riots in Spain with a previously announced decision to sell arms to Spain. Laborites Ernest Davies and George Jeger suggested that the British were appeasing Franco. British State Min. Selwyn Lloyd replied in the House Commons Jan. 25 that there was no "appeasement" intended and that the decision to sell arms to Spain was "governed entirely by commercial considerations." Jeger demanded to know "where the sense or logic comes in sending arms to our self-confessed enemies."

British Amb.-to-Spain Sir John Balfour presented 2 strong protests to the Spanish government but received no reply.

A Spanish government broadcast Jan. 26 said the demonstrations had indicated "the well-known unanimity with which the Spanish people condemn certain foreign policies."

The Spanish Information Ministry Jan. 28 released a statement claiming that the Madrid demonstrations were caused by "high patriotic motives" although they resulted in "distressing incidents which are deplored by all." The government was investigating the situation in order to "discover the facts and determine where the responsibility lies," the statement said. "Extraneous elements, following a plan of infiltration and agitation, had mixed with the students with the express purpose of spoiling their noble intentions and disrupting public order." The report concluded with the announcement that 18 among those arrested were individuals "with records that confirm their role as agitators" against the Franco regime.

The British Admiralty announced Jan. 28 that a visit the Home Fleet had intended to pay to Spain and Spanish Morocco during February and March had been cancelled. The admiralty statement concluded: "In view of the recent manifestations of anti-British feeling in Spain, the government have informed the Spanish government that, in the circumstances, they do not consider that any useful purpose can be served by these visits."

Meanwhile British Parliament members sent letters protesting the alleged persecution of 17 Basque nationalists then on trial. When the Duke Primo de Rivera, the Spanish ambassador in London, objected to such British interference in Spain's internal affairs, Britons informed the duke that he had interfered in Britain's internal affairs when he had objected to the visit of Elizabeth II to Gibralter.

Franco closed the Spanish consulate in Gibraltar Apr. 9, 1954. He ordered all Spaniards except those employed there to refrain from visiting the British colony, and he ordered Spanish customs officials at La Linea to make extensive checks of luggage entering Spain. The purpose of the last move was to deter tourists visiting Spain from making side trips to Gibraltar; there was no problem entering Gibraltar from Spain, but it could take 4 or 5 hours to clear La Linea customs on the turn. Tourist trade to Gibraltar was hurt.

Anti-British agitation then ceased for a while.

France & Morocco

Relations between Spain and France were growing increasingly bitter because of the Morocco issue. Reported to be disturbed by the generally acknowledged anti-French attitude of Lt. Gen. Rafael García Valiño, the Spanish high commissioner (resident) in Morocco, French Foreign Min. Georges Bidault summoned the Conde de Casa-Rojas, the Spanish ambassador to Paris, to a series of meetings Jan. 18 and 20, 1954 to discuss the intent of a proposed demonstration in Tetuan, the capital of Spanish Morocco. The French ambassador in Madrid, meanwhile, was seeking a statement on this subject from the Spanish Foreign Ministry.

Unable to secure assurances from Spain after the Jan. 18 meetings in Paris and Madrid, the French Foreign Ministry warned in a statement released later Jan. 18 that France would defend the unity of Morocco "by all the means in its power."

The 2d Paris meeting was in response to a note in which the cabinet of Mulay Muhammad bin Arafa, the recently enthroned pro-French sultan of Morocco, warned the French of the danger to Moroccan unity if the Spanish were permitted to proceed with the Tetuan demonstration.

García Valiño staged his demonstration of 30,000 in Tetuan Jan. 21, at which time he received an anti-French declaration signed by 430 Spanish Moroccan leaders. The declaration was given to him by Ahmed el-Haddad, grand vizir of Tetuan, who was acting for the khalifa, Hassan el-Mehdi, the deposed Sultan Muhammad V's representative in the Spanish Zone. Observers noted that even though the khalifa had sent his eldest son and his brothers to stand beside García Valiño, he, himself, was absent, obstensibly because of illness.

The declaration said: "We emphatically repudiate . . . the policy pursued in the French Zone and the procedure which led to the dethronement of the ligitimate sultan, Sidi Muhammad bin Yusef [Muhammad V], as a result of the intrigues of the French Residency . . . in opposition to the whole Moroccan population of that zone, in complete contempt for their views and feelings and in violation of the agreement under which the protectorate was established. We express our unconditional adherence to, and the gratitude of the whole Moroccan people for, the policy pursued in the Spanish Zone by your excellency [García Valiño]. We proclaim that we do not recognize the authority of Mulay [bin] Arafa as he was arbitrarily imposed by France in opposition to, and without regard for, the sentiments of the Moroccan people. We respect and reaffirm the fundamental idea, which has always been upheld by Spain, of the unity of the Moroccan empire. In these circumstances we demand the separation of the Spanish Zone for as long as the present political conditions remain in the French Zone. We wish the khalifa of our zone [Hassan el-Mehdi] to have full sovereignty over it, without any dependence on Mulay [bin] Arafa. . . ."

García Valiño replied: "The year 1953 has endangered the existence of the Moroccan nation. Ignoring her treaty obligations to support and strengthen the authority of the sultan legally elected by the Moroccan people, France imagined that the way out of the difficulties in which her own political mistakes had involved her lay in violent intervention and in support for a request by certain governmental authorities in her zone, which she herself had organized. France thereby took a step which can be described as irremediable and for which she must assume full responsibility, as at no time was our advice sought. The peace which now prevails in the Spanish Zone, in contrast to the unrest and anguish in the neighboring zone, bears eloquent witness to the succession of unpardonable errors committed by the strong hand of France." The Spanish commissioner concluded with the promise that the Tetuan declaration would be sent to Franco, who would "take what action he considered appropriate."

In honor of the declaration, García Valiño declared an amnesty Jan. 22: all those sentenced to prison for less than 2 years were liberated, while those with longer sentences had their terms reduced.

The French government, having received a copy of the Tetuan declaration almost immediately after its receipt by García Valiño, announced Jan. 21 that France would maintain its policy of defending a united Morocco and that France would defend the person of the new sultan. The French Jan. 22 sent to Franco what it described as a "firm and precise note" requesting Spanish cooperation in preserving the unity of the Sherifian Empire, as Morocco was legally called. The Spanish government refused to comment on the French note but did release a statement Jan. 22 to the effect that Franco had sent to García Valiño a cable expressing "great satisfaction" with the results of the Tetuan affair.

Gen. Augustin Guillaume, the French resident general (high commissioner), released to the press Jan. 23 a statement in which he claimed that not only had the Tetuan demonstration been organized by García Valiño but that Spanish officers had been sent among the various tribes to prepare the event. Furthermore, Guillaume complained not only was Spain the only country involved in Moroccan affairs who did not recognize the new sultan, but Spanish authorities had deliberately "paralyzed" all attempts within the Spanish Zone to galvanize support behind the new monarch. After dismissing the Spanish charge that Spain had not been informed of French intentions to remove Muhammad V on the ground that events had transpired so fast that there was no time to inform Madrid, the French resident charged that since Muhammad V's exile the Spanish had demonstrated "ever growing hostility" and that articles in the Spanish press and statements over the Spanish radio had carried "the most improbable stories and open appeals to revolt." Guillaume said that the Spanish campaign of undermining the government of the new sultan "was bound to lead to the manifestations of Jan. 21."

Sultan Mulay bin Arafa Jan. 24 issued a proclamation in which he asserted that he was the legal ruler of Morocco and warned that those who had "taken part in the Tetuan conspiracy" would be punished. The statement said there was evidence that those who had signed the Tetuan declaration had done so "under constraint and compulsion" and that "their actions and words were completely opposed to their thoughts and feelings." The sultan further charged that "occult influences" were responsible for Morocco's difficulties.

Meanwhile Muhammad V and his entourage had been billeted at L'Ile-Rousse on the northwest cost of Corsica. The deposed sultan, 2 of his sons and some of his wives were flown by the French Jan. 25, 1954 to Brazzaville, capital of the French Congo, where they stayed a few days. But the French said they feared an attempt to rescue the exiles, so Muhammad and his companions were flown to the French island colony of Madagascar, where they were lodged Jan. 29 at the interior mountain resort of Antsirabe, 100 miles southwest of Tananarive. The French government announced Feb. 3 that the exiles would be flown within a few weeks to the French colony of Tahiti. (But the French finally announced Apr. 23 that Muhammad, who had promised to refrain from further political activity, would be exiled permanently on Madagascar.)

Responding to Franco's continued friendly advances toward the Arab states, the Arab League Council in Cairo had announced Jan. 27 that it would not support Mulay bin Arafa and would continue to recognize Muhammad V as Morocco's legitimate sovereign. It expressed "the gratitude" of the Arab countries for the Spanish support of Muhammad V. The Council also expressed its support of the khalifa of Tetuan.

Franco welcomed Ahmed el-Haddad, the grand vizir of Tetuan, and various khalifan officials to Madrid Feb. 9. After the Spanish Moroccans had expressed their loyalty to the Franco government, Franco called it "not surprising that you should have raised your protest once the political basis of the [Moroccan] protectorate had been broken by the violent action of France." He said: "The fact that other interested powers maintain silence . . . does not mean that they approve of the violent and peculiar French action. For my part I can assure you that Spain will continue to be true to the treaties and loyal to her Moroccan brothers. She will inflexibly defend the unity of Morocco and the letter and spirit of the agreement, not accepting situations and facts which are contrary to our way of thinking and also to international morality and signed treaties. We are sure that the force of reason will in the end triumph over the unreason of force. Until that time comes, the Moroccan zone entrusted to our keeping will continue under the sovereignty of his imperial highness Prince Hassan el-Mehdi [the khalifa], assisted by our high commissioner, the authorities of the khalifa's government, pashas and *caids.*"

French Foreign Affairs Secy. Maurice Schumann accused Spain Feb. 11 of fostering anti-French moves. He denied a Spanish charge that France had violated international agreements on the Spanish Zone's sovereignty. But the French cabinet said Feb. 13, however, that there had been a favorable change in Spain's attitude toward anti-French agitation in Spanish Morocco.

With Franco's agreement, García Valiño had permitted Abd el-Khalek Torres, leader of Islah, to return to Tetuan Jan. 21. Khalek Torres reorganized the revolutionary Sociedad Hipica of Tetuan. Then, with the tacit approval of García Valiño and Ahmed el-Haddad, the grand vizir, he began to organize resistance to bin Arafa.

Meanwhile, Mark I. Cohen and Lorna Hahn reported in *Morocco, Old Land, New Nation*, French Morocco was torn by riots, terror and mass arrests, "several hundred each week." Many supporters of the deposed sultan died in jail; "14 of 45 suspects had died during a 16-hour imprisonment in an unventilated room 8 feet by 5."

French Premier Pierre Mendès-France removed Gen. Guillaume in June 1954, and Francis Lacoste, a career diplomat, became resident June 14.

Conditions in French Morocco were reported to be deteriorating, and French business began to suffer. Imports from France dropped 10%, and 130 French-owned shops went bankrupt. There was a major riot in Port Lyautey Aug. 9, "and nearly 300 fresh graves were counted the next day," Cohen and Hahn reported in *Morocco, Old Land, New Nation.* Moroccans began to attack all Europeans and even native Moroccan Jews, of whom there were 250,000 in the French Zone and 10,450 in the Spanish area. The attacks on Europeans and Jews were said to have convinced some Frenchmen that it had been a blunder to force Mulay bin Arafa on Morocco. In France there was a growing movement to force Pres. René Coty to make drastic reforms in Morocco, but the president of France had little real authority to initiate legislation. By September, it was reported, most Europeans in French Morocco went armed and Right-wing organizations began to organize counter-terror squads. According to Cohen and Hahn (in *Morocco, Old Land, New Nation*), some hired "Spanish, Corsican and French thugs to do their dirty work."

Lacoste flew to Paris in September for new instructions. He returned with a compromise plan: legislative authority was to be taken from the sultan and grand vizir and given to a 6-man council of

of 3 Moroccans and 3 Frenchmen. The nationalists, however, refused
to discuss anything until the return of Muhammad V.

Thami el-Glaoui, pasha of Marrakesh, was in Paris by Dec. 1954, attempting to persuade the French cabinet not to restore Muhammad V.
Mulay bin Arafa was reported to have purchased "property in Tangiers
as a possible refuge," and the French made an effort to secure Muhammad V's official abdication by offering him a residence in France.

There were frequent clashes in French Morocco. With what was
said to be García Valiño's tacit approval, terrorists hid in the Rif (in
Spanish Morocco) during the day and crossed into the French Zone at
night.

According to reports, some Spanish military leaders began to question the wisdom of Franco's policy, which, according to Arthur P.
Whitaker (in *Spain and Defense of the West*), was to keep Spanish
Morocco while pretending to support Moroccan independence. These
leaders speculated in private over whether the independence movement
in the French Zone would soon spread to Spanish Morocco. But, according to many authorities, Franco, convinced that France would
never surrender its hold over Morocco, doubted that the nationalists
could achieve their goals.

But France, under the 4th Republic, had already lost its empire in
Indochina and the Middle East. While most of French Africa remained
dormant, the French position in Algeria and Tunisia was being chal-
lenged by nationalists. For awhile some French leaders asserted that
France's position in Morocco was secure: Pierre July, minister for
Moroccan and Tunisian affairs, and the new French Premier, Edgar
Faure, asserted in Feb. 1955 that "there is no throne question in
Morocco," *i.e.*, Muhammad V was no longer sultan and bin Arafa was.
But Cohen and Hahn reported in *Morocco, Old Land, New Nation* that
at the end of May, Pierre July "acknowledged that there was after all a
throne question."

The French position eroded throughout the summer of 1955.
Troops supporting France and bin Arafa attempted unsuccessfully to
force Moroccan shopkeepers to end their strike and open their shops.
More and more Moroccan officials took quick trips from Rabat to
Madagascar, where the ousted Muhammad V lived in exile. By late
June French officials were suggesting that bin Arafa abdicate and a re-
gency be established.

Lacoste, unable to stem the tide of rebellion, was replaced as resident general by Gilbert Grandval, who arrived in Rabat July 7 and took
charge immediately although he did not officially take office until
July 20. Lacoste left Morocco July 17 and was officially removed from

office July 20. Grandval was dubbed "man of the last chance" by people who wanted France to remain in Morocco.

As Aug. 20, the 2d anniversary of Muhammad V's deposition approached, nationalist leaders were reported planning demonstrations to mark the day. They organized the Moroccan Liberation Army with headquarters in Spanish Morocco at Nador in the Rif Mountains. According to French charges, the rebels received material support from the Spanish resident, Lt. Gen. Rafael García Valiño. Terrorism and counter-terrorism plagued the French sector. Smala tribesmen Aug. 20 massacred the French population—about 200 men, women and children—of Oued Zem. France acted quickly and sent 110,000 troops to Morocco. But within a week the death toll in the riots, raids and massacres throughout the entire French sector had reached several thousand.

France protested Oct. 5 about Spain's alleged aid to the rebels, especially to those in the Rif, where the new Moroccan Liberation Army was being organized by Dr. Abd el-Krim Khatib, the Berber chief Mahjub Ahardane and the Communist Abd el-Krim bin Abdullah with the full support of the 74-year-old revolutionary hero Abd el-Krim, who was in Cairo. Calling on Spain to stop aiding guerrillas who had attacked French outposts in Morocco Oct. 1, the French Foreign Ministry told Spanish Amb. José Rojas y Moreno, Count de Casa-Rojas, that it had information that rebels had entered French Morocco from Spanish Morocco. García Valiño said in Tetuan Oct. 8 that the French charges were "unfounded." But he added that border patrols had been strengthened, following the French protest, to keep natives of Spanish Morocco from joining rebels in French Morocco.

About 8,000 French troops, supported by Vampire jet planes, opened an anti-rebel offensive in the Aknoul-Boured-Tizi Ouzli triangle near the Spanish Moroccan border Oct. 9. The objective was to encircle guerrillas in the Rif to cut their supply lines. The triangle was about 160 air miles northeast of Rabat, capital of French Morocco, and about 5 miles south of Spanish Morocco. (500 Berber tribesmen who had attacked Imouzzer-des-Marmoucha Oct. 1 had surrendered to the French Oct. 5.)

Spain Oct. 15 sent France a note protesting not only "the systematic campaign of false information conducted by the French press and radio" but the allegations by the French resident general, Lt. Gen. Pierre Georges Boyer de Latour du Moulin (who had replaced Grandval Aug. 31), and French Armed Forces Min. Pierre Billotte that the Rif-based Moroccan Liberation Army was receiving Spanish support. The Spanish claimed that they had prevented infiltration into the French zone by trouble makers and that García Valiño had closed the Gueznia region of the Rif. The Spanish warned that "if this campaign of false and baseless information continues in French organs of publicity—a campaign which could not be carried out without official backing—and if French authorities continue in their unfounded declarations . . . Spain will be obliged to denounce the facts before the UN," where it would show proof of "what is being attempted with this campaign and who menaces peace in this zone of the world."

Gen. Boyer de Latour, rejecting the Spanish note, said Oct. 16: "It is notorious that the Moroccan rebels have found help and refuge in the Spanish Zone of Morocco. . . . The most patent fact, which no one can deny, is that the French post of Bou Zineb which was only an observation post in the Spanish Zone, was attacked by rebels, and that the neighboring Spanish post, which is responsible for maintaining order in the area, did not intervene." A French unit had been fired on from Spanish territory Oct. 14 but did not return the fire. Boyer de Latour challenged the truth of García Valiño's assertion of Oct. 15 that he had invited a French officer to visit Spanish Morocco to "ascertain personally" the "falseness of the French accusations" that Spain was helping Moroccan guerrillas attack French outposts. The French statement said that Boyer de Latour had asked the Spanish high commissioner "to establish contact between the French and Spanish general staffs" and that he had "waited about 3 days for an answer that was not entirely positive."

A Spanish spokesman in Tetuan said Oct. 16 that he could "not understand" the French statement. He repeated that García Valiño had issued the invitation.

The Spanish Foreign Ministry Oct. 17 issued an official reply to Boyer de Latour's statement. The Spanish reply asserted that since the topography of the Franco-Spanish frontier in Morocco was so mountainous, the border had never really been defined with any exactitude and that, therefore, it would be difficult to prove that the French forces had been fired on from Spanish territory. Furthermore, the statement said, "the resident general complains that the Spanish position near the advanced post of Bou Zineb [a French observation post inside Spanish Morocco, Bou Zineb had been seized by rebels in the first week of October] did not help that post when it was attacked by rebels. Yet the French government, when it violated treaties to depose the legitimate sultan, cannot now call upon Spain for assistance in military operations intended to suppress the discontent provoked by this obtuse policy. . . ."

The Spanish consul general in Rabat complained to Boyer de Latour Oct. 18 that on 3 different occasions French aircraft or artillery had fired into Spanish territory. The French denied the allegations.

The French launched an offensive against rebel forces east of Tizi Ouzli Oct. 23, but the rebels escaped into the Spanish Zone. Rebels from Bou Zineb, the rebel-seized French observation post in Spanish Morocco, attacked the French outpost near Boured Oct. 25 and then returned across the frontier to Spanish Morocco. The French reoccupied Bou Zineb Nov. 3, and the rebels fled into the surrounding Spanish territory. French sources claimed that during the first 2 weeks of October the rebels had lost 143 killed and 2,115 wounded. No estimate of French and pro-government losses was given.

The French had called a conference with Moroccan nationalists at Aix-les-Bains Aug. 22-30, and Premier Edgar Faure had worked out this compromise: Muhammad V would be permitted to leave Madagascar for a dignified residence in France; Mulay bin Arafa would be deposed; Grandval would be replaced; some sort of representative legislative body would be established to ensure the Moroccans a greater degree of home rule, and a regency council, called the Council of Guardians of the Throne, would be established to settle the succession crisis. Gen. Georges Catroux headed a French delegation that called on Muhammad V in Madagascar Sept. 8-9 to explain the settlement plan.

Without consulting bin Arafa, the Council of the Guardians of the Throne was established Oct. 17, and Pasha Fatmi Ben Slimane was asked Oct. 19 to form a government. The Democratic Party for Independence (DPI) agreed to join a government, but Istiqlal representatives initially refused because Muhammad V was still on Madagascar. The Istiqlal resistance ended Oct. 22 after Council member M'Barek Ben Bekkai announced that Muhammad V approved of the composition of the Council and Ben Slimane announced the imminent departure of Muhammad V from Madagascar.

Ahmed Lyazidi, deputy secretary of Istiqlal said that the Council of the Throne would defend Muhammad V, not Mulay bin Arafa. By Oct. 25 Thami el-Glaoui, pasha of Marrakesh, had switched sides from Mulay bin Arafa to Muhammad V, and he made this declaration: "My visit to the members of the Council of Guardians of the Throne must not be interpreted as a recognition of the council, the legitimacy of which I have never ceased to deny. I share the joy of the entire Moroccan people at the announcement of his majesty Sidi Muhammad [V] bin Yusef's return to France. I associate myself with the desire of the Moroccan nation for the speedy restoration of Sidi Muhammad bin Yusef and his return to the throne, which alone can unify the nation in heart and spirit. . . ."

Mulay bin Arafa, in a letter to French Pres. Coty Oct. 29, announced his intention to abdicate as sultan. He said: "The situation in Morocco obliges us to take a further step along the path of self-effacement on which we have entered in our people's interests. In view of the unanimity of our beloved people, and of the will of a nation to which France has given unity and prosperity, we now consider it our duty . . . to renounce all our rights, whilst calling upon our subjects to rally, now that all obstacles have been removed, to the person of Sidi Muhammad bin Yusef."

Mulay bin Arafa abdicated Oct. 30, 1955. French government announced Oct. 31 that it was pleased with "the possibilities which are now offered of ensuring calm and orderly development in Morocco."

Muhammad V arrived in Nice, France Oct. 31 and was taken to a villa in St. Germain-en-Laye, near Paris. He met French Foreign Min. Antoine Pinay Nov. 1 and other French and Moroccan leaders, including Gen. Charles de Gaulle (who held no formal post). The French government Nov. 5 formally recognized Muhammad V's restoration as sultan, and he was flown to Rabat Nov. 16 by Air France.

France said in its Nov. 5 statement: "The French government is happy to state that the crisis which has long divided Morocco can now end with the unanimous agreement of the Moroccan people. With the return of his majesty Sidi Muhammad [V] bin Yusef to the sherifian throne, the way is now open for constructive negotiation. The sovereign, who is at present the guest of France, will soon return to Morocco. The French government, which remains faithful to the policy laid down in its declaration of Oct. 1, 1955 and to the principles expounded by the premier before the National Assembly Oct. 8, 1955, will work for the development of Morocco into a modern, free and sovereign state, within a framework of interdependence with France, in accordance with the guiding principles which formed the subject of the letters exchanged between Gen. [Georges] Catroux and his majesty Sidi Muhammad bin Yusef Sept. 8-9, 1955 at Antsirabé."

In his letter of Sept. 8, Catroux had held that France's policy was "to confirm by indisputable acts and principle of Moroccan sovereignty and to lead Morocco to the status of a modern, free and sovereign state, united to France by the permanent bonds of a freely accepted interdependence; with the reservation that, in view of the indissoluble nature of the bonds uniting the 2 countries, the rights and major interests of France in strategic, political, diplomatic, economic and cultural matters shall be guaranteed and that Frenchmen settled in the [sherifian] empire shall be granted a status proportionate to the important contribution which they have made and will continue to make to Morocco's general well-being." Catroux said in the letter that Muhammad V, indorsing this policy, had agreed that "the permanence of France's presence in Morocco and of her rights and prerogatives was not a subject for discussion, as the 2 countries were inseparable" and had confirmed that Frenchmen in Morocco should have "a different status from foreigners."

Istiqlal leaders meeting in Madrid Nov. 21 demanded the termination of the Treaty of Fez and the complete independence of Morocco. The Democratic Party for Independence Nov. 17 and the Moroccan Liberation Army, still in the field, also demanded complete independence. The Moroccan Liberation Army Nov. 28 demanded the end of the Spanish protectorate.

Muhammad V met Nov. 28 with leaders of the Spanish Moroccanbased Unity & Independence Party. After the interview the sultan expressed the hope that "Spain, which has never ceased to give promises to the Moroccan people, will carry out those promises now that France has recognized the principle of Moroccan independence."

Franco gave his reply in an interview with U.S. newsmen Nov. 30. He said it would be a "grave error" to "transplant pure and simple" a democratic system to Morocco. Political changes of this nature must be instituted gradually, "as we are doing in our zone," he declared, and complete self-government should be granted only when the Moroccans were ready.

A joint statement by Abd el-Khalek Torres, leader of the Reformist Party and minister of social affairs in the Spanish Moroccan cabinet, and Istiqlal leader Allal al-Fassi, who was visiting Tetuan, was issued Dec. 10. The Moroccan leaders called on the Spanish government to "take the measures which are now called for to help in the attainment of Moroccoan independence and territorial integrity."

Franco replied Dec. 14 in an interview with Pedro Gómez Aparicio, head of *EFE* (the letters stand for no word), the official Spanish news agency. In the interview, published Dec. 15, the *caudillo* said that it would be "regrettable for the future of the Moroccan . . . people to introduce . . . the suspicions and internal strife of political parties on the European model" and that freedom at this point would open the door to communism. "Nobody should wonder why we should not want for Moroccans that which is repugnant to us," Franco said. "We shall never consent to anyone replacing us in our mission of continuing to prepare the people entrusted to our protection and of guiding them along the path to independence and self government."

Meanwhile, García Valiño, who had been responsible for the implementation of Franco's program in Morocco sought a personal interview with the *caudillo*. He conferred with Franco Dec. 14. Then, at a press conference, he announced that Spain planned to reach "an immediate and total agreement with France with regard to Morocco." On returning to Spanish Morocco, García Valiño announced Dec. 19 that Spain planned to "increase the responsibilities of ministers of the native government" in Spanish Morocco "and intensify the transfer of administrative power to Moroccans." In an interview with the Tetuan newspaper *El Dia*, he said that "several long and complex steps must be taken before Spanish Morocco could become independent.

Spain & the UN

Spain's long struggle for UN membership ended Dec. 14, 1955, when the USSR voted with 54 other members to admit Spain.

The Cold War between the Soviet Union and the Western Allies had frustrated all attempts to increase the membership in the UN for 6 years. The USSR vetoed all non-Communist applications, while the Western powers rejected all Soviet allies. Throughout 1954 all Spanish efforts to gain admittance were blocked by the Soviet veto. Spain, therefore, had settled temporarily for a permanent observer at UN headquarters in New York.

Spain became the 8th nonmember state to maintain such an observer when Secy. Gen. Dag Hammarskjöld Jan. 25, 1955 sent an invitation to José María de Areilza, the Spanish ambassador in Washington, to send a permanent observer. Spain named José Sebastián de Erice Apr. 25 as its first observer.

Spain applied Sept. 26 for full UN membership, and U.S. Amb.-to-UN Henry Cabot Lodge Jr. announced the same day that the U.S. would support the application. Since no country could be admitted alone, the USSR and the U.S. began to consider a Canadian omnibus proposal. U.S. State Secy. John Foster Dulles and Soviet Foreign Min. Viacheslav M. Molotov held an informal meeting Nov. 13 at Molotov's request. Most of the discussion was devoted to UN membership for 18 applicant nations. Dulles was said to have told Molotov the U.S. would not oppose the admission of Albania, Bulgaria, Hungary and Rumania under the Canadian proposal, which would also admit Spain along with Austria, Ceylon, Cambodia, Ireland, Italy, Nepal, Libya, Japan, Portugal Laos, Jordan, Finland and the Mongolian People's Republic (Outer Mongolia).

There was one major problem: Nationalist China announced that it would veto the application of the Mongolian People's Republic on the ground that China claimed Mongolia as an integral part of China. Soviet

Deputy Foreign Min. Vasily V. Kuznetsov said in New York Nov. 17 that the USSR would veto all Western-sponsored countries if Mongolia were not included in any mass-admission proposal. Meanwhile, the U.S. informed UN delegations that it would not campaign against the admission of Mongolia and would abstain in the vote on all 5 Communist applicants.

Dr. Tingfu F. Tsiang of Nationalist China vetoed the application of Mongolia Dec. 13, whereupon the Soviet delegate, Arkady A. Sobolev, vetoed the 13 non-Communist states. After some discussion, the Soviets agreed to a compromise: If Mongolia remained out, so must Japan. Although the U.S. wanted Japan admitted, Japan was sacrificed.

The USSR and 54 other member states then voted Dec. 14 to admit Spain to the UN. Only Belgium and Mexico abstained; the delegates from Haiti, Paraguay and South Africa were absent. There was no negative vote.

Other Developments

Spain demanded Jan. 11, 1955 that the Soviet Union return $570 million worth of gold coins and bullion shipped to the USSR by the Spanish Republican government in 1936. An announcement by the government the following day stated that Spain had learned that the Soviets were using Spanish gold to make payments to "Czechoslovakia, Finland, and Western European countries." The Spanish also announced that they had requested that all governments trading with the USSR refuse Soviet gold payments until the Spanish gold had been returned. In separate notes to the U.S., England and France, the Spanish government claimed that the gold had been sent to Moscow for safe keeping and not in payment for Soviet arms, as Moscow contended.

Simultaneous announcements in Madrid and Bonn Dec. 15, 1954 had revealed that Spain and West Germany had concluded a cultural agreement calling for the exchange of students and teachers and the establishment of university chairs for the study of each other's language, history and institutions.

The Spanish and Austrian governments announced Oct. 4, 1955 the reestablishment of diplomatic relations, which had been severed when Hitler annexed Austria in 1938.

A Madrid statement Nov. 23, 1955 announced the reestablishment of diplomatic relations with Finland, which had been severed shortly after Finland had surrendered to the USSR in 1945.

Jews in Madrid had been denied permission in 1954 to hold Jewish

New Year services in a hall of a hotel. The refusal was under a law restricting all non-Catholic religious services to church buildings. Benjamin Welles reported in *Spain: The Gentle Anarchy*, however, that Jewish tourists in Madrid could attend services at the Castellana Hilton Hotel in 1954. Barcelona's first synagogue since the year 1492 was opened Sept. 27, 1954.

UNREST & ECONOMIC UNCERTAINTY (1956)

Spain's struggle to keep Morocco ended in 1956, and Franco reluctantly agreed to let Spanish Morocco go. This decision was reached during a period of growing unrest that brought clashes between pro-Falange and anti-Falange students in Madrid, strikes by workers and grumbling in the armed forces. The economy continued to record reverses as well as advancements.

Morocco Granted Independence

Spain agreed in Apr. 1956 to let Morocco have its independence. This reversal of Spanish policy, however, took place only after much bitter dispute.

Moroccan nationalists in the Spanish Zone had been increasingly showing dissatisfaction with Spain's earlier refusals to grant early independence to Morocco. Sheik Mekki el-Naciri, leader of the Unity & Independence Party, had criticized Franco's statements affirming the no-independence policy. El-Naciri said Jan. 2, 1956 that Franco's remarks—made toward the end of 1955—had caused "stupefaction in Arab circles" and that Moroccans were "beginning to feel reserved as to Spain's policy in Morocco."

El-Naciri, who had founded the Wahda (Unity Party) in 1936, was a political foe of the Spanish Zone's Social Affairs Min. Abd el-Khalek Torres, Spain's no-independence policy had brought them together. Torres and Justice Min. Abdellah Guenoun resigned Jan. 9 from the Spanish Moroccan cabinet of the khalifa of Tetuan, Hassan el-Mehdi. On receiving the resignations, el-Mehdi issued a statement expressing the hope that Franco would quickly "make a declaration recognizing the independence and territorial unity of Morocco and the sovereignty of the sultan [Muhammad V]."

Spanish High Commissioner Rafael García Valiño arranged a meeting in Palafito, Spanish Morocco Jan. 10 with André Dubois, the former police commissioner of Paris and the new French resident in Morocco. García Valiño requested that the French go slow on Moroccan independence, but Dubois refused. The Spaniard then requested a 3-way conference, and the Frenchman refused this request also.

Meanwhile Thami el-Glaoui, pasha of Marrakesh, France's most powerful ally in Morocco, became ill and was rushed to surgery. He resigned his post as pasha Jan. 13 and died Jan. 23.

As Spanish power in Morocco deteriorated, Spain adopted 2 courses. The first was an effort to tie northern Morocco to Spain

141

financially. The Cortes in Dec. 1955 had adopted a new economic and financial charter for Spanish Morocco. It took effect Jan. 1. The preamble, which described Ceuta and Melilla as of "inalienable Spanish sovereignty," stated that Spain was obliged to develop the "exceptional natural advantages of" the area. The Spanish, it said, were considering not only the present but "the possible consequences of today's decisions on the more or less near future, not only in these territories but also with regard to the evolution of the neighboring peoples and the permanent influence of Spain in North Africa." Important features of the charter were the establishment of a free customs zone for the whole Spanish Zone and a 50% reduction in profit taxes. The charter also outlined an extensive public works program.

Spain's 2d course called for the establishment of the khalifa of Tetuan as an independent sovereign by cutting all ties between Tetuan and the sultan's administration in Rabat. The khalifa, however, refused to collaborate. After García Valiño found that none of the Moroccan politicians would support an independent khalifa, he abandoned the plan.

In a statement issued Jan. 13, Madrid announced its decision "(1) to make known its firm intention to continue to defend, with the authority of the legitimate Sultan Muhammad V, the unity of the [Sherifian—or Moroccan] empire and the independence of Morocco; (2) to supply, in agreement with the khalifa and in collaboration with the [Spanish] Moroccan government and authorities, the means of attaining the self-government of the zone by its natural authorities in an orderly and peaceful manner; (3) to continue to assist and cooperate with the Moroccan people, so as to ensure that neither communism nor any other form of subversion will be able to disturb the peaceful execution of this task; (4) to follow attentively the development of the general situation in Morocco, as well as the policy pursued in the neighboring zone [French Morocco], so as to realize the aspirations of the Moroccan people without injuring Spain's legitimate interests."

Franco Jan. 14 recognized the impending independence of a united Morocco, but the Spanish position there continued to deteriorate. 50 Moroccan troops in the Spanish Legion deserted their battalion Jan. 15 at Larache, an important Atlantic coast port. The Beni Ourriagli clan rioted Jan. 16, and Spanish troops fired on them.

Some Moroccan nationalists, in an attempt to avoid further bloodshed, offered a compromise. Ex-Justice Min. Abdellah Guenoun and members of Islah (National Reform Party) expressed a willingness Jan. 17–19 to accept a Spanish-sponsored khalifa government provided it was understood that the government would be of transitional nature leading toward Moroccan unity. Garcia Valiño rejected this proposal Jan. 21, but a proclamation issued in Madrid Jan. 28 stated that the Spanish high commissioner would reorganize the Spanish Moroccan administrative system so that more power would be granted to the khalifa.

Meanwhile, France was undergoing a cabinet change. Edgar Faure's government had fallen in Dec. 1955. After considerable confusion, it was replaced by a cabinet headed by Guy Mollet, a Socialist, who promised to carry out the Faure policy of independence for Morocco.

Muhammad V arrived in Paris Feb. 11 to open negotiations for independence. The Moroccan sultan was greeted by Mollet and then by French Pres. René Coty, and they conferred informally for a week. Finally, a treaty terminating the 1912 Treaty of Fez was signed Mar. 2 by French Foreign Min. Christian Pineau and French Moroccan Premier M'Barek Ben Bekkai. (The Treaty of Fez had divided Morocco between Spain and France.)

The French-Moroccan treaty was an obvious defeat for Franco's Morocco policy. When the treaty was made public, riots erupted in the Spanish Zone Mar. 3–4. Mulay ben Hassan el-Mehdi, son and heir of the khalifa of Tetuan, flew to Rabat Mar. 5 to confer with Muhammad V, and García Valiño flew to Madrid Mar. 10. (The New York anti-Franco publication *Iberica* reported Mar. 15 that García Valiño "was recently a victim of an unsuccessful assassination attempt by Moroccan nationalists.")

Mark I. Cohen and Lorna Hahn reported in *Morocco, Old Land, New Nation* that "after ignoring 2 diplomatic invitations to Madrid that did not include a promise that talk would result in recognition of Morocco's independence, the sultan [Muhammad V] accepted a personal invitation from Franco that embodied such a statement."

Muhammad V and his entourage, which included Premier M'Barek Ben Bekkai, arrived in Madrid Apr. 4. He was greeted by Franco and Franco's Moorish Guard; for 2 days the sultan and his entourage were treated with lavish hospitality, and Franco awarded the sultan the Imperial Order of the Yoke and Arrow. In a speech noting the ties linking Spain and Morocco, Franco said Apr. 6 that "the flora and fauna of our geography are a continuation of those which your land has. And it is the wish of Providence that the very same seas bathe our coasts."

Meanwhile M'Barek Ben Bekkai discussed political matters with Spanish Foreign Min. Alberto Martín Artajo. During a private discussion, the Moroccan told Martín Artajo that Spain must recognize the complete independence of Morocco "in order to strengthen the friendship that unites the 2 states and to ensure a free and fruitful cooperation."

A "declaration and protocol" recognizing Morocco's independence was issued by the Spanish and Moroccan governments Apr. 7. *Text of the joint declaration and protocol:*

The Spanish government and his majesty Muhammad V, sultan of Morocco, desirous of reaching a particularly friendly treaty, on a reciprocal basis, to strengthen their ties of friendship and to consolidate peace in the area in which their countries are situated, have agreed to issue the following declaration:

1. The Spanish government and his majesty Muhammad V, sultan of Morocco, considering that the regime established in Morocco in 1912 no longer corresponds to present reality, declare that the agreement signed in Madrid on Nov. 27, 1912, can no longer regulate Spanish-Moroccan relations.

2. Consequently, the Spanish government recognizes Morocco's independence proclaimed by his majesty Muhammad V, and Morocco's full sovereignty with all the attributes appertaining thereto, including those relating to foreign policy and the army.

The Spanish government reaffirms its wish to respect the territorial unity of the empire, which is guaranteed by international treaties, and undertakes to adopt the necessary measures to render it effective.

The Spanish government also undertakes to grant his majesty the sultan such aid and assistance considered necessary by mutual agreement, notably in matters of foreign relations and defense.

3. The purpose of the negotiations opened at Madrid between the Spanish governemnt and his majesty Muhammad V, sultan of Morocco, is to lead to new agreements between the 2 sovereign and equal states, with the object of defining free cooperation in those spheres where their common interests are involved.

These agreements will guarantee, in the friendly spirit mentioned above, the freedoms and rights of Spanish nationals in Morocco and of Moroccans in Spain, of a private, economic, cultural, or social nature, on a basis of reciprocity and respect for the sovereignty of both countries.

4. The Spanish government and his majesty the sultan agree that until such time as the aforementioned agreements enter into force relations between Spain and Morocco shall be based upon the terms of the protocol annexed to the present declaration.

Protocol. 1. Legislative power will be exercised in a sovereign manner by his majesty the sultan. The representative of Spain in Rabat will be advised of projected decrees of the sultan that affect Spanish interests and will be allowed to make pertinent observations.

2. The powers exercised until now by the Spanish authorities in Morocco will be transferred to the Moroccan government in conformity with formulas established by common agreement. The position of Spanish civil servants in Morocco will be maintained.

3. The Spanish government will assist the Moroccan government in organizing its own army. The Spanish army will remain in Morocco during the period of transition.

4. Spanish currency shall remain in use pending the conclusion of a new agreement.

5. Visas and all administrative formalities required for passage of persons from one zone to the other are abolished.

6. The Spanish government will continue to be responsible for the protection abroad of the interests of Moroccans native to the zone defined previously by the Convention of Nov. 27, 1912, and residents abroad, until the government of his majesty the sultan assumes this function.

The treaty and protocol were silent on 3 matters of vital interest to Spain: Ifni, Spanish Sahara (or Río de Oro) and the Spanish towns in Morocco. The Spanish newspapers *Ya* and *ABC* declared that the Moroccan port cities of Ceuta and Melilla were "*plazas de soberania,*" *i.e.*, sovereign towns, which had been part of the Castilian kingdom since the 16th century and, therefore, not part of the Moroccan protectorate. Ifni, the papers claimed, had been ceded outright to Spain in 1860.

The Madrid agreement, furthermore, did not set a time table for Spanish withdrawl, although, in a subsequent letter, the sultan suggested that the transfer of authority begin May 7. Spain still administered its zone even after Muhammad V visited Tetuan Apr. 9 and was acclaimed sovereign by 250,000 people who had crowded into Tetuan (population 30,000) for the occasion.

Riots broke out Apr. 10 in Sidi Ifni, capital of Ifni. 2 demonstrators were killed, and 4 policemen and 2 demonstrators were injured.

García Valiño, meanwhile, attempted to find employment for his Moroccan troops in the new Moroccan army, but the sultan opposed a transfer of the Moroccan Legion into the Moroccan army. A compromise was reached: Muhammad ben-Mizzian ben-Kazem, leader of the Moroccan troops and a close personal friend of Franco, and 9,000 of the 30,000 Moroccan legionnaires were absorbed by the Moroccan army. (The Moroccans could not afford a large standing army. They had already taken 14,000 troops from the former French-controlled Moroccan army.)

Spanish-Moroccan relations grew further strained as Spain continued in control after May 7, the date the sultan had suggested for the transfer of sovereignty. Muhammad V appointed Abd el-Khalek Torres, who had extensive knowledge of Spanish affairs, as ambassador to Madrid June 4 in the reported hope of securing some agreement with Franco as to the date of Spanish withdrawl. To some degree the Spanish reluctance to reach an understanding with the sultan apparently was caused by what the Spanish seemed to consider slights by the Moroccans. For example, the Spanish government June 8 sent a note to Rabat objecting to the fact that French Amb.-to-Morocco André Dubois had been granted special privileges not shared by José Filipe

146 SPAIN & FRANCO 1949–59

Alcover y Sureda, the Spanish ambassador. The Rabat government refused to change.

The sultan did little to mollify the Spanish. During a reception June 6 for about 1,000 Ifni tribesmen, Muhammad V declared that "all territory which historically had been Moroccan must return to Morocco."

Moroccan nationalists began to make extensive territorial claims. Istiqlal leader Allal al-Fassi, speaking in Tangier June 19, said Morocco was "not completely unified" and must "continue the struggle until Tangier, the Spanish and French Sahara and Mauritania are liberated and unified." (The Instiqlal daily *al-Alam* July 5 printed a map of "Greater Morocco" that included the territories claimed by Al-Fassi plus French Sudan and the Tindouf and Tanezrouft areas of southern Algeria.)

Moroccan Amb.-to-Spain Abd el-Khalek Torres could not reach an agreement with the Spanish, so the sultan sent Crown Prince Mulay Hassan and Foreign Min. Ahmed Balafrej to Madrid June 17. The prince reached this compromise: Torres would oversee the transfer of authority from Spain to Morocco but, by an agreement ultimately concluded Aug. 1 between Spain and Morocco, Spain would maintain an active role in northern Morocco until 1958. The northern zone was to be tied to Spain economically until Feb. 1958. The Moroccans agreed to recognize that the cities of Ceuta and Melilla and the off-shore islands of Gomera, Alhucemas and Chafarinas were part of Spain. The Moroccan and Spanish governments agreed to table for an indefinite period all discussion as to the status of Ifni and Spanish Sahara.

Economic Advances & Weaknesses

Industrial progress was uneven during 1956. While rayon production, for example, increased to 14,720 tons, cotton cloth production fell to about 20% of the 1951–5 average. Overall textile production totaled 106% of the 1929–31 average in 1956 whereas in 1955 the figure had been 101%.

Shoe production increased to 24.2 million pairs. Paper production also increased—to 260,799 tons, but Spain's per-capita consumption of paper products was the lowest in Europe. The number of books published fell slightly to 4,419 titles. Movie production remained constant at 54 pictures.

Cement production rose to 3.9 million tons and steel production to 1.2 million tons. The number of locomotives produced fell to 45, but the output of rail coaches and freight cars increased to 2,598.

Automobile and truck output increased to 17,478 and 1.747, respectively, but bus and tractor production fell to 168 and 750, respectively. The output of both motorcycles (96,413) and bicycles (174,869) increased.

Shipbuilding increased to 181,000 tons; the number of ships on order doubled to 659,000 tons, and ship manufacturing capacity increased to 280,000 tons.

A record 2,728,000 people visited Spain, providing a profit of $94.8 million from tourism for 1956.

There was an increase in the availability of both electrical power and butane gas during 1956. There were 1,232 power stations, of which 1,002 were hydroelectric. Electric power consumption increased from 9.28 million kilowatt hours in 1955 to 10.58 billion kilowatt hours in 1956. The use of butane gas for heating and cooking trebeled during the year.

The record of the extractive industries was erratic during 1956. Cooper output reached an all-time high, but the production of wolfram (1,326 tons) and manganese (34,377 tons) declined. The output of mercury (1,404 tons valued at 30 million gold pesetas), potassium salt (1.4 million tons), potassium cloride (255,408 tons valued at 20½ million gold pesetas) and superphosphate (1½ million tons) increased, but phosphate production decreased to 11,300 tons. Iron extraction (5.2 million tons) and export (3½ million tons valued at 84.4 million gold pesetas) improved, as did the mining of zinc (22,835 tons) and lead (58,811 tons). The export of the latter (16,254 tons valued at 16.4 million gold pesetas), however, declined. Coal extraction increased to 14.8 million tons.

Agricultural production was also uneven. Wheat output increased but was below the 1954 level. Rice production decreased. Potato output rose but was below the 1951 figure. Onion production was also up, tomato production down. The cotton crop reached an all-time high (1½ million quintals valued at 1.85 billion pesetas), but tobacco output fell 20%. The sugar crop increased to 381,000 tons, but the government had to import 20,000 tons to meet demand.

In 1955–6, with 16.3 million sheep, there was an average yearly wool yield of 33,000 tons worth 1.9 billion pesetas. There were 3 million cattle, 2.3 million horses, mules and donkeys and 6 million pigs. Annual egg production during the period averaged 250 million dozen worth 5 billion pesetas.

Government attempts to broaden the use of fertilizers were frustrated because most farmers could not afford the price. Spain remained the lowest per-acre consumer of fertilizer in Western Europe, and Spanish farm production per acre was also the lowest. In 1956 the government helped irrigate only 30,000 acres of land, about half the 1955 total. The reparcelization program (most Spanish farmers did not hold a single farm but rather several plots scattered throughout the district; the reparcelization program aimed at consolidating the holdings of each farmer into one farm) and the support of cooperatives was continued by the government. About 340,000 acres were consolidated into 94 unified farms, while the number of coops increased slightly to 5,250 (with 1,139,975 families).

Production from Spain's forests increased in 1956. 5,358 million cubic meters of wood were cut and 58,344 tons of cork produced. While the tonnage of cork actually declined, the value, 62 million gold pesetas, rose. The production of resin and turpentine also increased. The government reforested some 313,000 acres.

There was also an increase in the fish catch.

A severe blizzard and cold wave hurt the Spanish economy. The value of the citrus crop loss was estimated Feb. 19 at $50 million. Orange exports (378,807 tons) were only half of the 1955 total, and their value fell to ⅓ (to 81,870,000 gold pesetas). Oranges' share of Spain's total exports fell from 17.9% to only 7.26%. (Figures reported by the Director General of Customs and the National Institute of Statistics vary. Exports of 7.26%, as stated by the Director General of Customs, would be valued at 98,285,880 gold pesetas, based on the institute's figures for total exports.) Spain's orange exports fell to only 31.6% of total Mediterranean orange exports.

The value of exports in 1956 was only 73% of the value of imports, leaving an unfavorable balance of 993 million gold pesetas, a serious burden on Spain's dwindling gold and foreign currency reserve. Of total exports valued at 1,353,800,000 gold pesetas, the bulk comprised foodstuffs (651.6 million gold pesetas), raw minerals and wood products (326.8 million gold pesetas), chemicals (76.2 million gold pesetas) and metals (73.9 million gold pesetas). Of total imports valued at 2,346,900,000 gold pesetas, the bulk comprised machines and vehicles (638.1 million gold pesetas), chemicals (419½ million gold pesetas) and various raw materials such as cotton and oil (749 million gold pesetas).

The government took various steps to solve Spain's transportation problem. Spain's substandard ports handled only 44.9 million tons of merchandise in 1956, and the government began a study of methods to modernize port facilities. (Port activity had almost doubled—from 20.6 million tons to 40.2 million tons—between 1945 and 1953.)

During 1956 Red Nacional de Ferrocarriles (RENFE), the government railroad agency, owned and operated 7,950 miles of Spain's 11,050 miles of track. It lost 2.9 billion pesetas (income 5.7 billion, expenses 6.7 billion, financial charges .6 billion, depreciation, .9 billion) in 1956. A 10 billion-peseta ($250 million) 7-year modernization program was announced: of the 1,845 freight stations, the number (947) servicing fewer than one car a day was to be reduced; the number of employees (125,000) was to be reduced 10%; the handling of traffic was to be increased 12% to 15%. (Spain's privately owned railroads, 2,600 miles of which are narrow gauge, are primarily used for hauling coal and other minerals to ports and factories.)

Of 74,994 miles of roads only 45,592 miles were hard surfaced in 1956. There was little modern road-building machinery, and the roads were still being "maintained" by *camineros*, day laborers who followed the medieval practice of repairing roads near their homes. A 5-year improvement program costing 750 million pesetas annually (about $18 million) was announced. The roads were used by 157,852 automobiles, 107,295 trucks and 9.143 buses, most of them foreign made and many pre-Civil War. 177,744 motorcycles, most of them made in Spain after the Civil War, were also in use.

Inflation rose by 10% during 1956—to 521.3% of the 1940 base. The government attempted to aid workers by ordering across-the-board wage increases. It announced Mar. 4 a 20% nationwide increase in wages effective Apr. 1 and an additional 7½% wage increase in October. These increases came at a time when many segments of the economy were stagnant. The result was increased pressure to raise prices, and the higher prices cancelled the benefits of the wage increase. For example, using 1940 as the base, wheat prices rose to 564.3 by the end of 1956.

The standard of living, still low, had just about managed to return to the level of 1935. While the Spanish government claimed that, using 1935 as the base, real wages stood at 108, ex-Republican diplomat Elena de La Souchere asserted in *An Explanation of Spain* that the living standard had not improved at all. Using as a base the year the Civil War started (1936), she said that the real value of salaries in 1956 was 15% to 35% below the pre-war level: while wages had increased 6 times, prices of meat had increased 10 times, of bread 12 times and of potatoes 18 times; furthermore, the Spaniard's per capita annual consumption of sugar, milk and meat was the lowest in Western Europe, even below that of such recognized impoverished nations as Greece and Egypt. But social services and housing had improved.

The government built 73,141 apartments in 1956. The infant mortality rate reached an all-time low of 4.64 per hundred live births in 1956 as a result of expanded medical facilities. There were 32,018 physicians, 10,033 pharmacists, 2,503 dentists, 5,338 midwives and an estimated 766 hospitals with a total of 116,000 patients (the National Institute of Statistics listed only "information received," not total information when listing hospital data).

There was a decline in emigration. The net loss of population in the immigration-emigration equation was 38,219 in 1956.

The government also took steps to improve educational facilities.

The first 4 of 10 projected workers' universities (*universidades laborales*) were opened in October at Cordova (Córdoba), Sevilla, Gijón and Tarragona. The universities (more like trade high schools or junior colleges in the U.S. than universities) were intended primarily to provide education for workers' sons, who would then be able to fill posts as managers, engineers and technologists on government-sponsored industrial and agricultural projects. The university concept had been originated by the popular Falangist labor minister, José Antonio Girón, and executed by the Labor and Education ministries in cooperation with the Falange. Each university was to have about 2,000 students and was to be a self-contained university city constructed along the model of Madrid's university city; students would be granted free tuition, books, housing, board and medical service plus a stipend. While most students were accepted only after passing an entrance examination, some students were admitted on the recommendation of the Falange labor unions. The students were all male, and the average age of entering freshman was 18, although special prevision was made to take certain students at the age of 10.

At Gijón, Workers' University José Antonio Girón was under the direction of the Society of Jesus; at Cordova, Workers' University Onesino Redondo was run by the Dominican Order; laymen controlled the teaching at Workers' University Virgen de los Reyes in Sevilla and at Workers' University Francisco Franco in Tarragona.

The government Jan. 11 approved the creation of a 348 million-peseta ($8.6 million) educational and cultural fund donated by Juan March, reportedly the richest man in Spain. The fund, called the March Foundation, was the largest philanthropic fund established in Spain.

Student Riots

Falange supporters clashed with opponents of the Falange on the campus of Madrid University and in the streets of the city Feb. 7-9, 1956 in disorders that, according to some sources, seriously threatened the Franco regime. Foreign observers reported that the Madrid riots marked the beginning of the politicization of the universities. In every Spanish university—even those directly controlled by the clergy— clandestine groups were established.

Yet as late as 1973, authorities on Spanish political events did not agree as to the cause and purpose of the riots. Their views ranged from the opinion that ex-Falangist Dionisio Ridruejo had organized the anti-Falangist riots to the speculation that the Falangist leader Tomás Romojaro had staged the disturbances in order to smash the growing anti-Falangist organizations within the university.

There seems to be agreement, however, on the fact that many Madrid University students had learned the results of an opinion poll taken by Madrid University Rector Pedro Lain Entralgo (the actual polling of students, 400 of whom responded, was taken by the social studies section of the Opus Dei-dominated Consejo Superior de Investigaciones Scientificas) and published in the *N.Y. Times* Jan. 4 and Jan. 7 in articles by Camille M. Cianfarra. Even though the Spanish authorities had prevented the sale of these papers, copies were available at the U.S. bases and from tourists. Within days of the *Times* article university students appeared to have become openly anti-Falangist.

Dr. Lain Entralgo sent the statistics on opinions to Education Min. Joaquín Ruíz Giménez along with his general overview of student feeling as of mid-1955. This report stated that the reasons for student dissatisfaction included the "restrictive and censorious paternalism" exercised by the authorities and the "sorry example" of large sections of Spanish society whose "preoccupation with immediate economic gain has become general and abusive." The rector indicated that many of the wealthy students had traveled abroad and had developed an "intense curiosity" about foreign intellectual currents and democratic processes—"things which have for them the irresistible attraction of forbidden fruit." To add to the student unrest, Lain Entralgo said, "the increase in jobs has not kept pace with the expanding university population." He warned that, although there was no sign of Marxism among students, "it would not be strange if it were gestating among those whose conscience tends toward radicalism."

The riots, according to most observers, were touched off by student elections. It had become a practice in the universities to elect, in February, student representatives to the SEU (Sindicato Español Universitario), a body that, in theory, had jurisdiction over the students and represented them before the university administration. Until 1956, the only organized list of candidates had been drawn by the Falange Youth Group. The Falange, however, had found it increasingly difficult to compile such a list since only about 2% of the student body had joined the Falange Youth (Frente de Juventudes). At the University of Barcelona's Law School, the Falange had imported non-law students to fill the list.

After the publication of the *Times* article and the organization by Ridruejo of a clandestine political club, Nuevo Tiempo, at Madrid University, various non-Falangist groups began to form. For the first time, Falangists were booed when they appeared at meetings.

Students of the Madrid University Feb. 1 issued an open letter to "the government of the nation, the minister of national education and the secretary-general of the Falange" demanding an end to Falange control over "thought, expression and corporate life" of university students. The letter denounced the SEU and demanded the convocation of a congress of university students to create an alternative to the current system, which was categorized as a "system of humiliating inertia ... in which all that is best in youth is being fatally lost year after year." The SEU was called "an artificial structure which prevents or deforms true student representation," and a barrier which "humiliates us in all international contacts with students of other countries." The letter also charged that many able professors were excluded from university life for "ideological or personal reasons."

Non-Falangists at Madrid University's Law School Feb. 4 elected a slate of non-Falangists to the SEU. The Falange Youth appealed to the SEU central organization, which was dominated by the Falange. The central organization Feb. 7 vetoed the election results on the ground that all candidates for office in the SEU must have prior approval of the SEU.

Falange Secy. Gen. Raimundo Fernández Cuesta was out of town, and his deputy, Tomás Romojaro, organized what Benjamin Welles (in *Spain: The Gentle Anarchy*) described as "goon squads." In an action that, according to George Hills (in *Franco*), was to be disguised as an anti-Bourbonist demonstration, some 200 "goons" invaded the university Feb. 8 and attacked 800 anti-Falangist students. (Max Gallo reported in *Histoire de l'Espagne Franquiste* that the Falangists were armed with "cudgels.") The Falangists shouted "we don't want a king," and the students shouted "down with SEU." After a brief fight the Falangists retired.

The anti-Falangists headed off Feb. 9 for a march of the Education Ministry to protest the voiding of the anti-Falangist slate of officers. After tearing down the Falange symbol from the Law School building, the students marched toward the ministry. Near the ministry they were attacked by armed Falangists. 20 students were wounded, and the anti-Falangists retired. While this clash was going on, 30 armed Falangists broke into the International Institute for Girls, a U.S. school; the Left-wing anti-Franco *Iberica* (published in New York) reported that several Falangists "pinned the arms of the directrice . . . , Miss Phyllis Turnball of Binghamton, New York, . . . the rest . . . broke up furniture, pianos, statues, pulled out telephone wires, etc."

1,000 anti-Falangist students and 500 armed Falangist students fought in the streets of Madrid Feb. 9. More than 50 students were wounded, one shot was fired, and a Falangist, Miguel Alvárez Pérez, was gravely wounded. (George Hills said in *Franco* that Alvárez Pérez was shot accidently by a fellow Falangist.) The police, according to observers, had refused to interpose Feb. 8 and 9 (the Institute for Girls is across the street from a police station, and *Iberica* said that the police saw the Falangists invade it and heard Miss Turnball's screams but "only looked on without doing anything"), yet they arrested 7 members of the Falange Youth Feb. 10 on charges of complicity in the riots.

The Falange Youth was reported to be infuriated by the arrests and by seeing stacks of the Falangist paper *Arriba* burned. Stanley Payne reported in *Politics and the Military in Modern Spain* that they planned to destroy the opposition by "slaughtering them in a 1936-style night raid." The murder plot had advanced to such a degree that "arms were distributed to a number of party activists."

When Franco had not acted by the morning of Feb. 10 (although university officials had announced the temporary closing of the university) the army, according to Payne, decided to intervene. Franco was visited at noon by Army Min. Agustín Muñoz Grandes, Lt. Gen. Miguel Rodrigo, captain general of Madrid, and Lt. Gen. Carlos Martínez an aide to Prince Juan Carlos. Payne reported that they informed Franco that unless he stopped the fighting and prevented the proposed slaughter, the army would take power, in Franco's name, in Madrid.

Franco then ordered the police to stop all demonstrations. A police statement issued in the afternoon of Feb. 10 and reported by *Arriba* the same day alleged that "elements affiliated with the Communist Party" had been responsible for the attacks on the Falangist students. *Arriba*, in the face of contrary evidence, claimed that Miguel Alvárez Pérez had been shot by "Communists or fellow-travelers." Meanwhile, the Education Ministry declared that university classes would be suspended until further notice and that Dr. Manuel Torres López, dean of the Law School, had been dismissed because of his anti-Falangist attitude. (Law School students Feb. 11 mailed leaflets describing the allegations of Communist responsibility for the riots as "farcical.")

The government Feb. 10 announced 57 arrests. Among those

arrested were Dionisio Ridruejo, Miguel Sánchez Mazas, the son of a Falangist writer, the economist Dr. Ramón Tamames and Francisco Bustelo, nephew of Calvo Sostelo, a Right-wing leader during the Republican era.

Franco Feb. 11 presided over a cabinet meeting at which it was decided to suspend Article 14 of the Bill of Rights, which allows residence in any part of Spain, and Article 18, which guarantees that no one may be arrested without warrant or detained for more than 72 hours without a hearing. Observers noted that the suspension of these articles permitted the government to banish individuals or detain them without warrant for an indefinite period. Later Feb. 11 the government announced that it intended to use its new powers against anyone who "directly or indirectly causes disturbances of the peace or who may in future attempt to disrupt peace and public order and foment disunity among the Spanish people."

In the midst of this turmoil, the first cabinet change since 1951 was announced Feb. 15. Jesús Rubio García Miña, 48, professor of commercial law at Madrid University, was appointed education minister to replace Joaquín Ruíz Giménez (or Jiménez; both are correct and used), a member of the clandestine Christian Democratic Party. Dr. Rubio, who had served as undersecretary of education from 1939 to 1951, had joined the Falange at the beginning of the Civil War but had spent the war as a political refugee in the Chilean embassy in Madrid. According to Benjamin Welles in *Spain: The Gentle Anarchy*, Rubio was "reputedly an arch-Republican." The outgoing minister, a political ally of Angel Herrera y Oria, bishop of Málaga, was, according to William Ebenstein in *Church and State in Franco Spain*, "too liberal" for some elements within the government.

The government continued to assert that the student disturbances were Communist-inspired. It charged Feb. 25 that the riots had been directed from the Soviet embassy in Paris. Antonio López Campillo, a chemistry student who had been studying in Paris since Oct. 1955 and who was specifically charged by the Spanish government with being the liaison between the Soviet embassy in Paris and the Madrid students, held a press conference Mar. 26 and denied the government's charges. Interviewed Apr. 6 by a reporter from *Iberica*, he again denied the charge and insisted that he was a Protestant, not a Marxist, that he had never been inside the Soviet embassy and that the government charge that he had held secret meetings with soviet agents at an Italian café on the Boulevard Saint Germain was a lie since there were no Italian cafés on the boulevard.

It was announced Feb. 20 that Madrid University would be reopened but that Dr. Pedro Lain Entralgo was no longer the rector. It was stated that Lain Entralgo's letter of resignation, which had lain on the education minister's desk since mid-1955, was accepted Feb. 9 and that the former rector had returned to his duties as professor of the history of medicine at the university.

Students were still being arrested in March, and members of the secret police were present. Because the police could keep individuals in jail for extended periods, it was difficult to determine who was in jail and for what reasons. After the beginning of a workers' strike Apr. 7, it became almost impossible to distinguish those arrested for student dissent from those arrested for supporting the workers. Reports from Madrid Apr. 11, for example, said that 4 young Spaniards, including Foreign Ministry employe Vicente Girbau Leon, 22, had been arrested Mar. 27 for "clandestine" propaganda and "offense to the authorities." The same report said that 4 other students had been arrested for preparing a manifesto calling for a general strike in Madrid Apr. 12. *Iberica* Apr. 15 listed 7 prominent Spaniards, including Vicente Girbau Leon, identified as chief of the code department of the Foreign Ministry, who were arrested for publicly protesting the dismissal of Lain Entralgo. (According to *What Is Happening in Spain?*, an official Spanish government work published in Madrid in 1959, Girbau Leon was convicted in Mar. 1956—before the announcement of his arrest—served 9 months in jail and then was exiled. According to the brief biography of Girbau Leon at the bottom of an article entitled "The Rebellion of the 'Generations Not Involved in the Civil War'," which he wrote for the Dec. 15, 1958 issue of *Iberica*, Girbau Leon was a member of the Foreign Ministry until May 1958, when he fled to France and was granted political asylum.) 2 trials of 4 students each were held Apr. 25–30 in Madrid. One of the trials was of students arrested for disturbances at the university, the other was for action involving the workers' strike. There apparently was a 3d trial of 4 students that started and ended Apr. 25. The confusion is compounded by the fact that the government charged all defendants with the same crime: clandestine propaganda and plotting.

Students involved in the university riot were defended at their trial in April by Christian Democratic leader and ex-Republican War Min. José María Gil Robles, who insisted that "when a regime denies its citizens normal means of expression, they have the right to resort to whatever means are in their grasp." Witnesses for the defense included Pedro Lain Entralgo, Manuel Torres López, former dean of Madrid Law School, and Dionisio Ridruejo (who had been arrested for his part in the riots, was reported to be in jail but was released sometime later).

Max Gallo said in *Histoire de l'Espagne Franquiste* that an irony of this trial was that 2 of the defendants were Francisco Bustelo, nephew of José Calvo Sotelo, Right-wing leader murdered by Republicans before the start of the Civil War, and Manuel Fernández Montesinos, nephew of Federico García Lorca, Republican poet murdered by the Falangists at the start of the Civil War. "The enemies of the Civil War were in the same box united against Franco," Gallo wrote. The students at this trial were convicted and sentenced to only 6 months in jail and a collective fine of 25,000 pesetas (about $600). Defendants at the other trials received one-year jail sentences.

Workers' Strike

Northern Spain was rocked by a series of strikes, lock-outs and demonstrations from Apr. 7, 1956 to the middle of May. Because of rigid censorship and because the government kept claiming, from Apr. 14, that the strikes were over, much of what transpired is unclear. The events are further beclouded by the fact that while hundreds of people were arrested, few were brought to trial during the period of the strike. Many arrested were released immediately, only to be rearrested later; many arrested were kept in jail or dentention camps without trial until late September. In many cases there were no arrest warrants.

The exact cause of the spring strikes is debatable. The role(s) of Madrid University students, Joseantonioists, priests, Communists or Socialists is also unclear, although observers credit these groups with playing "some part" in the demonstrations. Some observers also suggest that the initial action was a spontaneous demonstration generated by a belief that the government, which had just ordered, effective Apr. 1, a general 20% wage increase, was vulnerable because of open army dissatisfaction over Morocco. There was an unusual amount of open criticism of the Franco government from the army, the Church and, especially, the Falange. This agitation was believed to have had some bearing on a strike in which there appeared to be no leaders.

Jesús Díaz Montero, Falange party chief in Madrid, had said in a report to party leaders Feb. 26, 1956 that plans to restore the monarchy were causing "political ferment" in Spain. Díaz demanded liberal social and economic reforms as necessary to satisfy the Spanish people. One of the most outspoken Falangist critics was Labor Min. José Antonio Girón. Stanley Payne reported in *Falange* that Girón "took credit . . . for [the] across-the-board wage increase." Girón also made public his feelings that the increase was insufficient. Other Falangists, like Carlos Juan Ruiz de la Fuente, attacked the entire capitalist system, which, he claimed, was being forced on Spain.

Madrid University students Apr. 1 circulated a manifesto calling for a 48-hour general strike Apr. 12-13 to support demands for, among other things, the "reinstatement of our magnificent Pedro Lain Entralgo to his position as rector." A workers' manifesto, appearing Apr. 2, supported the students' position on the strike and also demanded economic reforms such as "a minimum daily wage of 75 pesetas [$1.75]; equal pay for women for equal work; free labor unions; unemployment insurance. . . ."

The Church leadership had also criticized the government's economic policies. The Church used both pastoral letters and the *Boletín* published by the Hermandades Obreras de Accíon Católica (HOAC), a labor arm of the Church. Because it cannot be sold to the public, the *Boletín* was permitted considerable editorial freedom to make its position known. The Madrid evening newspaper *El Alcázar* (which, until 1968, was controlled by Opus Dei) attacked the wage increases Mar. 9 on the grounds that, since between Dec. 1955 and Mar. 1956 food prices had increased by 40%, a 16%-20% wage increase was insufficient. Members of HOAC circulated reports by clerical investigators stating that Spanish wages were at least 50% below what was necessary for a decent living. According to William Ebenstein in *The Church and State in Franco Spain*, once the strike started, "hundreds of priests spoke up for the workers."

The strike started Apr. 7 among shoemakers in Pamplona, one of the most conservative, if not reactionary, centers in Spain. The walkout began with a peaceful demonstration in Pamplona's main square. Franco, however, ordered the police to disperse the strikers. The police marched to the sidestreets leading into the main square. When the workers saw the police they took out their rosaries and began to pray. The civil governor ordered the police into the square, but the police refused. The strikers eventually went home. They did not report to work Apr. 8 or 9, and the shoemakers were joined in the strike Apr. 10 by construction workers.

The general strike movement began to spread through northern Spain Apr. 11-17. Plants in Bilbao, Barcelona, San Sebastián, Valencia and smaller industrial centers were affected. At the peak of the movement, the strikes were supported by an estimated 60,000 to 80,000 workers. The strikes, illegal in Spain, were reportedly in protest against government wage policies and a rise in the cost of food and other basic items permitted after wages were raised Apr. 1. Strikers demanded that the 20% wage increase be doubled and that prices be held steady.

Affected plants in Navarra province and the Basque provinces of Vizcaya and Guipúzcoa were closed Apr. 12. Maj. Gen. Felipe Acedo

Colunga, Barcelona civil governor, said Apr. 12 that he had closed 2 struck plants and arrested some of the strikers. The Spanish cabinet, meeting Apr. 14 with Franco, ordered a lockout in all struck factories and the cancellation of strikers' contracts and social benefits.

Provincial governors warned Apr. 14 that employers paying strikers for time lost would be fined, but it was reported Apr. 14–17 that strikers were returning to their jobs after plant managers accepted demands for added pay raises ranging from 50% to 100% of the 20% Apr. 1 increase. Authorities were reported permitting full reinstatement with back pay for strikers returning to work immediately. San Sebastián plants were ordered reopened Apr. 20 after 16 had invoked lockouts for slowdowns Apr. 18.

4,500 workers in Bilbao were locked out Apr. 25 and then fired for "very serious professional faults," *i.e.*, a slow-down in work. 10,000 workers in Bilbao's Babcock Wilcox and General Electric plants walked out in sympathy. The strike spread Apr. 27 to Álava province. Reports in Madrid Apr. 30 and May 11 said that 30,000 to 40,000 workers were still either on strike or locked out in Bilbao. Sympathy for the Spanish strikers was expressed by AFL-CIO Pres. George Meany and the International Confederation of Free Trade Unions. The strike movement, however, was beginning to dissipate, and all plants were opened by May 20. Many workers, however, were still in jail while slowdowns in production were still reported.

The government, meanwhile, had begun a mass round-up of individuals whose connection with the strikes may or may not have been clear. Hundreds of Madrid University students were arrested, according to Madrid reports Apr. 11–12. Many of these arrested were released, but in September, 15 Catalan engineers were arrested on the orders of Barcelona Civil Gov. Felipe Acedo Colunga and sentenced to 3 months in jail. It was reported from Madrid June 5 that hundreds of workers and students were being held in a detention camp at Nanclares de la Oca in Álava province, while 70 workers from the Babcock Wilcox plant in Bilbao and scores of priests had been exiled from the Basque area.

Franco, meanwhile, spent the last week of April talking to various groups in southern Spain in an apparent attempt to reestablish harmony. At the opening of a new shipyard in Sevilla Apr. 24, he spoke in terms of a "crusade" for a better living, and he praised the Instituto Nacional de Industria "as the magnificent instrument of our revolution." The next morning the *caudillo* was at Huelva telling the people how his government "fought for . . . social justice for all workers." That afternoon, at the Rio Tinto mines, he told the workers "that there could not exist in Spain a regime more interested in raising the standard of living." Back in Sevilla Apr. 29, Franco said that his critics were "enemies of the state" who were attempting to disunite Spain. He promised that Spanish workers would soon have "something more important [than higher wages] —participation in management and a share of the profits."

Falange & Other Opposition

Franco appointed José Luis de Arrese Magra, 51, as secretary general of the Falange Feb. 15, 1956. Arrese, who also was appointed to the cabinet as a minister without portfolio, replaced Raimundo Fernández Cuesta. Arrese, an old-time Falangist, had joined the party at its inception, had been secretary general of the party 1941–5 and had been active in the Franco government, serving as Franco's ambassador to Berlin in 1943. During the waning days of the Nazi government, Hitler had approached Arrese in an attempt to overthrow Franco, but Arrese had refused to join the plot. Arrese, however, was anti-monarchist, and when Franco sought monarchist support, Arrese had resigned in July 1945. During his years out of power, Arrese wrote several works explaining the Falangist view on social and economic affairs. Arrese and the Joseantonioists (who had joined the party before 1936) remained in the shadows until the removal of Fernández Cuesta (who had been Falange secretary general since 1948) after the Feb. 10 Falange riots in Madrid.

35,000 new members had just joined the Falange. Brian Crozier asserted in *Franco* that the Falange's old guard, the Joseantonioists, felt at this time that "it was now or never. Either they made a successful bid for a share of power, or their identity was lost without a trace."

Observers generally agreed that the Falange was challenged by both the Christian Democrats and the Opus Dei. The Christian Democrats, whose organization was illegal, had apparently suffered a severe blow when Joaquín Ruíz Giménez was removed Feb. 15 as education minister. Observers, however, pointed out that Alberto Martín Artajo, the nominal leader of the clandestine organization, was still foreign minister. There was also what Elena de La Souchere (in *An Explanation of Spain*) called the "brilliant political comeback" of José María Gil Robles, the pre-Civil War leader of the Christian Democrats, during the trials of university students.

Many commentators on the Spanish scene suggested that in 1956 the greatest threat to the Falange came not from the Christian Democrats, but from the Opus Dei. It was said that this "3d force" had been preparing to take power ever since 1954. One of the leading intellectuals of the Opus Dei, Rafael Calvo Serer, had been publishing the anti-Falange *Escrits de Paris* from France since 1954. Madrid's monarchist newspaper *ABC* Jan. 12 and 21 had published articles indicating an alliance between Calvo Serer, a close friend of Don Juan, and the Bourbonist group for the purpose of hastening the reestablishment of the monarchy. To the Falange, the real danger of Opus Dei came from the fact that members of this secret organization were influential in the leading banks, industries, newspapers and universities. Opus Dei also had its own banks (Banco Popular and the Andorra Trust) and its own newspaper, *Madrid*. Elena de La Souchere indicated in *An Explanation of Spain* that she shared what she described as the Falange's conviction that Opus Dei was "discretly supported by the American embassy."

Carlist circles in Pamplona asserted Mar. 19 that a secret meeting had been held on an unspecified date in Madrid by Carlist pretender Francis Xavier and the pro-Carlist Justice Min. Antonio Iturmendi. At this meeting, it was said, Francis Xavier agreed to accept the regency of Spain with the understanding that, at his death, the Bourbon Juan Carlos would become king. The Carlists stated that Iturmendi was acting on "Franco's orders." The Catalan industrialist and Bourbonist leader Juan Claudio, Conde de Ruisenyada, visiting London in May, told the London *Daily Express* that Franco had given his word that Don Juan and not his son, Juan Carlos, would be the king. (In a speech before Falangists in Sevilla Apr. 29, Franco outlined his plans for the reestablishment of the monarchy, which most Falangists opposed, then asserted that "the monarchy cannot live without the Falange.")

According to Benjamin Welles, "Arrese proposed to retain Franco's monarchist succession plan while making the Falange the 'constitutional' power behind the throne." But the Francoists (as distinguished from the old-time Joseantonioists) within the Falange would not support him, and the radical Joseantonioists led by Luis González Vicen demanded a radical shift in the focus of the nation's economy. When Arrese tried to convince the radicals that they would have to accept a minimum program, González Vicen resigned June 8 from the Falange Central Committee. In his letter of resignation, González Vicen called for the subordination of the Church, army and economic order to the radical philosophy of José Antonio de Primo de Rivera y Sáenz de Heredia. Arrese and his supporters then proposed a series of "*anteproyectos*," or drafts, urging the elimination of the "army,

Church and opportunists" from the future governance of Spain. Stanley Payne reported in *Politics and the Military in Modern Spain* that when the army received word of the contents of the Arrese *anteproyectos*, a "delegation of generals" "protested personally" July 1. At a meeting of the Falange National Council in Salamanca Sept. 29, Arrese defended his *anteproyectos*. He was defeated by forces representing the army, the Church, the monarchists, Opus Dei and the Francoists. Arrese made his views public in a radio broadcast the night of Nov. 20, the 20th anniversary of the death of José Antonio. In a bitter attack on the government, Arrese charged that Spain was led by individuals who "run like thirsty madmen down the path of materialism and egotism [lusting] . . . for money." "You cannot be satisfied with this mediocre, sensual life," he declared. Franco summoned Arrese to Madrid and informed him of the united opposition. Arrese threatened to resign, but Franco refused to accept the resignation.

Franco was visited Dec. 16 by the U.S. ambassador, who, it was reported, informed the *caudillo* of Washington's displeasure with the pro-Nasser stand taken by Spain during the Suez crisis, and then by Gen. Agustín Muñoz Grandes, who, it was said, seconded the statement of the ambassador and added the army's complaint over the *anteproyectos*. Enrique Cardinal Plá y Deniel then sent Franco a secret note informing the *caudillo* of the Church's displeasure with the Arrese program.

Arrese appeared before the Falange National Council Dec. 29 in a final attempt to salvage his program. He pointed out that the opposition had little to fear since the Joseantonioists had little real power. He then listed the offices held by the old guard: 2 of the 16 ministers, one of 17 subsecretaries, 8 of 102 directors general, 18 of 50 civil governors, 8 of 50 presidents of provincial deputations, 65 of 150 members of the National Council, 137 of 575 deputies to the Cortes, 133 of 738 provincial deputies, 766 of 9,155 mayors, 2,226 of 55,960 municipal councilmen. Arrese said "that the original Falange occupies approximately 5% of the posts of leadership in Spain." Stanley Payne suggested in *Falange* that it was because of their weakness, documented in this fashion by Arrese, that the program of the Joseantonioists could be defeated.

Arrese submitted his program to Franco, but Franco never acted on it.

Spanish Communist Party (PCE) officials, according to Max Gallo (in *Histoire de l'Espagne Franquiste*), had been thrown into confusion by Soviet Premier Nikita S. Khrushchev's anti-Stalin speech at the 20th

Party Congress of the USSR Feb. 25, 1956. The PCE, according to Gallo, was forced to revise some of its policies. Members of the PCE Central Committee met in Prague, Czechoslovakia in August and adopted a platform, originally drawn up in June, that observers agreed was similar to the platform adopted by the Communist International in the 1930s. It called for the formation of a Popular Front. The leadership was still in the hands of Dolores Ibarruri (known as La Pasionaria), the most popular of the 1930-40 Communists. The Soviet crushing of the Hungarian uprising frustrated the program, and there were anti-Soviet demonstrations in Barcelona Nov. 29. Gallo reported that the demonstration quickly turned into an anti-dictatorship, *i.e.*, anti-Franco demonstration.

Arthur P. Whitaker wrote in *Spain and Defense of the West* that some Spaniards repatriated by the USSR in September and October 1956 were Communist agents and they helped strengthen the position of the CPE within Spain.

In a letter appearing in the *N.Y. Times* Dec. 30, Salvador de Madariaga disclosed that Ricardo Beneyto Sopena had been shot by a firing squad Nov. 19. Madariaga said that Beneyto had returned to Spain after receiving a promise of amnesty. (The Spanish government confirmed Jan. 4, 1957 that Beneyto had been granted amnesty for crimes committed during the Spanish Civil War but said he had been shot for crimes committed during 1945-7, when he was the chief Communist agent in Andalusia.)

Max Gallo reported in *Histoire de l'Espagne Franquiste* that several gun battles took place in Barcelona in December between police and members of the Anarchist Confederación Nacional del Trabajo.

An organization calling itself the Catalan Resistance announced that it was responsible for setting off a bomb in Barcelona Dec. 29. It also announced that the explosion was only the initial action of the group.

The Dec. 15 issue of the New York anti-Franco magazine *Iberica* printed a copy of a manifesto issued by ex-Falangist Dionisio Ridruejo announcing the formation of the "Democratic Social Action Party."

Julio Ceron Ayuso founded the FLP (Frente de Liberación Popular or "Felipe") toward the end of 1956. It was reported to be a Left-Wing Catholic group that, in its constitution, called for "violent seizure of power by the working class, the liquidation of the capitalist system of production, the suppression of private ownership of the means of production and the creation of a classless society." FLP's publication *Revolución Socialista* declared in the winter of 1956 that "there exists in Spain a revolutionary situation" that should be exploited.

The Church

Angel Herrera y Oria, bishop of Málaga, continued his criticism of social conditions during 1956. In a pastoral Jan. 12, the bishop attacked the social injustice of the government and the "collective unconsciousness" of "our upper class." Father José María Díaz Alegria, S. J., charged Apr. 5, in a speech before the Madrid Chamber of Commerce, that "the Spanish worker is treated as an inferior being" and "has no effective means within his reach for defending his rights."

The government in April arrested the entire organizing committee of the church-sponsored Juventud Obrera Católica (Catholic Labor Youth, JOC) in the towns of Sabadell and Tarressa. Many observers commented on the fact that Enrique Cardinal Plá y Deniel did not respond to this or to Falange attacks on HOAC (Hermandades Obreras de Acción Católica), both organizations being under the cardinal's protection. Plá y Deniel, however, did respond obliquely. In a pastoral letter May 5, he attacked "totalitarianism and centralization by the state of all functions." He and a number of other prelates Aug. 15 circulated what Arthur P. Whitaker (in *Spain and Defense of the West*) called "a discreetly worded but definite indictment of the government's social policy for its failure to provide workers with a decent living wage and for its intervention in the country's life in a manner contrary to the teachings of the church as established by papal encyclicals." The document was entitled "The Right and Duty of the Church to Intervene in Social Problems." Msgr. Rafael González Moralejo appended a statement attacking the entire Falangist syndicalist concept.

A pastoral letter signed by all Spanish archbishops said Sept. 22 that "workers pay should be sufficient for the needs of himself and his family . . . today there are many . . . in Spain who can pay for necessities only with the utmost difficulty."

Many younger members of the priesthood were active in supporting the strikers during Apr. and May. Starting in early May several priests were exiled from Guipúzcoa province. William Ebenstein reported in *Church and State in Franco Spain* that "about 200 priests were removed from their parishes on the intervention of the government with the local bishops."

The Press & Censorship

The only members of the press to challenge the government during 1956 were the editors of the literary reviews *Indice* and *Insula*. When José Ortega y Gasset died in 1955 the Information & Tourism Ministry had announced that newspapers and periodicals could publish "up to 3 articles . . . , a biography and 2 commentaries [on Ortega y Gasset but that] . . . every article . . . must underline his errors." *Indice* and *Insula* exceeded the limits and were closed in Jan. 1956.

According to the New York Anti-Franco publication *Iberica* (edited by ex-Republican jurist Victoria Kent and having as honarary chairmen ex-Republican diplomat Salvador de Madariaga and U.S. Socialist leader Norman Thomas), Foreign Min. Alberto Martín Artajo asked the cabinet unsuccessfuly to reopen *Indice* and *Insula* because their suppression had created "an unfavorable impression outside of Spain." Ex-Falangist Dionisio Ridruejo had brought the affair to world attention by publishing in France a letter he had written to Martín Artajo protesting the closing of the journals. (*Indice* remained closed to the end of 1956, and *Insula* did not reappear until 1957.)

Army Dissatisfaction

Franco was faced during 1956 with what was reported to be serious disaffection in the army stemming from Spain's difficulties in Morocco. Many observers agree that Morocco had a special meaning in Spain's internal politics and an even stronger meaning for the army. It was said that generals had become involved in Spanish politics to protect the position of the army in Morocco. Young Francisco Franco had made a name for himself in Morocco, and many army officers had proved their abilities and received promotions there. Many officers were reported infuriated with Franco's Moroccan policy, which, they charged, had led to the loss of Spanish Morocco.

Yet, it was widely held, Franco could ill afford to anger the officer corps. According to Arthur P. Whitaker in *Spain and Defense of the West*, the army "could send him [Franco] packing without firing a shot, as they did Primo de Rivera in 1930, and Alfonso XIII the next year." Moreover, students of Spain asserted, Franco needed the army as a counterweight to the Falangists. In Feb. 1956, when Falangists demonstrated noisily in the streets of Madrid, the army expressed fear of a Falangist revolt. Army Min. Agustín Muñoz Grandes informed Franco Feb. 10 that if he did not take control of the Falange extremists, the army would seize Madrid. It was reported that Muñoz Grandes was a loyal supporter of Franco and the threat was not *against* the *caudillo* but against the Falange. Muñoz Grandes was said to be warning that the army intended to be the arbiter of Spain's future.

Franco sought to canciliate the army in several ways. He praised the army in Sevilla Apr. 29 "as one of the true columns of the state." "The army has as its mission the enforcement of the constitution, the defense of peace and internal order," Franco declared. "It has a holy mission." Franco announced in February and authorized May 9 a substantial increase in military salaries, effective June 1. The new scale:

Lieutenant general....	68,000	pesetas	(55% increase)
Major general............	57,700	"	(55% increase)
Brigadier general.......	48,500	"	(74% increase)
First lieutenant.........	19,000	"	(90% increase)
2d lieutenant............	16,100	"	(83% increase)
Sergeant...................	14,000	"	(88% increase)

(It was announced July 3, that Franco's salary was being increased by 12.8% to 1,185,000 pesetas and that his expense account was being raised 11% to 7 million pesetas. His total income, therefore, rose to about $170,000.)

Despite the military pay raise, a continued decline was reported in army morale. 50 native troops had deserted Jan. 14 at Larache, Spanish Morocco. 149 Spanish troops in Ifni deserted in April and fled to Casablanca. (There was no official word of this event, but the Jan. 15, 1958 issue of the New York anti-Franco publication *Iberica* carried a request for funds to help refugees who had deserted 20 months previously.) Some junior officers organized the "Juntas de Acción Patriotica" in Madrid, Barcelona, Sevilla, Valladolid and Valencia.

According to Stanley Payne (in *Politics and the Military in Modern Spain*), the Juntas were nothing more than "grumbling societies." But other observers said Franco was worried by them. For the first time since the Civil War, anti-Franco action originated in the Right-wing of the army. The Oct. 15, 1956 issue of *Iberica* carried the text of a Juntas manifesto blaming Franco for all of Spain's ills, including "the latent division between the younger clergy who are identified with the people and the hierarchy; the creation of insoluble probelms in the university . . . , the scandalous immorality of certain cabinet ministers." The manifesto ended with the following: "The ruling class must prevent the realization of the tremendous dilemma which can be foreseen on the horizon: SPAIN OR GENERAL FRANCO, and must force him to surrender his powers to people which manfully raises its voice to choose, without any vacillation in favor of its country. Spaniards Be Strong! Viva España!"

The Falange, workers and students had demonstrated at various times throughtout 1956. Many observers said that dissention in the army could be the final blow that would overthrow Franco, and powerful forces in the Army were not pacified by the pay raises; it was reported that they insisted on keeping Spain's "empire" in Africa intact. In the face of such army pressure, as well as pressure from traditional forces within Spain, Franco did not agree to a rapid evacuation of the northern zone of Morocco and insisted on the *status quo* for Ifni and the 5 Spanish enclaves in the northern area. As useless as the Spanish African empire then might seem (later discoveries showed that Rio de Oro did have economic value) some authorities held that Franco had to maintain the empire to prevent either an army coup or a Falangist revolt.

Spain & the Suez Crisis

Egypt nationalized the Suez Canal July 26, 1956. Franco made his position known through the Falangist newspaper *Arriba*, which attacked Britain's Mid-East policy July 29 and said that Spain would support Egypt if the seizure came before the UN.

The British, French and U.S. governments Aug. 2 issued a call for a 24-nation conference to meet Aug. 16 to discuss the affair. After a few days the Spanish government agreed to attend. Spanish Foreign Min. Alberto Martín Artajo arrived in London for the opening, but he suddenly left Aug. 16 for San Sebastián, where, according to *Iberica*, he met Franco. He returned to London early Aug. 23, rejoined the conference and supported a U.S. proposal, conditional on its acceptance by Egypt. Martín Artajo said that if Gamal Abdel Nasser of Egypt rejected the U.S. plan, negotiations should be attempted on the basis of Spain's plan for operating the Canal by an Egyptian company whose board would include both Egyptian and foreign members.

60 Spanish pilots had announced Sept. 4 that they were ready to go to Egypt "to defend Egypt against foreign aggression."

The Franco government Sept. 17 insisted on direct talks with the Egyptians rather than unilateral action by a projected Suez Canal Users' Association (SCUA). Martín Artajo reportedly urged Sept. 17 that other Western governments attend an Egyptian-proposed conference.

SCUA was formally inaugurated Oct. 1 by British Foreign Secy. Selwyn Lloyd at the opening session of a new (the 3d) London conference on the Suez dispute. The conference was attended by ambassadors of the 15 SCUA member states, including Spain.

Franco was reported to be undecided in an argument between the anti-capitalist and anti-imperialist Falange, which supported Nasser (after the Anglo-French-Israeli invasion of Suez and the Sinai, the Falange organ *Arriba* said Nov. 4 that Anthony Eden of Britain, Guy Mollet of France and David Ben-Gurion of Israel should be tried as war criminals), and members of the Spanish officer corps, who feared that by supporting Nasser, Spain would encourage Arab nationalist attacks on Río de Oro. Despite the fact that the closing of the Canal (after the Anglo-French-Israeli attack) had forced the Spanish government to institute fuel rationing Nov. 12, Franco initially permitted the Spanish press to continue to attack Western imperialism.

As the Mediterranean situation deteriorated, U.S. pressure on Franco increased. The U.S. ambassador and Army Min. Agustín Muñoz Grandes called separately on Franco Dec. 16 to object, according to observers, to the press, pro-Nasser attitude, and, observers noted, within 2 days all attacks on Western imperialists disappeared from the Spanish press.

U.S. Relations

Because of the poor performance of the Spanish economy, the Spanish sought more aid from the U.S. Spanish Foreign Min. Alberto Martín Artajo said in a speech at Fordham University in New York Apr. 16 that he had requested an extension of the U.S. military agreements with Spain to cover the complete re-equipping of the Spanish army and its installations. Martín Artajo also asserted that economic aid afforded Spain under the 1953 agreement was insufficient and should be supplemented by heavy U.S. capital investment in Spanish industry.

U.S. aid to Spain in the fiscal year 1956-7 was budgeted at $60 million or 5½% of the Spanish government's total revenue of $1.1 billion (44.1 billion pesetas at the official rate of 40 pesetas to the dollar). (Spain's total revenue consisted of 20 billion pesetas [$500 million] from direct taxes, 16.8 billion pesetas [$420 million] from indirect taxes and excise duties, miscellaneous receipts of 3 billion pesetas [$75 million] and customs duties of 2.4 billion pesetas [$60 million].)

The U.S. aid, some Spanish economists pointed out, was equivalent to one of the least significant items of Spanish income. But American economists noted that U.S. aid figures did not include millions of dollars contributed to the Spanish economy by U.S. servicemen and their dependants, the salaries paid by the U.S. government to 5,000 Spaniards employed at the U.S. establishments and the military equipment granted to the Spanish armed forces. (By April Spain's armed forces had received 130 shiploads of military hardware and a squadron of F-86 Saberjets.) Neither did they reflect the fact that the U.S. permitted Spain to buy surplus U.S. items at prices below market value. In September the U.S. government announced this distribution of the year's economic aid to Spain: $15 million for cotton; $12 million for other agricultural products; $4.6 million for raw materials other than coal; $1.3 million to aid the cement industry; $9 million to help Spanish railroads buy new equipment and coal; $8 million for the purchase of electrical equipment, steel plates, various machines and diverse items needed to improve non-rail transportation; $10 million for other items.

With the end of the Korean War, the military need for Spanish bases lessened. During a hearing before the House Committee on Appropriations in February, U.S. Air Force Secy. Donald A. Quarles had said that while the U.S. had originally planned 8 or 9 bases in Spain, the 4 bases then under construction seemed sufficient. Arthur P. Whitaker asserted in *Spain and Defense of the West* that the pace of construction of the U.S. bases had been kept slow for fear that a crash program "might cause a severe shock to Spain's very weak economy and thus reduce the value of the alliance by discrediting its government and provoking strong antagonism among its people." By the end of 1956 Spain had received, in one form or another, over $500 million in U.S. aid. But Ramón Tamames wrote in his 3d edition of *Estructura Economica de España* that "the American aid had little significance in the development of the equipment necessary for our economic well being."

Several other problems strained U.S.-Spanish relations. Many Spaniards objected to non-Catholic U.S. servicemen marrying Catholic women, even though the law courts held civil marriages legal. Another problem was caused by the influx of American tourists who were not sensitive to Spanish attitudes. For example, Harry Whitney, 31, a U.S. bullfighter from Austin, Tex., received a 6-year prison sentence in Madrid June 8 for violating Spanish law against "insulting the nation" with remarks against Spain during an argument over a traffic incident. (But he was released Sept. 21 by order of the Spanish cabinet at the suggestion of the Spanish Supreme Court.) While he was in "jail" he was permitted to leave to fight a bull. In July he killed a bull, which he "dedicated to the Spanish people." He also explained to the audience that he "never intended to insult the people of Spain."

Tensions were caused by what Benjamin Welles, in *Spain: The Gentle Anarchy*, described as "occasional rapes, bar brawls and attacks on taxi drivers." Spanish authorities and Maj. Gen. August W. Kissner,

head of the U.S. military mission in Madrid, constantly tried to eliminate these barriers to U.S.-Spanish friendship.

Spain & the Communist Bloc

Despite recrimination in the Spanish and East European press,
Spain continued to do business and increase its contacts with the Soviet
bloc.

At the beginning of January 200 Polish tractors were put on sale in
Barcelona.

A delegation from the Soviet Academy of Science attended the
International Union of Crystallography held in Madrid in April, and
Agriculture Undersecy. Aleksandr N. Askotchevskii led a trade dele-
gation to Madrid in mid-June.

The Russian ship *Crimea* (*Krym*) arrived in Valencia Sept. 28 with
557 Spanish repatriates. Many had been sent by their parents to the
USSR during the Civil War. Others were former members of the Spanish
Blue Division who had fought against the USSR. The *Crimea* returned
to Valencia Oct. 22 with another 461 repatriates.

DISCONTENT, REFORMS & ECONOMIC GAINS (1957-8)

Demonstrations, boycotts and strikes during 1957 gave evidence of serious discontent prevalent in many sectors of Spanish society. A major revision of the cabinet was undertaken by Franco in a move to put new forces to work on the nation's problems. Reforms were taken up in the Cortes. Improvements were made in Spain's economic position and in its relations with its neighbors during 1957-8.

Dissatisfaction Spurs Cabinet Change

Widespread discontent was becoming increasingly obvious in Spain during Jan. 1957. This dissatisfaction, which led to a cabinet change toward the end of February, was shown in various ways: Students and workers demonstrated against an increase in transit fares. Students rioted in Barcelona Jan. 14-15 and in Sevilla Jan. 18 and staged boycotts of city transit services in opposition to fare increases. While the students created a disturbance, the workers of Barcelona expressed their discontent in a peaceful boycott. Benjamin Welles reported in *Spain: The Gentle Anarchy* that "foreign observers were struck by the sight of orderly masses of Barcelona metal and textile workers leaving home at 5 or 6 in the morning to walk to work, then trudging silently home again at the day's end. No violence took place . . . not even a stone was thrown."

By Jan. 1957 authorities on Spain seemed to agree that Franco intended to change the cabinet and to dispense with José Luis de Arrese Magraz and the Joseantonioist wing of the Falange, whose program Franco had rejected in 1956. Franco was said to have had 3 choices for leadership in the forthcoming regime: the illegal Christian Democratic organization, headed by José Maria Gil Robles and Foreign Min. Alberto Martín Artajo; the Opus Dei; or a non-party group led by the military. It was generally assumed that Franco would give the military a prominant place in order to still the anger caused by the loss of Morocco. The pro-Franco segment of the Falange was widely regarded as having little to offer in the way of leadership. The major question was considered to be whether he would pick Christian Democratic politicians or Opus Dei technocrats to form the core of the government.

Arrese had already offered his resignation as secretary general of the Falange, but, according to Brian Crozier in *Franco*, "Franco coldly turned it down." Benjamin Welles added in *Spain: The Gentle Anarchy* that "Franco wanted no martyrs. No one resigned in Spain except on his orders." And it was reported Jan. 22 that Arrese had withdrawn his resignation.

171

Franco interviewed candidates for government posts for 4 weeks before he announced Feb. 25 the composition of a new cabinet. Its members were (*designates new cabinet member): *Pedro Gual Villalbi, minister without portfolio and president of Council of National Economy. *Dr. Fernando María Castiella y Maíz, foreign affairs. *Gen. Camilo Alonso Vega, interior. *Gen. Antonio Barroso Sanchez-Guerra, army. *Adm. Felipe José Abárzuza Oliva, navy. *Gen. José Rodríguez y Díaz de Lecca, air. *Mariano Navarro Rubio, finance. *Cirilo Cánovas García, agriculture. *Prof. Alberto Ullastres Calvo, commerce. *Gen. Jorge Vigón Suerodiaz, public works. *Fermín Sanz Orrio, labor, *José Solis Ruíz, secretary general of the Falange and minister without portfolio. Antonio Iturmendi Bañales, justice. Jesús Rubio García Mina, education. Gabriel Arias Salgado, information and tourism. Joaquín Planell, industry. José Luis de Arrese, housing. Rear Adm. Luis Carrero Blanco, ministerial undersecretary of the Presidential Office.

Some of the cabinet changes surprised observers. The first major surprise was the removal of Foreign Min. Alberto Martín Artajo, titular leader of the clandestine Christian Democratic Party, who had served Franco since 1945 (when Franco needed a Christian Democrat to deal with the European Christian Democrats Konrad Adenauer of Germany George Bidault of France and Alcide de Gaspari of Italy) and had concluded the military agreement with the U.S. and the new Concordat with the Vatican. Commentators suggested 3 possible reasons for the removal of Martín Artajo: Some saw it as intended to reduce the influence of the Christian Democrats who, since the return of José María Gil Robles, had become "too liberal." Others saw it as Franco's way of indicating that he was rejecting the anti-French and pro-Arab policies of Martín Artajo. The 3d reason advanced was that Franco had a personal argument with his foreign minister: on a good will trip with Martín Artajo to the Middle East in 1950, Franco's daughter Carmencita and her new husband, the Marques Cristobal de Villaverdes, had been placed on the bottom of the list of precedence; Benjamin Welles reported in *Spain: The Gentle Anarchy* that Franco was annoyed and that his daughter "not only cut [Martín Artajo] dead but refused to speak with him for weeks."

A 2d major surprise was the removal of José Antonio Girón, minister of labor for 16 years. Stanley Payne reported in *Falange:* "It had been said that with his demagogic radio speeches and his injurious but impressive wage increases, he was building too strong a position ever to be ousted."

The appointment of Dr. Fernando María Castiella y Maíz as foreign minister was a surprise. Castiella had been professor of international law at Madrid University before being appointed ambassador to the Holy See where he arranged the 1953 Concordat. During World War II he had been decorated by Adolf Hitler. (Castiella was a member of the Spanish Blue Division, which fought on the Russian front.) He had served as director of the Falangist Institute for Political Studies in 1943. And he co-authored an anti-British book, *Reivindicaciones de España (Spanish Claims)*. (Benjamin Welles reported that the book disappeared from Spanish book stores soon after the appointment, and those interested in it were told that it was out of print.) When Franco had planned to send Castiella as ambassador to London in 1951, British Prime Min. Clement Attlee had informed the Caudillo that Castiella was *persona non grata*. (Attlee had served in the Republican International Brigade during the Spanish Civil War.) Technically Castiella was a monarchist yet at the same time a member of the Falange, which is republican. But Welles described this "burly, square-shouldered, square-featured Basque" as a "technician rather than a politician."

The new army minister, Antonio Barroso, was described by Stanley Payne in *Politics and the Military in Modern Spain* as "one of Franco's most trusted personal adherents." Arthur P. Whitaker intimated in *Spain and Defense of the West* that he was dishonest. Barroso was chairman of the board of Telefunken Radiotecnica Iberica, a member of the board of Fabrica Turbos Electricos, Standard Electrica S.A. and of Vias y Construcciones. There was said to be no political significance in the change from Agustín Muñoz Grandes to Barroso. (Muñoz Grandes was appointed army chief of staff June 8, 1958 and was promoted to the rank of full captain general. The only other captain general in the army was Franco.)

The appointment of Gabriel Arias Salgado as information and tourism minister surprised many observers: Arias Salgado was an old-time Falagist; during World War II he had been noted for his anti-Allies position, and in 1955 he had a public argument with Bishop Angel Herrera of Málaga over the question of censorship. Benjamin Welles described him as having "loyalty bordering on servility; an ignorance of the outside world exceeded only by his contemp for it." Henry F. Schulte said in *The Spanish Press, 1470-1966* that Arias Salgado had "used his powers [as press and propaganda chief of the Falange] to muzzle the press, stifle initiative and independence."

José Luis de Arrese's appointment as housing minister was analyzed by Stanley Payne as "depriving Arrese of his personal independence by retaining him in an innocuous position." Arrese disliked his new position and, according to Payne, "found courage to circulate a clandestine pamphlet in which it was declared that the Falangists had been 'cast aside by the priests and the military, who are the ones who have governed from the very beginning. . . . The Falange cannot be responsible for the situation of our *patria*.' "

Rear Adm. Luis Carrero Blanco, appointed ministerial undersecretary, was described by both Brian Crozier in *Franco* and George Hills in *Franco* as "a gray eminence" who performed some of Franco's unpleasant duties. (It was the admiral who phoned Alberto Martín Artajo and informed the foreign minister of his removal from office.)

3 of Franco's appointments reflected his concern with the economic situation: Dr. Alberto Ullastres Calvo, a leader of the Opus Dei, held the chair of international economic history at Madrid University until being appointed commerce minister. Finance Min. Mariano Navarro Rubio, who had been an officer of the military juridical corps and then the administrator of the Banco Popular, was an Opus Dei member. The 3d economic appointee, who did not admit his membership in Opus Dei, was Pedro Gual Villalbi, who had been professor of political and economic science at the University of Barcelona; he became minister without portfolio and president of the Council on Economic Affairs.

Commentators also noted the appointment of Dr. Laureano López Rodo, 37, who was professor of administrative law at Madrid University; to the non-cabinet post of technical, secretary general to to the presidency. Brian Crozier reported that López Rodo was also a member of Opus Dei.

The new cabinet was said to have a distinctly non-party character. The majority was from the armed forces or the universities. The military and naval men were old friends of the *caudillo*, while the university people were technocrats.

The appointments, however, were considered more a reorganization of the government than a simple cabinet change. Some observers said this apparently was confirmed by a decree issued Feb. 25, the day the changes were announced. 5 committees, under the direct supervision of Franco or Adm. Carrero Blanco, were established to deal with these interministerial problems: defense, cultural affairs, health and welfare, transportation and communications, economics. The last named interministerial council was placed under the direction of Gual Villabi. Franco, in an interview in the *N.Y. Times* Mar. 19, said that the change was a natural result of the needs of reorganization.

The new cabinet promised Feb. 28 that it would "intensify its contact with the people through the institutions already existing, into which the government will endeavour to infuse a greater vitality."

The cabinet gave an outline of its goals, which included a defense of the purchasing power of the peseta and new measures to combat inflation, encourage private enterprise, intensify production, improve labor conditions and to eliminate the housing shortage. The cabinet also promised to try to strengthen Spain's links with the U.S., Portugal and the Arab states.

Franco's '12 Principles'

A political declaration later known as the "12 Principles" was issued by Franco May 17, 1958. In this declaration, Franco reaffirmed his belief in the Falangist system. In the 1964 edition of *Pensamiento Politico de Franco* (*Franco's Political Thought*), the "12 Principles" were called "The Law of May 17, 1958." Franco's declaration:

I, Francisco Franco Bahamonde, *caudillo* of Spain, conscious of my responsibility before God and before history, in the presence of the Cortes of the kingdom, promulgate as Principles of the National Movement . . . the following:

1. . . . Service to the state should be the sacred and collective task of all Spaniards.

2. The Spanish nation considers as a stamp of honor the acknowledgement of the laws of God, following the doctrine of the Holy Catholic, Apostolic and and Roman Church, the only true faith, inseparable from the national conscience, which inspires its legislation. . . .

3. Spain, root of a great family of peoples, with whom there is an indissoluable feeling of brotherhood, aspires to the institutions of justice and of peace among nations.

4. The unity between the people and the land of Spain is intangible. The integrity of the nation and its independence are the supreme necessity of the national community. The armed forces of Spain, the defender of its security and the expression of the historic virtues of our people, should possess the necessary force to be of optimum service to the nation.

5. The national community is based on man, as the carrier of eternal values, and on the family, as the base of social life; but the individual and collective interests always have to be subordinated to the communal good of the nation. . . .

6. The national entities of social life: family, city and sindics, are the basic structure of the national community.

7. The Spanish people, united in a regime of law, . . . is the national state. Its political form, following the immutable laws of the national movement is . . . the traditional, Catholic, social and representative monarch.

8. The representative character of our public order is the basic principle of our political institutions. The participation of the people in the legislative tasks and in other functions of general interest [is carried out by] organic representation.

9. All Spaniards have rights. . . . The Christian ideal of social justice, reflected in our labor constitution, will inspire policy and laws.

10. . . . Private property in all its forms [is] a right conditioned by social function. . . .

11. The relations between [labor and industry] should be based on justice, . . . and economic value should be subordinate to human and social order.
12. [The state is the protector of all Spanish virtues.]

Monarchist Activity

The presumed pro-monarchist attitude of the new cabinet appeared to some observers to be confirmed July 15, 1957 when Rear Adm. Luis Carrero Blanco, ministerial undersecretary of the Presidential Office, told the Cortes: "When the *caudillo* is no longer with us, the destinies of Spain will be directed by a monarchy which is neither liberal nor absolute but traditional, popular and Catholic. The person who embodies the monarchy will have to serve loyally the principles of the [Falangist] regime."

Considerable monarchist political activity was reported. At a meeting in Estoril, Portugal Dec. 20, 1957, 46 Carlist leaders headed by Arauz de Robles pledged loyalty to Don Juan, 43, exiled Bourbón pretender to the Spanish throne. At the meeting, Don Juan, who had placed a red *boina* (beret, symbol of the Carlists) on his head, said: "3 essential factors make traditionalism useful to Spain at the present moment. They are popular roots, distaste for party politics, and the certainty of support for a real policy of social justice which is vitally necessary in our century and must be carried out in Spain, not for reasons of political tactics, but because it is the duty of our Christian conscience. . . . I want to be a very human king, in contact with my people, and not a symbolic mummy preserved in court protocol. . . . I want to be the king of all Spaniards and do not reject anyone, even my enemies. I want to establish a solid basis for the state and the government, and to give peace and true liberty to Spain."

When Don Juan finished speaking, the Carlists shouted "Viva el rey!" Theo Aronson reported in *Royal Vendetta* that at this meeting "Don Juan agreed to the traditional principles laid down by [the conservative Carlist pretender] Don Alfonso Carlos." (Carlist circles in Spain and France, however, rejected any "deal" with Don Juan and maintained their support for Carlist pretender Francis Xavier of Bourbon-Parma and his son Hugo Carlos. According to Alan Lloyd in *Franco*, Hugo Carlos had entered Spain in 1957 and secretly met with Carlist leaders in Bilbao.)

The rapprochement between Don Juan and the Carlists, according to Arthur P. Whitaker (in *Spain and Defense of the West*), alienated Christian Democratic leader José María Gil Robles, a supporter of parliamentary government. Whitaker reported that in the spring of 1958, when it seemed that Don Juan might accept the throne and the Falange in a "package deal," Gil Robles "threatened a rupture," "Don Juan drew back, and the restoration was dropped."

Gil Robles' action, according to observers, split the pro-Bourbon monarchists into 3 groups. The first, on the Right, was led by José Rodríquez Soler, who, according to Whitaker, was opposed to the Falange but had "no other serious differences with the present regime, and many of the members [of this group] are called 'collaborationists.'"

Tangentially allied to this group, according to observers, was Opus Dei intellectual leader Rafael Calvo Serer, who was a close friend of Don Juan. From 1953 to 1958 Calvo Serer had been both the leading Opus Dei monarchist and anti-Falangist and, as a result, endured brief periods of temporary exile. In 1958 he published a collection of his articles (under the title "*La Fuerza Creadora de la Libertad*") in which he called for the reestablishment of a monarchy in which the Cortes would have only advisory and consulting power.

The 2d group, the Left-Center, led by Gil Robles, Basque industrialist Joaquín Satrustegui and Socialist Prof. Enrique Tierno Galvan, organized the Union Española.

Whitaker cited another monarchist group on the Left, led by Manuel Giménez Fernández, which "support[s] a restoration of the monarchy on condition of its prior endorsement in a free national referendum."

Mrs. Carmen Franco, the *caudillo*'s wife, visited Lisbon in May 1958. Don Juan sent her an invitation to tea. According to Benjamin Welles in *Spain: The Gentle Anarchy:* Mrs. Franco, Spanish Foreign Min. Fernando María Castiella y Maíz and his wife, and the wife of Interior Min. Camilo Alonso Vega accepted the invitation. When Mrs. Franco "entered the royal home-in-exile" at Villa Giralda, she "dropped Don Juan and Doña María [his wife] a deep curtsy, addressing them both as 'majestad.' Her aides . . . had no alternative but to follow suit."

Franco, meanwhile, had permitted Don Juan's son Juan Carlos, 20, to sail with his fellow classmates to the U.S. The prince, who had no legal status in the Spanish government, found himself toasted at a banquet given by the Spanish embassy, welcomed by Pres. Dwight D. Eisenhower and State Secy. John Foster Dulles and given a luncheon by the *N.Y. Times.* Don Juan, according to Welles, was "so heartened" that he joined his son in New York. Juan Carlos left the U.S. May 16, and his father went to Connecticut to visit friends.

Political Opposition

Following the defeat in Oct. 1956 of the Falange program of José Luis Arrese and the removal in Feb. 1957 of both Arrese and Labor Min. José Antonio Girón from their positions of power, radical elements of the Falange reportedly began to engage in clandestine activity.

In the spring of 1958 a group of young Falangists who called themselves "Hedillistas" was arrested in Madrid's Atocha railway station. No reason for the arrest was made public. (The Hedellistas were named in honor of Manuel Hedilla Larrey, who had become head of the Falange following the murder of Falange founder José Antonio Primo de Rivera. Hedilla was arrested by Franco Apr. 25, 1937, threatened with execution and then incarcerated until pardoned in 1947. Despite the use of his name, Hedilla, who had returned to private life, not only refused to support the clandestine activity, but also refused to engage in any Falangist activity.)

In Santander, Hedilla's home province, a group of young Falangists organized the Haz Iberico. Stanley Payne reported in *Falange* stated that this "semiclandestine neo-Falange [movement] attracted several thousand followers scattered throughout northern Spain, but on a national level it had no significance."

Since 1957, Benjamin Welles reported in *Spain: the Gentle Anarchy*, the "emphasis" of the Spanish Communist Party (PCE) "has been on penetration of Franco's bureacracy. . . . Even the Spanish police concede that the PCE has had considerable success."

The PCE proposed Sept. 7, 1957 that all parties unite in a "Day of National Reconciliation" and a peaceful general strike. The other anti-government parties, however, refused to ally themselves with the Communists.

Gen. Camilo Alonso Vega, the interior minister, announced Jan. 18, 1958 that 44 persons had been arrested in Madrid, Zaragoza and Valencia for conspiring to organize an anti-Franco "Day of National Reconciliation" general strike and for plotting to recussitate the PCE. According to Alonso Vega, some of those arrested were students who had attended the World Youth Festival in Moscow in the summer of 1957. The Spanish police were aware of all who had visited Moscow, Alonso Vega said. Of 193 Spaniards at the meeting, only 90 were Spanish residents; these 90 apparently had been recruited by Soviet agents in Paris. Among those arrested was Associate Prof. Javier Pradera Cortazar of the Madrid University law school, son-in-law of Falangist philospher Rafael Sánchez Mazas. Pradera was charged with being a member of the PCE Central Committee. Bogdan Raditsa, writing in *Commentary*

(1959), said that 25 priests, "including Franco's own chaplain," came to the defense of the accused.

(Franco Jan. 24 appointed Col. Enrique Eymar Fernández as military judge to deal with extremist activity throughout Spain.)

The PCE's "Day of National Reconciliation" ultimately took place May 5, 1958, as scheduled. There were confusing reports as to its effectiveness. It was reported that the government had prepared for an open insurrection. (Someone had issued a bogus copy of *Mundo Obrero*, the PCE clandestine newspaper, calling for violence.) Sergio Vilar reported in *Protagonistas de la España Democratica* that there were strikes in the Basque provinces, Barcelona and Madrid. Because of censorship, there was no disclosure of such events in the press. Franco declared in a speech to the Cortes May 16 that the Communist plan had failed to inflame the workers. The police continued to round up "Communists." Many were quickly released because of lack of evidence. Some however, were tried and imprisoned.

Communist activities in Spain were said to have been hindered by the fact that the French police watched Spaniards who made contact with the Soviet embassy in Paris and informed the Spanish police. A result of growing Hispano-French friendship was the removal from Paris of Radio España Independente, which, Arthur P. Whitaker reported in *Spain and Defense of the West*, was "financed and controlled by Moscow." After being forced to leave Paris, the station moved to Prague, Czechoslovakia.

The outlawed Partido Socialista Obrera Español (PSOE) was reported divided during 1957–8 between the Spanish Socialists in Spain and the old pre-Civil War leaders living in France (the 7th Congress of the PSOE was held in Toulouse in Aug. 1958). Max Gallo reported in *Histoire de l'Espagne Franquiste* that the Socialist leadership had reafirmed its opposition to any deal with either the Communists, the Trotskyites (Partido Obrero Unificado Marxista, or POUM) or the Anarchists (Confederación Nacional del Trabajo, or CNT). The Catalan Socialist Party (Moviment Socialista de Catalunya), meeting in Perpignan in Aug. 1958, called for unity of all anti-Franco parties in Catalunya.

The Socialist intellectual Prof. Enrique Tierno Galvan had attempted to organize a broad-based anti-Franco group in Spain. In 1957 he formed the "Association for the Functional Unity of Europe," but it was supressed by the government. He then joined with the Basque industrialist Joaquín Satrustegui and others to form the pro-monanchist Unión Española. Financed by Satrustegui, Tierno Galvan maintained contact with Manuel Giménez Fernández of the Left

Christian Democrats and with ex-Falangist Dionisio Ridruejo. Tierno Galvan, Ridruejo, Antonio Menchaca Carega, 36, a Basque liberal, and Raúl Morode, 22 a Galician Socialist, were imprisoned briefly in April and May 1957 for anti-government activity. Tierno Galvan was picked up again in June and again released, but this time, according to reports, he was informed that charges against him would not be dropped and that the government eventually would bring him to trial.

Antonio Amat (described by Benjamin Welles in *Spain: The Gentle Anarchy* as the "chief Socialist organizer in Spain") was arrested Nov. 6, 1958. (According to Sergio Vilar in *Protagonistas de la España Democratica*, Amat had spent the past 4 years in organizing PSOE and Union General de Trabajadores [UGT] groups throughout Spain.) Son of a wealthy family from Basque province of Álava, Amat was known as "Guridi" to the Socialist underground. Amat was taken to Burgos jail and held there for 2 years without trial.

Within 2 weeks of Amat's arrest the police began to round up suspected Socialists. 50 members of the Spanish Socialist Party, among them Prof. Juan Reventos y Carnera of Barcelona University were reported to have been arrested Nov. 18–21. The arrests of 80 prominent anti-Franco Spanish Socialists were reported by the *N.Y. Times* Nov. 30. Those arrested were said to include Antonio Villar, associate of monarchist leader Antonio Garrigues, the future Spanish ambassador to the U.S., Prof. Juan Rion of Barcelona University; Luis Torres Sole, Francisco Casares Potav, Antonio Pisserer Sabater and Edmundo Valles, Barcelona lawyers; Drs. Vicente Urcola and José Leon Careche of San Sebastián; Joaquín Pradera, grandson of Falange martyr Victor Pradera. The arrests were said to be linked to renewed Socialist efforts to reunite a Leftist faction led by Indalecio Prieto, in exile in Mexico, and Rightists headed by Luis Araquistan, living in Switzerland.

Rejecting U.S. and Western European protests against the arrests, the Spanish government charged that the "Spanish Socialists [were] allied to communism in all subversive actions against Spain."

The Church

The appearance of at least 3 and possibly 4 members of the lay-Catholic organization Opus Dei (Sociedad Sacerdotal de la Santa Cruz y del Opus Dei) in the cabinet did not, according to observers, end clerical opposition to the regime. According to some observers, Opus Dei membership in the cabinet increased clerical opposition to the government's social and economic policies. Church officials were reported to object to the fact that Opus Dei was independent of the Spanish hierarchy. Some clerics, it was said, considered Opus Dei to be a political organization opposed to the Church-sponsored Catholic Action, long held to be the most powerful element in the clandestine Christian Democratic Party. Father Julian Herranz, writing in the Opus Dei publication *Nuestro Tiempo* in Apr. 1957, denied that Opus Dei had any political orientation.

Bishop Angel Herrera y Oria of Málaga, considered an opponent of the Franco regime, was disclosed Jan. 29, 1958 to have been named president of the governing board of Editorial Católica, the agency controlling the Catholic Action press in Spain. When Herrera took control of the firm, the post of editor-in-chief was given to ex-Foreign Min. Alberto Martín Artajo, the Christian Democratic Party leader, while Javier Martín Artajo became business manager. Under Herrera's direction, Editorial Católica began to publish "liberal" theological works by Jacques Maritain as well as lay sociological studies. Part of the new direction in publication, some observers assert, was caused by Catholic Action's desire to compete with the Opus Dei-sponsored *Biblioteca de Pensamiento Actual*, edited by Rafael Calvo Serer, which published works by Etienne Gilson, considered by many to be the leading academic defender of Aristotelian-Thomistic Catholic liberalism. The Opus Dei had also published *The Theory of Militarism* (*Teoria del Militarismo*), by Public Works Min. Jorge Vigón Suero Díaz.

Bishop Herrera y Oria supported direct action by priests. The Instituto Social Leon XIII (Leo XIII Social Institute) in Madrid and the Escuela Social Sacerdotal (Social School for Priests) in Málaga were used to train priests for social action. One of the chief text books in both schools was written by the liberal auxiliary bishop of Valencia, Rafael González Moralejo, who had studied in Brussels.

Franco, according to observers, usually did not interfere with the clerics' social criticism. But when clerics acted through Church-supported institutions such as Hermandades Obreras de Acción Católica (HOAC) or publicly opposed government policies by writing articles in Church-controlled newspapers and periodicals, the government treated the clerical opposition no different than any other political opposition. Church publications such as *Tu* and *Boletín Verde* have been suspended for brief periods and HOAC organizers jailed. (According to William Ebenstein in *Church and State in Franco Spain*, in 1957 Bishop Herrera's brother Francisco spent several months in jail for anti-government activity.) A Spanish priest told this editor that the government does not like to arrest priests and so has developed another method of "getting rid of trouble makers": The priest is summoned to the police station and informed that "Communist literature has been found in his room and that he will be arrested within 24 hours. This gives the priest time to flee."

Sometimes clerical authorities have supported the suppression of criticism. Father Carlos Martín Castañeda of Campuzano (Santander Province), in a sermon delivered the morning of May 11, 1958, defended strikers and announced that he was collecting money for the strikers' families. That night the provincial vicar-general ordered Martín Castañeda to go to a monastery and remain silent.

A confrontation between clerics and government officials took place in Dec. 1958 over the question of the right of clerics to preach in non-Castilian languages. Gen. Felipe Acedo Colunga, the civil governor of Barcelona, delivered a speech at a Falangist rally at Granollers Dec. 1 and, according to Elena de La Souchere (in *An Explaination of Spain*), "accused Catalonyan* [sic.] clergy of fomenting secession by preaching in Catalonyan. The abbot of Montserrat, Dom Aurelio María Escarre, reported Dec. 8: "The Church always speaks the truth. If this truth is not pleasant to the ears of those who govern us, then it is up to them to change." The civil authorities refused to permit the press to carry the abbot's words, but members of the Christian Democratic Party, HOAC and Catalan nationalist organizations circulated "thousands of pamphlets reproducing the words of Dom Escarre." Soon other pamphlets appeared defending the abbot and declaring that "all of us feel that Montserrat is, as always, our Sinai." By Feb. 1959 this dispute became a *cause célèbre* involving the entire archdiocese of Tarragona, the press, the Catalan nationalists and the central government.

The clerical opposition involved still another factor: The election of Pope John XXIII (Oct. 28, 1958), Brian Crozier reported in *Franco*, "had a profound effect on the Spanish Church's attitude toward social problems." Under the new pope, Archbishop Enrique Cardinal Plá y Deniel of Toledo, Archbishop Marcelino Olaechea of Valencia, Bishop Pablo Gurpide of Bilbao and the new archbishop of Sevilla, José María Bueno Monreal, who had replaced the decreased (Apr. 8, 1957) Pedro Cardinal Segura y Sáenz, joined Bishop Angel Herrera in demanding social reforms. According to observers, the pope's position on reforms in Spain was made clear when Bueno Monreal was made cardinal Dec. 14, 1958.

---

*Catalan is the name usually used for both the people and the language of Catalunya.

Reforms & Press Restrictions

Various reforms were discussed by the Cortes, during 1958, and some were enacted. A 3-day Spanish Cortes session ending Apr. 17 modified traditional restrictions on Spanish women and granted married women the right to control of their own property. Franco was reported June 27 to have formed a cabinet committee charged with drafting laws to permit more freedom to the Cortes and to ensure Spain's transition to a monarchic government when Franco's rule ceased.

Censorship of foreign news reports and comment appearing in Spanish newspapers was ordered ended Mar. 5, 1958 by the Direction General of the Press. But Henry F. Schulte indicated in *The Spanish Press, 1470-1966* that this order did not reduce government control of the press. In May, for example, the censors permitted the Madrid pro-monarchist daily *ABC* to carry a full account of the meeting in Lisbon between Bourbonist pretender Don Juan and Franco's wife, but the magazine *SP*, was "forbidden to report on the event." According to Schulte, the government had 3 effective methods of controlling the press:

(1.) The government controlled the distribution of newsprint. In the summer of 1958 the Information & Tourism Ministry cut by 10% the newsprint available to *Informaciones* because its "political nuances" were offensive to the government. The authorities then divided the newsprint between *ABC* and *Madrid.*

(2.) The government could order the publication of certain items. This had 2 consequences. First, since the government controlled the newsprint and since required government material had to be published before other items, the government could force a paper into bankruptcy by ordering the publication of items and restricting the newsprint available for advertisment. 2d, the government could force the publication of fabrication. Schulte, who had been United Press' Madrid bureau chief, reported that the Information & Tourism Ministry distributed reports of a United Press interview with Foreign Min. Fernando María Castiella y Maíz of which he had no knowledge.

(3.) The government could force the editor of a newspaper to hire an assistant acceptable to the government. The Marques Torcuata Luca de Tena, editor and owner of Madrid's *ABC*, had been forced, according to Schulte, to hire such an individual in 1954, and the Count de Godo, owner of Barcelona's influential *La Vanguardia*, had to hire Luis de Galinsoga in 1957.

In honor of the election of Pope John XXIII Oct. 28, 1958, the government reduced the prison sentences of 16,000 prisoners.

Strikes & Labor Problems

The dissatisfaction of the workers continued to be a major problem in Spain. Considerable discontent with working and living conditions was reported. The 8½ million worker members of the Falange-controlled syndical organization had been told of their misery and poverty for years. (The Falange labor paper *Pueblo*, for example, described Sept. 22, 1952 how 11,000 caves were being used as homes by migrant workers, and it reported that a "belt of filth and poverty" ringed Madrid. 5 years later, after 324,708 new living units had been built by the government, the office of the archbishop of Barcelona estimated that 300,000 people in the diocese were living in shacks. According to ex-Republican diplomat Elena de La Souchere in *An Explanation of Spain*, Spain needed 1,067,452 new homes in 1957. The Falange party organ, *Arriba*, reported Nov. 20, 1955, that while Spain spent only $2.22 per capita on education, backward Egypt was spending $3.98 per capita on education.)

Some observers described the shop-steward elections of 1957 as a peaceful revolution. According to Benjamin Welles in *Spain: The Gentle Anarchy*, "approximately 70% of the 350,000 stewards elected . . . were newcomers. About half were in their mid-20s, while the rest were old workers with a background of trade unionism in the old Anarcho-Sindicalist CNT [Confederación Nacional del Trabajo] and the Socialist UGT [Union General de Trabajadores]." Max Gallo reported in *Histoire de l'Espagne Franquiste* that Communist members of PSUC (Partit Socialista Unificat de Catalunya) were also elected in Barcelona.

By 1957, it was reported, worker protests were supported by Communists, Socialists, the Church-supported Hermandades Obreras de Acción Católica (HOAC) and university students. Sergio Vilar said in *Protagonistas de la España Democratica* that by Mar. 1957, students from the universities of Barcelona, Madrid and Zaragoza were actively backing strike action and agitating for strikes. According to informants it was the student agitation in conjunction with the HOAC, CNT, UGT and Communist organizations that led to further industrial strife.

About 5,000 Asturian coal miners struck Mar. 4, 1958 in protest against low pay scales and the suspension of 8 pitmen. Cracking down on the strikers, Franco Mar. 14 suspended constitutional guarantees against arbitrary search and arrest. But the strikers did not return to work until Mar. 17, after the government announced that all strikers would be drafted into the army.

2 Barcelona factories were closed Mar. 25 by Gen. Felipe Acedo Colunga, Barcelona governor, after 500 workers struck in response to

clandestine appeals Mar. 24 for a Barcelona general strike. Textile, metal and other industrial workers struck Mar. 26-29 in the Barcelona and San Sebastián districts in sympathy with the earlier Barcelona strikers and Asturian miners. 30 shop stewards were reported under arrest and an estimated 30,000 workers idle in Barcelona by Mar. 29. Basque workers in Guipúzcoa Province joined the walkouts Apr. 1. Government officials blamed the initial Barcelona strikes on agitation from leaflets and clandestine broadcasts by exiles employed on the French Toulouse radio. An estimated 25,000 Barcelona strikers finally returned to work Apr. 8 after local authorities ordered an end to the lockout at affected plants and paid salaries for part of the strike period.

Spanish police Mar. 30 had announced the arrest of 11 "Communists" who had allegedly organized the Asturian coal miners strike. And a Spanish Security Directorate communiqué said Apr. 12 that 34 more alleged Communists had been arrested for leading the strikes in Barcelona. It named Miguel Nuñez Gonzáles, a philosophy student said to be a member of the PCE (Spanish Communist Party) Central Committee, as leader of the group. (Nuñez was later sentenced to 15 years in jail.) Another arrested as a PCE leader involved in the strikes was Emilion Fabrego Arroyo. 31 Asturian miners were sentenced to prison terms of 2 to 20 years Dec. 22 on charges of organizing Communist groups.

A major concession was granted to Spanish workers when the Spanish Cortes Apr. 15 approved a law giving the workers the right to negotiate directly with employers on disputes involving wages and working conditions. Observers described this new law as a major defeat for Falangism and the Falange-controlled syndicals and a major victory for HOAC.

Economic Progress

The economic upturn in Spain continued in most areas during 1957-8. Although the picture in agriculture was spotty, the industrial situation was largely good. Industrial output (using 1929 as a base) rose from 279 to 305 in the 2-year period.

Spain produced 49 locomotives in 1957 and 65 the following year, 2,285 coaches and freight cars in 1957 and 2,714 in 1958. Production of automobiles rose from 23,325 to 33,201, tractors from 1,508 (double the 1956 output) to 1,943, motorcycles from 127,603 to 153,176, bikes from 187,936 to 194,000, buses from none to 239. For the first time consumer goods began to play an important role in industrial production and acceptable statistics were compiled. (According to the International Bank for Reconstruction & Development mission, one of

Spain's many problems was its lack of an adequate, accurate statistical system.) In 1958 Spain produced 262,305 radios, 3,993 TV sets, 21,325 refrigerators, 67,099 washing machines and 57,665 gas stoves.

Shipbuilding continued to improve although observers noted what appeared to be a danger sign: Actual construction during 1957-8 increased from 116,000 tons annually to 146,000 tons; ships in construction increased from 265,000 tons to 304,000 tons, and the capacity of Spanish shipyards increased from 315,000 to 360,000 tons. But new orders decreased from 959,000 tons to 877,000 tons.

Cement production increased from 4.1 million tons to 4.8 million. 27 million liters of beer were produced in 1958, or 11 million more than in 1955.

The value of textile production increased from 14.9 billion pesetas in 1957 to 15.7 billion pesetas the following year. But while the production of synthetic rayon increased from 15,934 tons to 16,746 tons, the export of cotton cloth, a major item in the Spanish economy, fell from 1,020 tons with a value of 7½ million gold pesetas to only 191 tons with a value of 1.8 million gold pesetas. By the end of 1958 the London *Economist* reported that Catalunya was in a "grave recession" and that Catalan textiles, the most important part of the Spanish textile industry, had declined 25% in sales while future orders were 59% below normal.

Shoe production fell from 25.3 million pair in 1957 to 20.4 million in 1958, a figure below that of 1952.

Paper production increased from 286,791 tons to 320,981 during the 2-year period, while book production increased from 4,243 titles to 5,183, which was still below the 1953 level.

The production of new motion pictures fell to 50 in 1957, but rose slightly to 52 in 1958.

The consumption of electricity increased from 11.3 billion kilowatt hours in 1957 to 12.8 billion in 1958; the consumption of butane gas went from a little less than one million kilograms to 2.2 million during the same period.

Spanish ports handled 50 million tons of goods in 1957 and 53 million tons in 1958.

Tourism *seemed* to improve. The number of people who visited Spain increased from 3.2 million to 3.6 million, and the amount of money spent in Spain increased from $212.9 million to $263.1 million but the actual profits to Spain decreased from $76.9 million to $71.6 million. Part of the reason for the low yield was the need for Spain to reinvest money in tourist facilities.

The agricultural picture was mixed during 1957-8. The agricultural index rose slightly from 113% of the 1931-5 average to 117.4% in the 2 years. Wheat production, however, declined slightly in 1957 to 4.4 million metric tons, then rose a small amount in 1958; rice production increased in 1957 but in 1958 fell below the 1956 level; the potato crop, which fell sharply in 1957, recovered slightly in 1958 but was still below the 1956 crop; onion and tomato production rose in both years and reached all-time highs in 1958; the amount of cotton produced fell in 1957, then rose slightly in 1958 but was still below the 1956 crop; tobacco output fell in both years, and the government began to import large quantities of tobacco.

Orange exports rose from 429,322 tons, worth 117.9 million gold pesetas, to 709,375 tons, worth 175 million gold pesetas. Oranges' share of total exports rose from 8.1% to 11.7%. Sugar production fell from the 1956 level. In 1957, 367,000 tons were produced and 36,000 tons imported (including beet sugar from eastern Europe); the following year 326,000 tons were produced and 137,000 tons imported. The per capita consumption of sugar continued to increase from 13.6 kilograms to 16.5 kilograms. Milk production in 1958 was 2,405,500 tons, or below the 1953-7 average of 2,450,000 tons.

Wood manufacture fell from 4.6 million cubic meters to 4.3 million cubic meters. Cork production rose from 43,388 tons valued at 34.3 million gold pesetas to 53,590 tons valued at 45.9 million gold pesetas. The production, however, was below 1956 levels.

The fish harvest increased from 694,407 tons in 1957 to 721,570 in 1958.

Production of the extractive industries was unstable during 1957-8. Coal output increased from 16½ million tons to 17.1 million; iron production decreased from 5.2 million tons (of which 3.3 million tons, worth 96.4 million gold pesetas, were exported) to 5 million tons (of which only 2.2 million tons, worth 58.9 million gold pesetas, were exported). Lead production increased from 61.2 tons (of which 11.6 tons, worth 9½ million gold pesetas, were exported) to 70½ tons (of which 23½ tons, worth 13.9 million gold pesetas, were exported). Copper output increased from 144,334 tons to 149,526 tons, but copper export decreased from 64,630 tons (worth 11.7 million gold pesetas) to 54,611 tons (worth only 4.7 million gold pesetas). Aluminum production increased from 14,925 to 16,148 tons, but imports also increased from 31,565 tons to 41,265. The production of wolfram continued to decline—from 1,215 tons to 1,160 tons—while exports decreased from 1,526 tons (worth 12 million gold pesetas) to 538 tons (worth only 2 million gold pesetas). Manganese production fell from 41,388 tons to 36,350. The export of mercury increased from 1,596 tons to 1,748 tons, but its value decreased from 33 million gold pesetas to 31.8 million gold pesetas. Salt production increased from 1.4 million tons to 1.54 million tons—an all-time high. The export of potassium, however, fell from a record 328,653 tons valued at 28.6 million gold pesetas in 1957 to 264,674 tons worth 24 million gold pesetas. The phosphate industry disappeared: in 1956 11,300 tons were produced, in 1957 100 tons, and in 1958 nothing. Superphosphate output, however, increased from 1.6 million tons to 1.8 million tons.. The production of sulphuric acid increased in both years.

Because chemicals were available in Spain, Bayer, Ciba, and Schering opened offices and plants in Barcelona and Madrid.

The government continued efforts to improve the economy. The number of government-financed houses increased from 75,203 built in 1957 to 77,064 completed in 1958 (private home construction increased from about 5,000 units built in 1957 to 5,100 units completed in 1958).

The land-reform program was pursued. 140 parcels of 841,600 acres were created in 1957 but only 134 parcels of 606,700 acres in 1958. The number of government-sponsored cooperatives in Spain increased from 5,336 with 1,168,823 families in 1957 to 5,612 with 1,183,359 families by the end of 1958.

The reforestation program suffered a set-back; 340,800 acres of land were reforested in 1957 but only 225,000 acres in 1958.

One of the most impressive accomplishments of 1957–8 was the completion of the huge Entrepeñas-Buendia reservoirs. Claude Martin described them in *Franco Soldado y Estadista* as "the greatest in Europe"—with a capacity of 2,462,000 cubic meters. The system was inaugurated July 14, 1958. The dams can hold water capable of irrigating 400,000 acres of land, and they make possible the exploitation of the Tagus and Guadiela rivers for hydroelectricity. The 2 dams cost an estimated 750 million pesetas (about $20 million). A government press release said 90 other dams were under construction.

Infant mortality, which rose slightly in 1957 to 4.72 per 100 live births, reached an all-time low of 4.19 in 1958.

The number of individuals leaving Spain decreased from 58,260 to 47,179, while the number of foreigners seeking to reside in Spain increased from 18,618 to 22,888.

Stanley Payne reported in *Franco's Spain* that "by 1957 . . . galloping prices were getting completely out of hand." Using 1940 as the base, prices in 1957 jumped from 521.3 to 608.4; by the end of 1958 the index was 668.2. Some economists blamed the inflation on government borrowing (between 1951 and 1957 the national debt had more than doubled to 139 billion pesetas). To pay for its expenditures the government printed vast quantities of paper money; between 1953 and 1957 the value of paper in circulation jumped from 36 billion pesetas to 67 billion. Economists said that prices were rising faster than production.

One result of the inflation was a thriving money black market that gave 62 pesetas to the dollar instead of the official 40. As the value of the peseta declined, more-affluent Spaniards converted their paper into gold or dollars and sent the money to Switzerland. (By the end of 1958 it was estimated that $250 million had been sent from Spain to Swiss banks.) This "Swiss Bank Scandal" helped increase the flight of the peseta. It was not until Dec. 1958 that the government began a crackdown on black marketers, many of whom were either government officials or their relatives. It was reported in Madrid Dec. 16 that the government had begun to recover foreign currency held in illegal Swiss bank deposits by at least 1,000 prominent Spaniards. The illicit deposits totaled an estimated $125–$400 million.

It was generally acknowledged that the inflation had all but wiped out the effects of 1956's 20% wage increase. This was so despite the fact that the workers' per capita annual earnings in terms of 1953 pesetas had increased from 9,862 pesetas in 1957 to 10,166 pesetas ($242.05 at the official rate, $195.50 at the tourist rate and $163.90 at the black market rate) in 1958 and, using the depression year 1935 as a base, personal incomes had risen from 122.2 to 126 during 1957–8. Arthur P. Whitaker asserted in *Spain and Defense of the West* that by the end of 1958 the worker was worse off than before the 1956 wage increase.

Spain's import-export balance remained unfavorable. In 1957 2.64 billion gold pesetas worth of goods were imported while only 1.46 billion gold pesetas worth were exported; in 1958 2.67 billion gold pesetas worth were imported and only 1½ billion worth exported. Spain's monetary reserves fell to $96.8 million by the end of 1957 and to $65 million by the end of 1958. Whitaker noted that the Spanish gold reserve had reached its "untouchable" minimum as set by law. Furthermore, the Spanish government was faced with the need to pay $68 million on debts due at the end of 1958 and another $50 million on debts due in mid-1959.

The cabinet was revised in Feb. 1957 in an effort to bring in experts and other individuals who could solve the economic ills. The experts found, according to some observers, that the various forces constituting the Franco regime would not permit a radical repair of the situation. Franco himself refused to admit the seriousness of the economic situation. In response to a question from the *N.Y. Times*, Franco said Mar. 13, 1957 that "what is called a crisis, is only a small difficulty . . . in our economic progress." In these circumstances, the technocrats attempted what was described as stop-gap remedies.

Action was taken to reduce imports and increase exports. To make imports expensive and exports cheaper the government Apr. 9, 1957 announced a devaluation of the peseta: the rate was raised to 42 pesetas to the dollar from 40. Many experts held that the devaluation was too small (the black market rate was 62 to the dollar). The government virtually admitted then that it had not devalued the peseta sufficiently when it announced that tourists could buy pesetas at a rate of 52 to the dollar while U.S. servicemen stationed in Spain were permitted to receive 55 for a dollar at U.S. bases. But many tourists and servicemen preferred to buy pesetas at even better rates "on the street" or in Tangier.

Since, in 1958, 22.4% of Spain's imports were petroleum, gasoline and tobacco, the government attempted to discourage such imports by increasing the taxes on these particular imports in 1958. This action failed to curb the imports but did increase government revenue.

The government sought foreign grants and low-cost loans. During 1957-8 the U.S. gave or lent Spain $400 million, but this was not enough to solve the economic problems.

The cabinet also attacked government expenditures and alleged internal mismanagement. It sought to impede the ease with which certain government agencies borrowed capital; and it tried to make private borrowing more expensive.

The cabinet's technocrats soon discovered that some budgetary items could not be changed. Spain's military and naval appropriations supported a 461,000-man army, 23 warships and 6 submarines—the world's 5th largest fleet and 7th largest standing army—and the cabinet as a whole refused to cut these appropriations. Maintaining the Spanish colony of Ifni became expensive in mid-1957. Until 1956 expenditures for Ifni had been negligible, but with the granting of independence to Morocco and the demand of Ifni natives for unity with Morocco, Spain began to fortify the colony. By mid-1957, Benjamin Welles reported in *Spain: The Gentle Anarchy*, the government was spending 10 million pesetas a day to defend Ifni from rebel forces. Besides direct military expenditures, the army, navy and air force departments had attached to them quasi-autonomous civilian agencies that spent billions of pesetas a year to build housing, airports and port facilities. The cabinet was said to have little control over these agencies.

Spain's transportation system was another drain on the treasury.

The antiquated railway system lost 3.6 billion pesetas annually in 1957–8 but Spain had neither the money nor the technological skills to overhaul it. Up to 1956 Spain's airlines had been profitable even though the government had subsidized internal air fares. By 1957, however, the airports were becoming obsolete and the airports at Madrid, Barcelona, Palma de Mallorca, Las Palmas in the Canary Islands and Málaga had to be enlarged and modernized for the increased tourist trade. In 1958 the government announced a 1.4 billion peseta revamping program, but it did not raise fares on internal trips.

Faced with an antiquated and decentralized government bookkeeping system, the cabinet July 26, 1957 ordered a massive reorganization of the system of accounts so that the cabinet could see where money was being spent. The implementing of this reform according to a report of the International Bank for Reconstruction & Development, took several years.

One of the most expensive single projects in Spain was the Valley of the Fallen. Started in 1942, but periodically abandoned for lack of funds, the Valley is a huge mausoleum cut into the Guadarrama mountains 33 miles west of Madrid. The mausoleum was to house the bodies of soldiers who fought on either side during the Civil War. When the government opened the Valley to visitors Sept. 7, 1958, it became obvious, according to viewers, that the builders had ignored cost: at the entrance to the crypt are 2 bronze doors each weighing 11 tons; the altar is marble; the granite interior had been softened by generous use of marble facing; the monument is topped by a 450-foot granite cross visible for miles. Even though much of the work on the Valley had been done by prison labor (Republican prisoners were able to get a reduction in sentence for working at the Valley), critics held that poverty-stricken Spain could ill afford such a luxury. No government cost figures were released. Alan Lloyd in *Franco* estimated the cost at $27 million, Bogdan Raditsa in *Commentary* estimated the cost at $200 million, but Benjamin Welles said in *Spain: The Gentle Anarchy* that "only Franco and a few intimates know the cost."

As part of their anti-inflationary program the cabinet's technocrats examined the tax-exempt Instituto Nacional de Industria (INI), a 19 billion-peseta "private" company (financed by government funds) that controlled 50 of Spain's leading firms (including the SEAT automobile works) and had interests in 25 other establishments. Various aspects of INI practices were made public by government officials. One of the charges against INI was that INI officials made "private deals" with bankers and industrialists to conceal the cost of INI projects. (Spanish businessmen complained, Benjamin Welles reported in *Spain: The Gentle*

Anarchy, that INI "was squandering public funds on showy but uneco-
nomic projects, that it was concealing huge losses and competing un-
fairly with private industry." This charge appeared to be substantiated
in part by a report of the International Bank for Reconstruction &
Development that there was "little evidence that investment proposals . . . are examined and analyzed in terms of cost and objective in
any systematical way. . . . The consequence of not obtaining the highest
economic returns for the investment of public money are extremely
serious.")
    The dispute between INI and the cabinet's technocrats was said to
involve a clash of ideas. Claude Martin reported in *Franco Soldado y
Estadista* that Juan Antonio Suanzes y Fernández, director of INI, believed in autarchy but that the technocrats did not share his convictions.
According to Benjamin Welles, Suanzes, "a brilliant naval enginer,"
conceived the idea of making Spain an industrial power and persuaded
his childhood friend Franco to give him a blank check. Suanzes once
said that it would cost a lot of money to industrialize Spain but after it
was done "no one will question the cost." Writing in the 1963 edition
of the government publication *El Nuevo Estado Español*, Suanzes
boasted of INI accomplishments during the period 1945–53 because
these successes were achieved without "the river of gold" from the U.S.
(Even the anti-Franco former Republican diplomat Elena de La Souchere
said in *An Explanation of Spain* that INI's "achievements under Suanzes'
direction are considerable.") The technocrats, on the other hand, were
very much interested in costs and claimed that INI projects used funds
needed elsewhere. (A 1958 UNESCO report stated that 45% of Spanish
industry used pre-1920 equipment and 28% used equipment installed
between 1920 and 1931; only 27% had post-1931 equipment. 65% of
the Spanish merchant marine was pre-1939; some ships were pre-1898.)
    INI was removed from the government budget Dec. 22, 1957.
Observers noted, however, that, while the separation of INI from the
government cut government expenses, it did not hinder INI's ability to
expand. Deprived of government funds, INI was able to borrow sufficient capital from the Banco de España at 0.75% interest. It was reported that the inflationary aspects of INI were not curbed. (A prime
target of the cabinet's technocrats had been the Aviles steel plant complex, whose cost had been reported at 7 billion pesetas but which, some
observers hold, had actually cost much more. In order to build the
plant a marsh had to be drained and a road, railroad and river had to be
relocated. The cost of the changing of the landscape was not charged
to the plant. The plant was supposed to produce 4 million tons of steel
a year, but in 1958 its output was only 600,000 tons.)

In another attempt to control the inflation, the government in 1957 ordered interest rates raised from 4½% to 5%. Then, by the so-called *Law of 1958*, the government permitted only 6 official medium- and long-term credit institutions dependent on the Finance Ministry for their funds to advance credit for industrial expansion. Because of the complex interrelationship between Spanish banks and industry, observers expressed doubt that these reforms would curb the inflation. The Banco de Vizcaya had interests in the Bilbao Blast Furnaces; the Banco de Bilbao was said to control the Iberduero hydroelectric company and the Papelera Española paper cartel; the Banco Hispano-Americano dominated the Estrella Insurance Co., while the Banco Central controlled Cia Minerosiderurgicia de Ponferrada. Because of the interrelationship the banks made loans at low rates that permitted industrial expansion but contributed to inflation.

Ramón Tamames, in *Estructura Economica de España*, stated the widely held view that "the [economic] reforms did little to solve" Spain's economic problems. Arthur P. Whitaker said in *Spain and Defense of the West:* "As 1958 drew to a close it became clear that the reforms as a whole had not succeeded in halting the deterioration." Finance Min. Mariano Navarro Rubio had warned in a speech before the Cortes July 28, 1958 that unless there was progress, drastic measures would have to be taken. The government asked the Organization for European Economic Cooperation (OEEC) to send representatives to Spain to study the country's economic position, and OEEC representatives arrived Dec. 1958. (Spain had become a member of the Paris-based OEEC Jan. 10, 1958.) The Spanish also asked the International Bank for Reconstruction & Development to send a mission to help (and the mission arrived in early 1959).

U.S. Relations, Rejection by NATO

The U.S., busy completing its military bases in Spain, tried unsuccessfully to persuade its Atlantic Pact partners to admit Spain to NATO.

The *N.Y. Times* reported Mar. 8, 1957 that $290 million of $313.7 million appropriated for the U.S. base program in Spain had been committed in contracts and that $170 million worth of facilities had been completed. The 4 U.S. air bases, linked by a 485-mile underground pipeline, said to be 80% complete and near operational status (figures are final costs), were: Zaragoza (16th Air Force Headquarters), $75 million; Moron de la Frontera, $45 million; San Pablo (Air Force supply depot), $9 million; Rota (Naval Air Force and carrier base), $83 million. (Maj. Gen. August W. Kissner, retiring commander of the U.S. military-base construction program in Spain, was succeeded by his deputy, Maj. Gen. Stanley J. Donovan of the Strategic Air Command.)

The U.S. effort to win NATO membership for Spain received considerable support from some U.S. Congress members, especially after Feb. 14, 1957, when Britain announced its intention to seek NATO permission to reduce its military committments to NATO. Assistant U.S. State Secy. Robert C. Hill wrote Sen. Theodore F. Green (D., R.I.) Mar. 8 that U.S. policy aimed at creating a "climate favorable to eventual Spanish participation in NATO." Hill, informing Green that the State Department had no objections to a draft Senate resolution favoring NATO status for Spain, conceded that it would take "improvement in relations between Spain and certain NATO powers." The House Foreign Affairs Committee Mar. 18 unanimously approved a resolution urging Spanish entry into NATO. When it appeared that the U.S. *might* persuade its allies to replace British troops with Spanish, Radio Moscow May 19 broadcast a warning to Spain that it risked "atomic retaliation" if it did not reject U.S. moves to incorporate Spain in NATO.

As it turned out, Spain had little chance of admittance. Dr. Halvard Lange, the Norwegian foreign minister was quoted as having said at a press conference Apr. 16 that "a Norwegian veto was to be expected if Spanish membership should be suggested by any country— whether it should be the U.S.A. or any other member-country—at the next meeting of the Council in Bonn." The Spanish government made it known that it was "hurt" by Lange's remarks and considered them "unnecessary" and "unfriendly."

Some members of the U.S. Congress expressed interest in what one could expect from Spain. During a June 4, 1957 session of the Senate Foreign Relations Committee, Sen. Wayne Morse (D., Ore.) asked Brig. Gen. John Guthrie of the Defense Department: "Can anybody . . . tell me how much help you think we can get from Spain?" Guthrie suggested that "perhaps Gen. [Lauris] Norstad . . . can enlarge on the NATO side of it; Spain . . . is important in the NATO concept."

English Labor MP Denis Healey asserted in the Nov. 1957 issue of *Western World* that Spain was "militarily useless and an affront to our principles." But Spanish Army Min. Antonio Barroso, in a speech before the Cortes Dec. 21, 1957, provided reasons that Spain was of great military value to NATO. Among these reasons: the Canary Islands could serve as a base for naval concentration; Rio de Oro could provide air bases.

Meanwhile U.S. Senators were investigating aid to Spain. At a hearing before the Senate Appropriations Committee July 29, 1957,

Sen. Allen J. Ellender (D., La.) asked Assistant State Secy. C. Burke Elbrick: "Why is [the economic aid] necessary? . . . We were led to believe . . . that the base construction would prime the [Spanish economy, but] . . . now we are requesting aid grants. . . . What has happened?" Elbrick denied that anything had happened in the way of a "new course" and stated that "this aid program . . . is very closely connected with the base program."

The USSR sent *Sputnik 1*, the first man-made satellite, into orbit Oct. 4, 1957. There was some question among military men, however, about whether the Soviet military position had improved. In any event, the U.S. Dec. 10 announced plans to stop shipping short-range guided missiles to Western Europe and to begin preparations for establishing bases for intermediate range balistic missiles (IRBMs). Observers held that the U.S. military considered Spain more important than ever since Spain appeared to be an excellent location for IRBM bases. U.S. military leaders were said to feel that with the growing understanding between the USSR and Morocco, Spain would not reject a U.S. request for missile sites. According to observers, the only factor that prevented an immediate establishment of IRBM bases in Spain was the objection of the U.S.' NATO partners.

At a NATO meeting in Paris in December, the questions of Spain and the IRBM were raised. After the meeting U.S. State Secy. John Foster Dulles flew Dec. 20 to Madrid for a 3-hour talk with Franco before returning to the U.S. Dec. 21. Dulles and Franco, accompanied by Spanish Foreign Min. Fernando Maria Castiella y Maíz and U.S. Amb.-to-Spain John Davis Lodge, reviewed decisions of the Paris NATO meeting that particularly affected Spain but, according to a report in the *N.Y. Times*, that did not touch on the possible construction of IRBM sites on Spanish territory. Dulles said that Spain's economic needs and the recent fighting in Ifni were also discussed. Franco was said to have broached preliminary requests for an additional $30 million in U.S. aid above the $40 million in defense support and $70 million in farm surpluses that Spain was scheduled to receive in 1958.

Failing to convince its NATO allies of Spain's significance both as a military power and as a secure base for missiles, the U.S., nevertheless, expressed determination to maintain a stable regime in Spain. In order to prevent Spanish food riots, the U.S. not only permitted Spain to purchase surplus U.S. farm commodities at bargain rates but also permitted the Spanish to pay for these items in non-convertible pesetas. A non-convertible peseta was no drain on the Spanish treasury since the owner could not convert the currency into either gold or dollars (Spain had practically none left) and could be spent only in Spain.

A U.S.-Spanish agreement signed in Madrid Jan. 27, 1958 provided for the purchase in pesetas of $69.1 million worth of surplus U.S. farm commodities, with 55% of the currency to be returned to Spain as a 30-year loan at 5%, the remainder to be held for future U.S. use in Spain. The pact brought U.S. aid to Spain since 1953 to over $1 billion ($400 million in military aid, $260 million in surplus food accords, $340 million in defense support). And an additional $15 million U.S. defense-support allocation was made to Spain Mar. 25. Totals of other U.S. Export-Import Bank loans and credits, $106,600,000; 1954 Commodity Credit Corp. wheat sales, $20 million; agricultural surplus sales, $254,800,000; food grants to charities, $89,500,000. Spain also was reported to have been given $200 million worth of U.S. military equipment.

As tensions mounted in the Middle East, more U.S. funds were made available to Spain. The Export-Import Bank June 18 approved $24½ million in loans to finance purchases of U.S. electrical equipment by Spanish firms building power projects on the Duero River, near Portugal, and in Ponferrada, Spain.

During the Lebanon crisis in July 1958, when France and Italy prevented the U.S. from using bases on their territory to transport troops to the Middle East, Franco announced that the U.S. could use its bases in Spain. The value of the U.S. bases were underscored when Sultan Muhammad V of Morocco, angered at the use of U.S. bases in Morocco to transport Marines to Lebanon, began to demand the evacuation of those bases.

Spanish Army Min. Antonio Barroso had been reexamining the posture of the Spanish army. Military observers generally seemed to agree that Spain, because of the economic crisis and the loss of Morocco, could not afford a large standing army. It was held that Spain needed a relatively small, well-trained army equipped with expensive hardware. Barroso's plan, according to Stanley Payne in *Politics and the Military in Modern Spain*, was to cut the army force by at least 25% by reducing the number of standing divisions from 18 to 12. 5 of the new divisions, however, "might even be armed with tactical atomic weapons." According to Arthur P. Whitaker in *Spain and Defense of the West*, the plan called for higher salaries and better living conditions for the military. Since "almost all the money for the proposed reorganization would have to come from the" U.S., according to Payne, Barroso made special trips to Washington in August and October 1958.

Meanwhile, the U.S. government found use for the unconvertible paper pesetas beginning to pile up as a result of its deals with Franco. The U.S. agreed Oct. 16 to award 60 scholarships a year to Spaniards to study in the U.S., and other funds were made available for 40 "Fulbright" awards for U.S. students to study in Spain.

As 1958 drew to a close, the U.S. announced a further loan. U.S. aid accords revealed in Madrid Dec. 27 pledged $27 million for railway and farm development.

Ex-Foreign Min. Alberto Martín Artajo, who had negotiated the Pact of Madrid with the U.S., called for a revision of the pact because the volume of U.S. aid was "wholly inadequate." He did so in an article published in the March/April issue of *Revista de Estudios Politicos*, and he had expressed similar views—which many Spaniards seemed to share—in a speech he had delivered before the U.S. Chamber of Commerce Feb. 5, 1958.

Morocco & Ifni

2 treaties were signed by Franco and Moroccan Sultan Muhammad V in Madrid Feb. 11, 1957. The French embassy in Rabat charged Feb. 23 that the agreements violated a previous Franco-Moroccan convention.

The first treaty: called for close consultation between Madrid and Rabat on matters of mutual interest; promised Spanish support for Moroccan membership in international organizations; agreed that Moroccan and Spanish representatives in each other's countries would be raised to the ambassadorial rank; recorded a Spanish promise to represent Moroccan interests in areas where Morocco had no official representation.

The 2d treaty stated that: Spanish legal officials were at the disposal of the Moroccan government; Spanish and Moroccan lawyers could practice in each other's country; Spanish would remain as a valid language in the courts in the former Spanish Zone for as long as necessary; Spain would help train Moroccan lawyers; Spaniards would aid Morocco in developing a new legal code for all of Morocco.

The Spanish Foreign Ministry announced Feb. 12 that Spain would represent Moroccan interests in Argentina, Bolivia, Brazil, Chile, Colombia, Cuba, Dominican Republic, Ecuador, El Salvador, Guatemala, Haiti, Honduras, Nicaragua, Panama, Paraguay, Peru, the Philippines, Uruguay and Venezuela.

Spanish troops and Ifni rebels (allegedly aided by Moroccan irregulars) clashed in Apr. 1957 in Sidi Ifni, capital of the Spanish African province of Ifni, a wasteland with ill-defined frontiers. (Juan Pérez de Tudela Bueso and Tomás Pérez Sáenz, in *Geografia Economica de España* gave the area as 1,700 square kilometers, but the Instituto

Nacional de Estadistica claimed only 1,500 square kilometers. In 1958 there were 4,618 Europeans and 42,285 natives registered in the province. Sidi Ifni had a population of 5,910.) The revolt was supressed, but the population was continually inflamed by the Istiqlal newspaper, *al-Alam*, which hailed delegations of Ifni Berbers who saught reunion with the fatherland. Spanish authorities closed the Sidi Ifni branch of Istiqlal but could not prevent either *al-Alam* from entering the province or the Moroccan Istiqlal from organizing a strike in Sidi Ifni in July.

Meanwhile Moroccan Foreign Min. Ahmed Balafrej went to Madrid where he and Spanish Foreign Min. Fernando María Castiella y Maíz agreed June 4, 1957 to terminate the Spanish-Moroccan trade treaty of 1861.

Spain and Morocco signed 4 treaties July 7. The first called for the purchase by Morocco of all Spanish Moroccan pesetas with Moroccan francs, thus giving Morocco a uniform currency. (Morocco had been forced to issue 2 sets of stamps: one in franc values and the other in pesetas.) The 2d agreement called for Spanish technical assistance to Morocco; the 3d detailed trade and payments; the 4th was a cultural exchange agreement.

Reliable sources stated that during the meeting that led to the July 7 treaties there had been some discussion on the various interpretations of the Treaty of Uad-Ras (1860), which had ended a brief Moroccan-Spanish war. According to the Moroccan version of the treaty: in 1860 Sultan Muhammad bin Abd al-Rahman had granted the Spaniards only fishing rights off Ifni and the possession of an old fort that had been built by Spaniards in 1476; the fort was destroyed 50 years later, and Spain abandoned claims to Ifni until 1860. The Spanish version was that the 1860 treaty had surrendered to Spain full sovereignty to the province of Ifni. Since no agreement could be reached on the meaning of the treaty, according to informants, discussion ended. Franco said in an interview with *Le Figaro* of Paris June 14, 1958 that "the sultan conceeded in perpetuity sufficient territory to construct a fish factory plus . . . the region where Spain had historically exercised its authority."

The revolt then raging in French-held Algeria was said to affect Spanish dealings with both Morocco and France. Because of the events in Algeria, it was reported, Muhammad V took a tougher stand toward Spain. The sultan recalled his ambassador to Spain for talks Aug. 20–23 on the possibility of negotiations for the incorporation of Ifni into Morocco. The Moroccan government announced Oct. 16 that Spain was prepared to transfer sovereignty of Southern Morocco (Tarfaya Province) to Morocco. Madrid did not comment. France was reported to be willing to forget some of its anger at Spain's former pro-Arab policy. Maurice Faure, French state secretary for Moroccan and Tunisian affairs, met in San Sebastián 'Aug. 24 with Spanish Foreign Min. Castiella for talks on Hispano-French economic cooperation in North Africa.

While these discussions were taking place, Allal al-Fassi, who with Ahmed Balafrej had organized the original Moroccan Nationalist Party in 1926, was busy, Mark I. Cohen and Lorna Hahn reported in *Morocco, Old Land, New Nation*, with "political harangues in the south." According to Cohen and Hahn, because of al-Fassi's "intensive propaganda effort," the Sahara Liberation Army (also called the Army of Liberation, Liberation Fighters or Mujahidines), prepared to invade Ifni. The backbone of this force, according to Benjamin Welles (in *Spain: The Gentle Anarchy*) and Brian Crozier (in *Franco*), was 1,000 troops trained by the ex-Spanish resident in Morocco, Rafael Garcia Valiño, "to harass the French in 1956."

The Moroccans attacked at 5 a.m. Nov. 23, 1957. Stanley Payne reported in *Politics and the Military in Modern Spain* that the Spanish "garrison was, as usual, unprepared." Welles said that "despite the presence of 1,500 Spanish troops, . . . 'Moroccan Liberation Army,' led by a local bravo named Ben Hammum, penetrated the barbed-wire defenses, stole past the Spanish sentries, and came within an ace of seizing an important arms dump on the beach." The attack apparently took everyone but the Istiqlal paper *al-Alam* by surprise. *Al-Alam* claimed that the Spanish had "provoked" the assault by first attacking Moroccan outposts. (Crown Prince Mulay Hassan said Nov. 28 that he knew nothing of the attack. In a broadcast to his people he admitted complete "surprise" at the events and denounced the "adventursome people who act contrary to the interest of the government.") There is no exact information as to the size of the attacking force. Figures range from "1,200 troops from Ifni, together with Moroccan irregulars," as reported by Cohen and Hahn, to "8,000," as estimated by Arthur P. Whitaker in *Spain and Defense of the West*. For several days no official word reached the world, although *al-Alam* made many claims, including the capture of Sidi Ifni. The Spanish Army Ministry announced Nov. 27 that Ifni had been attacked by individuals seeking to foment unrest. An appeal was issued to Crown Prince Mulay Hassan, in view of the sultan's absence (on a trip to the U.S.), to maintain Moroccan authority in areas bordering the Spanish provinces. Spanish Army Min. Antonio Barroso announced that 100 attackers had been killed or wounded and that 5 Spaniards had died and 34 were wounded.

Although the attackers failed to take Sidi Ifni, the rest of the

Spanish territory was in trouble. (The 1963 edition of the official government publication *El Nuevo Estado Español* admitted that the attackers had "obliged the Spanish garrison to retire to the coast, where they fought heroically until the arrival of reinforcements.") At Teliouine, on the southern perimeter, 120 Spaniards reportedly held off "thousands" of attackers until they received reinforcements from paratroopers, who enabled the garrison to fight its way back to Sidi Ifni Dec. 5. Other outposts like Tiourza held out for 2 weeks before being relieved.

Franco had hurried back to Madrid to organize defenses. But, it was reported, the U.S. had vetoed the use of any U.S. equipment against the invaders. Franco did not use his new American jets but sent up old Junker and Heinkel bombers and Messerschmitt fighter planes of World War II vintage and deployed a quarter of the Spanish fleet, including the 1912 cruiser *Canarias* (10,000 tons) and the smaller cruisers *Miguel de Cervantes* (7,500 tons) and *Mendez Nuñez* (4,500 tons). Initially, however, a 5-day storm prevented the use of air power; when the weather cleared, the airport at Sidi Ifni could not handle most of the planes (supplies could be landed, but the war planes had to use the airport in the Canaries); and there was neither a pier nor a dock in Ifni so that troops and supplies had to be brought ashore by small craft, or troops had to wade ashore.

Yet by Nov. 29 a Spanish communiqué stated that all that was left was "a mop-up operation" and that the several hundred invaders, none of them apparently inhabitants of either Ifni or Rio de Oro, had been killed, wounded or captured. Spain Dec. 8 issued another communiqué in which it stated that the Spanish garrison, which by then had been reinforced by 4,000 troops from the Canary Islands, had defeated "every coordinated enemy action" and was engaged in reestablishing law and order. The report said the additional troops would remain to "clear bandits out of all the villages and mountains of Ifni until peace and order had been restored." The report admitted that several outposts had been abandoned for defensive purposes. While claiming that several hundred bandits had been killed or wounded, the communiqué stated that only 61 Spanish officers and men had been killed, 128 wounded. Franco said in a New Year's report Dec. 31: "The [Spanish] military force . . . completed its mission with the spirit and heroism of those who know that the defense of the national sovereignty constitutes a glorious and most noble calling."

Crown Prince Mulay Hassan Dec. 3 had rejected a Spanish charge that the fighting had been started by the Morocco-based Sahara Liberation Army. The prince insisted that the attack was started by

Ifni natives (the Ba Amrane tribe) who had been "provoked" by Spain's refusal to return Ifni to Morocco. Mulay Hassan added that "if Gen. Franco, in whose word I have complete confidence, announces his intention to transfer Southern Morocco [Tarfaya province of Spanish Sahara] immediately to the sherifian [Moroccan] authorities, I will appeal to the Ba Amrane to put their trust in his majesty [Muhammad V] and the government to settle their case through diplomatic channels."

The Spanish government replied Dec. 6 that a "prior condition" for any "present or future" consultation on Ifni was the restoration of peace.

A Spanish flotilla of 2 ancient cruisers, 5 support ships and a submarine anchored Dec. 7 off the Moroccan port of Agadir, about 100 miles north of Sidi Ifni. Reporters commented that Agadir seemed to have been the gathering point of the Istiqlal organization, and *al-Alam* had reported that Spanish warplanes had bombed and strafed the area several times, killing several women and children. When word reached Mulay Hassan of the flotilla's arrival, he sent a "polite note of protest" and suggested that if Spain would evacuate Southern Morocco (Tarfaya) immediately, he would use his good offices to arrange a cease-fire. The Spanish did not reply to the note, but the fleet left Agadir Dec. 8.

Sporadic fighting was reported in Spanish Sahara (Rio de Oro) in December, but there was little accurate information. Information & Tourism Min. Gabriel Arias Salgado had prevented reporters from entering the danger zones. When most of the fighting in Ifni was over, he permitted Benjamin Welles of the *N.Y. Times*, Eric Olivier of *Le Figaro* of Paris and Gilbert Graziani of *Paris-Match*, but no Spanish reporters, to visit Sidi Ifni. The reporters, however, were still barred from Spanish Sahara.

The Ifni incident had these consequences for Spain. First, according to Stanley Payne in *Politics and the Military in Modern Spain*, "the Ifni-Sahara build-up provided new colonial employment and higher pay for many of the officers relieved from the [Morocco] Protectorate 18 months earlier, and it may have hastened the dissolution of the [Right-wing anti-Franco military group called] Juntas de Acción Patriótica." 2d, the war cost the almost bankrupt Spanish treasury $250,000 a day and added to Spain's economic woes. 3d, according to Benjamin Welles in *Spain: The Gentle Anarchy*, the fighting placed a new strain on U.S.-Spanish relations because of the U.S. veto of the use of equipment supplied by the U.S. The Spaniards viewed the Ifni battle as part of the general war against communism. The attackers had been armed with

Czechoslovak weapons and had been supported by Morocco, which was becoming friendly with the USSR. Thomas F. Brady of the *N.Y. Times* had spent 10 days with the Sahara Liberation Army, and he reported that the invaders had been accompanied by "unofficial" Moroccan advisers. (The 1963 edition of the official Spanish *El Nuevo Estado Español* asserted that "the bands were armed, but apparently not controlled, by the Rabat government.")

The Spanish government Jan. 14, 1958 announced that the Spanish colonies in Northwest Africa would be reorganized as provinces of Spain: Lt. Gen. Mariano Gómez Zamalloa, the former governor of Spanish Sahara and commander of the Ifni garrison, was appointed Governor General of Ifni; Maj. Gen. José Hector Vazquez was appointed Governor General of Spanish Sahara, which included the former colony of Rio de Oro (or Spanish Western Sahara as it was called in the 1920s) and the district of Saguia el Hamra; Lt. Gen. López Valencia was appointed commander of all troops in the 2 African provinces and the Canary Islands. It was announced that the provinces would be administered by the Dirección General de Plazas y Provincias Africanas in Madrid.

Meanwhile fighting had broken out in Spanish Sahara. Spanish troops and members of the Sahara Liberation Army clashed Jan. 3, 1958 near Villa Cisneros in southern Spanish Sahara. There were no reports of casualties. The 2 forces fought a major battle Jan. 12–14 at El Aiun, capital of the province. 241 Moroccans were reported killed and 51 Spaniards killed or wounded.

The increasing threat of Moroccan irredentism was said to have convinced the French government that it would be wise to cooperate with Spain in this phase of the conflict. Hispano-French forces struck Feb. 10, 1958 at attacking rebels not only in Spanish Sahara but also at rebel camps in southern Algeria, Mauritania and Morocco itself. The reason given for the wide scale of the operations was that many members of the nomadic Regueibat tribe had joined the insurgents. The bulk of the Hispano-French force was 10,000 Spanish troops and 5,000 French troops supported by 70 modern French warplanes and 60 antiquated Spanish aircraft. The chief bases for the allied forces were the old French forts of Tindouf, Fort Tringuet and Fort Gouraud in southern Algeria and Mauritania. In the Hispano-French attacks, planes would spot a group of insurgents and begin strafing, with most of the fire aimed at the rebels' camels; meanwhile other planes would drop paratroopers and jeeps near the insurgents. Since the camel was usually the only transportation the rebels had, the jeeps and paratroopers would soon catch up with them and either chase them into Morocco or

kill or capture them. Sahara Liberation Army communiqués charged
Feb. 25 that poison gas dropped by Spanish and French aircraft had
killed 600 civilians in Western Sahara.

Moroccan Sultan Muhammad V, who had returned from his trip to
the U.S., was reported under pressure from Istiqlal leaders to support
the rebels openly. The sultan announced in Mhamid (a hamlet on the
Morocco-Algerian frontier about 200 miles north of Tindouf) Feb. 25
that Morocco intended to recover "our Sahara" in accord with its
historic rights and the wishes of its "faithful subjects" living in the area.
(The *N.Y. Times* reported Mar. 21 that Moroccan claims extended to
the Senegal River and included not only Spanish Sahara but all of
Mauritania, and large parts of southern Algeria and northwestern
French Sudan.)

Spanish propaganda quickly responded to the Moroccan charges
and claims. Spanish newspapers and magazines began to carry stories
about the bravery of Spanish troops in their battle with "Communist
agents." (West European commentators, who had expected the Spanish
African empire to collapse at the first blow, indicated surprise at the
ability of Spain to withstand the Liberation Army.) The March issue of
Ejercito published a propagandistic article by Col. Hermengildo
Tabernero Chacabo called "Ifni, the Creation of Spain."

By the end of Feb. 1958 the rebels, having lost most of their
camels, sought sanctuary in Morocco. About 12,000 members of the
Regueibat tribe found refuge near Agadir in Morocco.

The Spanish War Ministry claimed Mar. 1 that a 3-week air and
ground campaign led by Lt. Gen. López Valencia had cleared "invading
elements of the Moroccan guerrilla Sahara Liberation Army from "the
central Spanish Sahara." It said that "French units in Mauretania . . .
carried out cleaning-up operations in cooperation with our troops."
Casualties were placed at 214 rebels killed but only 5 Spanish killed and
27 wounded.

The French, facing increasing difficulty in Algeria and Tunisia,
proposed an alliance of western Mediterranean powers, including
France, Spain, Italy, Tunisia, Morocco, Libya and possibly Britain. The
proposal was made Mar. 7 by French Premier Felix Gaillard. Speaking
in the French National Assembly, Gaillard said such a grouping would
form "a north-south axis for the common defense which would be the
natural and necessary complement to the Atlantic Pact." He stressed
that the planned alliance, to include "French Algeria," would involve
joint economic development of the Sahara by France, Morocco and
Tunisia. Gaillard's cabinet unanimously approved the proposal Mar. 10.
He had said Mar. 9 that the response to his call for a Mediterranean pact

would show "if these chiefs of state [presumably Tunisian Pres. Habib Bourguiba] who proclaim themselves attached to the West" were honest or "wanted to try blackmail." Tunisian and Moroccan newspapers criticized the alliance proposed Mar. 9-10 on the ground that it contained no provisions for settling the Algerian war or for the departure of French troops from their countries. Spanish newspapers lauded the proposal Mar. 9 but chided Gaillard for taking credit for what they termed a 1947 Turkish plan elaborated by Spain in 1952.

The Spanish government was considering ways to increase the Spanish population in its African provinces. One suggestion, which was placed into effect, was to offer salaries double those of metropolitan Spain. While that plan did attract some settlers, the economy of West Africa was so underdeveloped that there was little for the workers to do. The chief occupation was that of day laborer on government construction jobs. Another program, suggested by Army Min. Antonio Barroso, was to settle 30,000 Spanish colonists in Spanish Sahara.

Spain and Morocco had been discussing the Spanish evacuation of what was called Southern Morocco or Tarfaya by the Moroccans and Cape Juby (or Yubi) by the Spanish. (The area of 10,000 square miles had only 6,000 inhabitants. According to Mark I. Cohen and Lorna Hahn in *Morocco*, *Old Land*, *New Nation*, the area was part of "Morocco's historic sphere of influence" but prior to 1912 was free of Moroccan rule.)

Spanish Foreign Min. Fernando María Castiella y Maíz and Moroccan Foreign Min. Ahmed Balafrej Apr. 1 signed an agreement stipulating the evacuation of Spanish troops from Tarfaya. The Moroccans, however, soon found that it was not simple to take over their land. A force of about a thousand Moroccans marched on the capital, Villa Bens (sometimes called Cabo Yubi or Cape Juby, the name used by the Spanish for the whole area), only to discover that the only road ran through Spanish Sahara, and the Spanish refused crossing rights. The Moroccans, therefore, had to go through the desert and did not reach Villa Bens until Apr. 18. Meanwhile, the small Spanish garrison at Villa Bens had apparently made no preparations to vacate the post.

Sultan Muhammad V, under pressure from Istiqlal leaders to get all Spaniards out of Morocco, had demanded the withdrawal of the Villa Bens garrison as early as Apr. 12. Muhammad V, however, faced with a cabinet crisis caused by the resignation of Premier M'Barek Ben Bekkai Apr. 16, was unable to enforce his demands. When the Moroccans finally stationed themselves in most of the provincial hamlets but not yet in Villa Bens, the sultan announced the appointment of Ali Bou

Aida as the new governor. The Spanish objected because Bou Aida was known for his anti-Spanish views. Muhammad V, however, refused to cancel the appointment. The Moroccan cabinet crisis ended May 8 when Ahmed Balafrej agreed to serve as premier. One of his first tasks was to secure the evacuation of Villa Bens. The Spanish ambassador in Rabat informed Balafrej May 10 that Villa Bens would soon be evacuated and that all administrative buildings turned over to Morocco.

Rapprochement with France

Relations between Spain and France seemed to be improving throughout most of 1957-8. Observers said that the chief cause of the rapproachement was the asserted growing danger from Moroccan expansionism.

Spanish Foreign Min. Fernando María Castiella y Maíz and French State Secy. (for Moroccan & Tunisian Affairs) Maurice Faure met at San Sebastián and Biarritz in the last week of Aug. 1957 and discussed, according to Arthur P. Whitaker in *Spain and Defense of the West*, a wide spectrum of affairs ranging from North Africa to the European Common Market. One of the points of chief interest was the French desire to build a railroad from Tindouf and Fort Gouraud in French West Africa (southern Algeria and Mauritania) to El Aiun in Spanish Sahara. Geologists had discovered a reserve of more than 2 billion tons of iron ranging from 33% to 66% pure in West Africa. It would have been easier and cheaper to build the railroad to the Moroccan port of Agadir, but since the ore reserve was in lands claimed by Morocco, the French, according to observers, considered it politically expedient not to do so. The Spanish would benefit from the French project since the French proposed to build a rail line through the virtually uninhabited Spanish Saharan northern province of Saguia el Hamra and also to build a port because the port facilities of El Aiun were unsatisfactory. Spain had another reason to cooperate: According to Benjamin Welles in *Spain: The Gentle Anarchy*, the Spanish hoped to find ore in Spanish Sahara (they eventually did so), and the railroad and port facilities would aid their exploitation of the minerals.

Observers pointed to several other signs of Hispano-French friendship: In June 1957 Gen. Charles de Gaulle had called for the admission of Spain to NATO; in December José Felix de Lequerica, Spain's delegate to the UN, for the first time supported France during a debate on the Algerian questions; in Feb. 1958 a group of French parliamentarians visited Spain. In a 2-day interview June 13-14, 1958 Franco told George Groussard of *Le Figaro* of Paris that, among other things, there should be closer cooperation and understanding between Paris and Madrid. *Le Monde* of Paris noted ·favorably July 18 that many of the new men brought to the Spanish Foreign Ministry by Castiella y Maíz had been educated in France.

Other Foreign Developments

Spain had no formal diplomatic relations with the Communist nations. Since 1955, however, there has been economic and cultural ties. Spain bought aluminum and celulose from the USSR and coal from Poland, while the East purchased a variety of Spanish products, especially citrus fruits. In late 1958 negotiations were opened with Czechoslovakia for tractors, and with Hungary for aluminum. Several teams of Soviet scholars and scientists attended international meetings in Spain, and in July 1958 a Spanish delegation attended the Moscow meetings of the International Union of Architects.

The Spanish demand for the return of about 500 tons of gold that the Spanish Republic had sent to the USSR in 1937 had been refused consistently. *Pravda* denied Apr. 5, 1957 that the USSR owed Spain anything. The Soviets claimed that the gold was sent to Moscow to pay for shipments of war materiel; they said they had a letter from Dr. Juan Negrin, the last Republican premier, dated Aug. 8, 1938, confirming their position. The *Pravda* article said the Spanish Republic still owed Russia $50 million for arms shipments.

Franco and King Ibn Saud of Saudi Arabia had met in Madrid Feb. 10, 1957. At a gala party for visiting Pres. Camille Chamoun of Lebanon Oct. 30, Franco said: "Spain wishes to reaffirm now its traditional friendship with the Arabs."

During Apr. 1957 Spain received the balance of the $5½ million that Japan had agreed to pay (Jan. 9, 1951) as compensation for damage to Spanish property and injury to Spanish nationals suffered during the Japanese occupation of the Philippine Islands 1942-5.

A Spanish-West German agreement signed in Madrid Apr. 9 by Foreign Mins. Fernando Castiella of Spain and Heinrich von Brentano of West Germany provided for the settlement of an assets dispute arising from the Spanish seizure and sale of German property in Spain in 1948.

Franco met with Shah Muhammad Riza Pahlavi and Empress Soraya of Iran May 23 and expressed the hope that Spain and Iran would continue their friendship, which had remained unbroken since the 14th century.

After raising the level of representation to that of ambassador,

Spain appointed Count Luis de Olivares y Bruguera de Artaza Amb.-to-India Aug. 1957. (The resumption of Indo-Spanish diplomatic relations had been announced May 23, 1956.)

Pres. Muhammad Ayub Khan of Pakistan visited Spain Nov. 15. Franco reminded him that Cordova and Lahore were once the frontiers of the califate of Damascus. Franco then quoted the Pakistani poet Muhammad Iqbal (1877–1938), who said that the "marvelous coast of the Indian Ocean ends in the gardens of Al-Andalus."

Spanish Foreign Min. Castiella visited Athens June 21–3, 1958. After meetings with Greek Premier Constantine Karamanlis and Foreign Min. Evanghelos Averoff, it was announced in a joint communiqué that Greek-Spanish trade would be increased, that both states would work for world peace and that "the traditional friendship which links both Greece and Spain with the Arab countries constitutes an important factor of equilibrium which it would be desirable to reinforce."

Spain became a member of the International Bank for Reconstruction & Development (World Bank) and the International Monetary Fund (IMF) Sept. 18, 1958. Spain's contribution to the IMF was fixed at $100 million, while its subscription to the Bank stock was 1,000 shares, or $100 million.

The UN General Assembly filled Economic & Social Council vacancies Oct. 8 by electing Afghanistan, Bulgaria, New Zealand, Spain, the U.S. and Venezuela.

ECONOMIC REFORM, POLITICAL STAGNATION (1959)

Spain embarked on a serious economic stablilization program in mid-1959 after measures described as stop-gaps appeared to have done little to improve a worsening situation. Early results of the new measures appeared only partly promising. The political picture remained unchanged. Franco let it be known that he intended to have no king on the Spanish throne while he was alive, and he reiterated his opposition to liberalism and political democracy. In what was regarded as a diplomatic coup, Franco was host to U.S. Pres. Dwight D. Eisenhower toward the end of 1959 when Eisenhower arrived for a visit that began with some coolness but ended in apparent warmth and good-fellowship.

Economy Lags

A widely acknowledged need for economic reforms in Spain appeared to be confirmed by the economy's poor performance in 1959. The industrial production index for the year was virtually unchanged from the 1958 figure. Using 1929 as a base, industrial production reached 319; but with 1958 as the base, it was 100.1.

Locomotive production declined to 47 units and rolling stock production declined to 2,482 cars during 1959. The decline was caused by a plan to concentrate on the repair of existing equipment rather than produce new equipment: 338 locomotives and 5,677 coaches and freight cars were overhauled. (During 1959 the government invested 3.1 billion pesetas in the railroads. There was an 8% reduction in railroad traffic. But operating expense exceeded income by 3.444 billion pesetas.)

Automobile producion increased to 37,763 units; truck output rose to 10,454 units; tractor production increased 50% to 3,319 units, but motorcycle output fell to 124,250 units.

The production of radios (269,845 units), TV sets (25,729 units, almost 7 times the 1958 figure), refrigerators (26,477 units) and gas stoves (90,144 units) increased. Shoe production reached an all-time high of 25.8 million pair. Paper and cardboard production increased to 340,752 tons, and 12,833 different books were produced. Spain sold 557 million pesetas worth of books; 497 million pesetas worth of these books went to Latin America, and 109 million pesetas worth of books was imported; Spain thus had a 448 million-peseta ($21 million) favorable balance of trade in books.

Coal production declined to 15.642 million tons in 1959. Iron production fell to 4.6 million tons, and iron exports declined to 1.8

209

million tons worth 42,975,000 gold pesetas. Lead output increased to 71,200 tons, and the lead exports rose 29,858 tons worth 17.6 million gold pesetas. Zinc ore production increased to 157,745 tons, and zinc-ore exports rose to 131,604 tons worth 15.3 million gold pesetas. Aluminum output climbed to 21,073 tons, and the government imported another 36,825 tons. Wolfram production fell to 716 tons, and wolfram exports declined to 605 tons worth 1.6 million gold pesetas. Manganese (40,754 tons), salt (1.6 million tons), phosphates (300 tons) and superphosphate (1.8 million tons) production increased. There was an increase in potassium chloride exports to 295,598 tons worth 25.1 million gold pesetas.

Refined iron production increased to 1.8 million tons in 1959, but exports of refined iron fell to 985,897 tons worth 25.9 million gold pesetas. 24,529 tons of refined zinc were produced and 413 tons of refined zinc worth 264,000 gold pesetas were exported. Cement production increased to 5.2 million tons. The manufacture of nitrogen fertilizer increased 40% to 71.856 tons. The export of mercury dropped to 1,483 tons worth 26.7 million gold pesetas.

Movie production remained relatively stable with 51 pictures produced; in 1958 52 movies had been produced.

Textile production was generally down. Rayon output fell to 15,055 tons. Cotton cloth output fell slightly, but the export of cotton cloth increased to 7,137 tons worth 39 million gold pesetas. Wool cloth output declined to 12,151 tons, but the production of silk cloth increased to 527,791 kilograms.

Electrical production increased to 16.7 billion kilowatt hours in 1959 and electrical consumption to 13.5 billion kilowatt hours.

Wood production declined to 3,870,000 cubic meters, and cork output increased to 55,697 tons worth 49,257,000 gold pesetas. The government reforested 310,000 acres of land in 1959.

The fish catch increased to 751,600 tons, but profits were low. Spain had the lowest ratio of catch to fisherman—9 tons of fish to one fisherman—in Europe. Spain's ratio of catch to ship tonnage—2.4 tons of fish for each ton of shipping—was the 2d lowest in Europe (France had the lowest). The chief causes of the low profit yield, according to economists, were the antiquity of the Spanish fishing fleet and the lack of modern processing facilities.

The Spanish merchant marine was also considered inefficient by economists. 47% of all Spanish merchant ships were over 25 years old, while 28.6% were less than 5 years old.

The total volume of merchandise handled by Spanish ports fell by 600,000 tons to 53 million tons in 1959. This was caused almost entirely by restrictions placed on imports after Aug. 1. Total import unloading fell from the 1958 high of 30.7 million tons to 29.9 million tons.

The tourist trade continued to improve. There were 82,698 hotel rooms of varying quality available, and 4,195,000 people visited Spain during 1959. They spent $297 million, from which the government received $150 million in foreign exchange. But the currency black market, which until July 17 offered a tourist 50% more than the official rate, prevented the government from receiving the full foreign exchange benefit of tourism.

Agricultural production was little changed from 1958. Wheat production fell to 4½ million tons but wheat exports increased to 565,000 tons. Orange exports increased to 755,377 tons worth 195 million gold pesetas (12.6% of Spain's total export). (Despite increased competition from Israel and North Africa, the demand for Spanish oranges, tangerines and mandarins increased. In 1959 the government prepared an additional 22,000 acres for eventual orange production and 6,500 acres for tangerine cultivation.) Meat output increased to 516,232 tons. Milk production declined to 2,314,100 tons. Sugar production increased to 428,000 tons and imports of cane sugar declined to 39,000 tons; per capita comsumption fell to 15½ kilograms during the year. With some 5.3 million acres under cultivation, the production of both olives and olive oil increased.

Agronomists agreed that government aid was needed to improve the agricultural sector. Specific projects mentioned included more irrigation, land redistribution and the creation of cooperatives.

The 16½ billion-cubic-foot Yesa Dam on the Aragon River (in northeastern Spain) was inaugurated by Franco Apr. 8. The project was designed to irrigate 648,000 acres of land. But only 76,000 new acres were irrigated in 1959. Only 5 million of Spain's 55 million acres of farm land were irrigated. While irrigated land usually produce 2 to 3 times the yield of unirrigated land, agronomists estimate, all types of crops do not benefit equally from irrigation: the potato crop, for example, hardly benefits from irrigation, but the yield of irrigated cotton fields is 4 times that of non-irrigated fields.

(Even irrigation efforts can cause danger and tragedy. A dam burst at the Vega de Tera Reservoir in northwestern Spain Jan. 9 drowned 132 of the 500 residents of the Zamora province mountain village of Rivadelago, 3 miles downstream on the shore of Lake Sanabria. About 125 of the village's 150 buildings were destroyed. The break was caused by a sluice gate's collapse under pressure of month-long rains. The break, which took place at 4 a.m., sent an estimated 230 million cubic feet of water sweeping down the river.)

The government continued to support the reparcelling program by redistributing land to create 100 parcels totaling about 260,000 acres. The reparcelling program, while acknowledged helpful, was also considered insufficient. (Since 1955 there had been an 8% reduction in the number of parcels under 5 acres and a 20% increase in the number of parcels above 450 acres.)

The Spanish farm land was divided into some 54 million parcels owned by 6 million people. 41.8 million parcels were of an acre or less each; 6.9 million parcels were from 1 to 2 acres each; 4.2 million parcels were from 2 to 12 acres; a million parcels were from 12 to 125 acres; 110,000 parcels from 125 to 650 acres; 14,000 parcels were greater than 650 acres each. In Badajoz Province, 1% of the owners controlled 38% of the land; in Cádiz Province, 2½% of the owners held 57½% of the land.

In theory, but not in practice, each owner worked 9 parcels. In Tarragona Province, the average owner worked 26¼ small scattered plots; in Barcelona Province the average owner worked 2.32 plots, while on the Balearic Islands 43% of the parcels were over 7,500 acres each. According to agronomists, the small size of the parcels prevented the industrialization of agriculture. It was said that wheat production especially, would benefit greatly from industrialization. 43.4% of the wheat farms were of less than 15 acres each, but they employed 90% of the labor force. 4.2% of the wheat farms had more than 450 acres each, and they employed only .06% of the labor force.

The government-sponsored cooperative program was not very popular and had limited success. There were 5,926 cooperatives with a total of 1,223,499 families in 1959. The coops varied in size and wealth. In Salamanca Province there were 422 coops with a total of 27,390 families; poverty-stricken Navarra had 391 coops with a total of 46,756 families; in Huesca Province, where between 1950 and 1960 there was a net loss in population, there 284 coops with a total of 116,906 families; in Valencia Province, which accounts for 5% of Spain's industrial output and has one of the higher standards of living in Spain, there were 279 coops with a total of 149,289 families.

Economic Problems Attacked

Despite a seemingly healthy economy, many economists held that Spain faced serious economic problems. These included: (1) failure to adopt a clear plan for economic development, (2) uncontrolled inflation, (3) an antiquated and inefficient banking and credit system, (4) a multiplicity of national, local, religious and guild holidays, and

(5) a balance-of-payments deficit that might bankrupt the country before the end of 1959.

To solve the first problem, the government had invited various economic groups to visit Spain during the latter part of 1958 and report their findings. Experts from the Organization for European Economic Cooperation (OEEC) had arrived in Dec. 1958 and were at work. In Feb. 1959 a team from the International Monetary Fund arrived. Franco asked French Pres. Charles de Gaulle to lend Spain the services of French economist Jacques Rueff, who had stabilized the French economy in 1958; Rueff arrived in Feb. 1959. Meanwhile, a U.S. economic mission headed by Richard S. Aldrich, according to Benjamin Welles in *Spain: The Gentle Anarchy*, "urged the regime . . . to end deficit spending."

Demands for reform also came from Spaniards. Spanish industrialist Alejandro de Araoz warned that "we have spent more than we have earned. . . . We have invested and pledged more than we have saved." The annual report of the Banco de España bolstered its demand for fiscal reform by demonstrating that while the private sector of the economy showed a profit of 20.1 billion pesetas, the public sector showed a deficit of 14 billion pesetas. Both Spanish and foreign economists criticized the national budget, which had forced the government to increase the public debt from 8.1 to 8.2 billion pesetas. An 81.4 billion-peseta ($1.7 billion) 1959 state and private investment budget, disclosed Mar. 13, provided 18 billion pesetas for the construction of 140,000 new housing units, 16½ billion pesetas for basic industry, 15.7 billion pesetas for agriculture, 11½ billion pesetas for public works. (Total Spanish government expenditures in 1959 were estimated at $795 million, income at $692 million, including $68 million in foreign credits and $127 million in U.S. aid.)

Government attempts to solve the economic problem by what were called stop-gap measures achieved only minor results. A request to various guilds, for example, that saint's days be celebrated on Sunday instead of during the week was rejected by the guilds. The government discovered during 1959 that the 1958 banking law that was supposed to have permitted the government to control credit did not work because the private banks were permitted to issue bonds. In 1959 Spanish banks floated 37.4 billion pesetas worth of bonds and used the capital to invest in industry. By the end of 1959 Spanish banks had invested a total of 88.9 billion pesetas in industry. Furthermore, the government discovered, it had no control over either who received loans from Spanish banks or in what industries the banks invested. Because of the interrelationship between the boards of directors of banks and industrial firms, the larger industrial firms had no problem securing capital for expansion. On the other hand, because of a 1936 law that had prevented the establishment of new banks, firms that did not have contacts with the lending banks found it impossible to secure loans. By mid-1959 government economists admitted privately that the 1958 law did not give the government sufficient power to control the Spanish banking industry.

Government authorities claimed that they had stopped the flight of gold and convertible currency from Spain. 369 prominent Spanish businessmen and professionals were disclosed Mar. 9 to have been fined a total of nearly 117 million pesetas ($2,786,000) for maintaining unregistered foreign currency deposits in Swiss banks. The heaviest fines were $520,000 against Madrid coal merchant Carlos Sobrino Alvarez, $170,000 against Ricardo Gorina Oliver of Barcelona, $100,000 against Anselmo Bengel López Martín, $70,000 against Antonio Sabates Vila and $60,000 against Constantino Villar Soria, all of Madrid. Unauthorized foreign assets, including $1,198,715 in dollars, £8,000 ($22,400) and 5,506,213 Swiss francs ($1,266,500), also were confiscated. Officials said the unregistered accounts totalled 300 million pesetas (about $6 million), not the $280 million–$1 billion originally reported to be involved.

Yet by spring, according to economists, Spain was on the verge of economic catastrophe. As of Jan. 1, 1959 Spain had only $57 million in gold and $4 million in convertible currency in reserve. Unless the government acted quickly, economists warned, Spain would be bankrupt by July 1.

The Organization for European Economic Cooperation (OEEC) May 14 issued a preliminary report that, among other things, criticized the unrealisticly high exchange value of the peseta. According to the findings the 40-peseta-to-the-dollar rate contributed to both Spain's unfavorable balance of trade and the inflation. The OEEC report held, however, that "the problem of reestablishing equilibrium in Spain can be solved in a comparatively short time by vigorous and coordinated action."

An economic stabilization program was introduced in 1959 on the prodding of the cabinet's 3 Opus Dei members. Commerce Min. Alberto Ullastres Calvo, Finance Min. Mariano Navarro Rubio and Pedro Gual Villalbi, president of the Council on Economic Affairs, convinced not only the bankers and industrialists but, according to Arthur P. Whitaker in *Spain and Defense of the West*, José Solis, head of the Falange, and José Antonio Suanzes, head of INI (Instituto Nacional de Industria), who needed $4.4 million in U.S. aid for equipment for the Aviles steel plant, that radical reforms were necessary. The ministers approached the *caudillo*. "Franco turned wearily, angrily to the Opus Dei ministers," according to Benjamin Welles in *Spain: The Gentle Anarchy*, " 'Hagan lo que les de la gana,' he snapped." ("Do it the way you will!") That, according to Bernhard Schütze in *Rekonstruktion der Freiheit Die Politischen Opposi-. tionsbewgungen in Spanien*, "was the signal for the [introduction] of the stabilization program."

Spain sought immediate foreign credits to pay due bills, but the international banking community demanded signs of positive reform first. Agreements finally initialled in Madrid June 26 by Spanish officials and Per Jacobsson of the International Monetary Fund (IMF), René Sargent of the OEEC and H. K. von Mangoldt of the European Monetary Agreement provided for the devaluation of the Spanish peseta and a strict austerity program in return for substantial international credits and Spanish entry into the OEEC.

A 22-page "Memorandum to the International Monetary Fund and the European Organization for Economic Cooperation" was issued by the Spanish government June 30. The memo outlined this program, called "The Plan for Stabilization" or simply "The Plan":

(1) The budget was to be limited to 80 billion pesetas; the prices the government charged for public services were to be raised by as much as 50% (Decree 1,302/1959 of July 17 raised rail rates 40% effective Oct. 10; a ministerial order of July 28 raised phone rates); prices charged by government monopolies were to be increased (petroleum prices were increased July 27; tobacco prices were raised July 28); loans by private banks were to be reduced by at least 3.4 billion pesetas.

(2) There were to be no new government bond issues, and a limit was to be placed on the value of bonds issued by the Banco de España.

(3) A ceiling was to be placed on the total volume of loans issued by individual banks. (To discourage loans, the Banco de España Aug. 6 raised the rediscount rate from 5% to 6½%.)

(4) A 25% deposit would have to be placed with the Banco de España on all orders for imported goods. (Decree 1,300/1959 of July 27 put this into law.)

(5) The peseta was to be devaluated to a realistic free market level and the various rates for individual items abolished. (Decree 1251/1959 of July 17 set the peseta at .0148112 grams of gold or 60 pesetas to the dollar. The decree carried out an agreement signed the same day in Washington by Commerce Min. Alberto Ullastres Calvo and the IMF. Bills from Spain, however, were calculated at 59.79 pesetas to the dollar and not 60. Commerce Min. Ullastres July 22 declared the peseta freely convertible into the currencies of the U.S., Britain, West Germany, Belgium and Luxemburg, Switzerland, Canada, Austria, the Netherlands, France, Italy, Denmark, Norway and Sweden.)

(6) The importation of meat was to be subsidized by the government to prevent inflation; there was to be an export tax on oranges to keep the internal price down. Both the import subsidy and the export tax were to be gradually reduced over a period of 3 years.

(7) Government controls on both Spanish and foreign investments were to be reduced in order to stimulate venture capital. (A ministerial order July 28 raised from 25% to 50% the amount of stock foreign investers could own in any one Spanish enterprise and provided for repatriation of profits and capital within short periods. 7 government agencies that had regulated prices and production in various industries were abolished Sept. 16.)

The Plan called for about $546.3 million in loans and grants of which the U.S. was expected to supply $285.3 million: $45 million for defense, $60 million for agricultural surplus, $30 million from the Export-Import Bank, $123.3 million (7.4 billion pesetas) as counterpart funds for Spanish expenses, and $68 million in loans from private banks.

The OEEC Council announced July 20 that Spain, which had been an associate member of the council, would be admitted to full membership. Spain had been a full member of the European Nuclear Energy Agency, an OEEC subsidiary, since Jan. 1959, when Spain had contributed $1½ million to the construction of the agency's irradiated nuclear fuel plant at Mol, Belgium. The council also announced that $145 million in credits would be made available to Spain in view of these circumstances: Spain had "expressed its desire to reorient its economic policies to bring them into line with Western countries." Spain "indicated its intention progressively to fulfill the various obligations contained in the Convention for European Economic Cooperation" of Apr. 16, 1948. Spain had announced "a number of economic reforms necessary to enable Spain to take on these commitments."

The OEEC credits took 2 forms: The first was a credit of $100 million (advanced through the European Monetary Agreement), of which $75 million was available immediately "to enable Spain to undertake her measures of liberalization without risk to her balance of payments" and the balance to be made available Feb. 1, 1960 after the OEEC had reviewed the Spanish reforms. The 2d OEEC credit was for $45 million, which, according to Arthur P. Whitaker in *Spain and Defense of the West*, "permitted Spain to pay its commercial and other obligations over a period of 4 years."

The IMF announced credits to Spain totaling $75 million: $25 million in dollars, $25 million divided between French francs and sterling and $25 million in "stand-by" credits. The Chase Manhattan and First National City banks of New York extended loans to Spain totaling $70 million. Spain received U.S. government aid in various forms: Under U.S. Public Law 480 the U.S. authorized Spain to buy an additional $60 million worth of surplus farm commodities at bargain prices with non-convertible pesetas, and the money would remain in Spain. The Export-Import Bank advanced $30 million.

The U.S. announced that, subject to Congressional approval, $40 million would be advanced for defense.

The total face value of the international credits and loans came to $420 million. But in addition, the U.S., which had accumulated 7.4 billion non-convertible pesetas as a result of farm surplus sales to Spain, announced that it would spend the money ($123.3 million) in Spain. Spain thus received $543.3 million worth of aid. The total of U.S. non-military aid to Spain since the signing of the 1953 pact (excluding the sums spent by U.S. servicemen and tourists and the salaries paid to Spaniards employed by the U.S. government) reached $929.2 million by Dec. 1959. And the U.S. Congress Sept. 15 voted Spain an additional $45 million for defense in 1960.

Ramón Tamames reported in *Estructura Economica de España*, "the effects of the plan were immediate and in many cases encouraging." According to Arthur P. Whitaker in *Spain and Defense of the West*, during "the first 11 months of 1959, currency in circulation had decreased by more than 2.7 billion pesetas. . . . From August to November 1959 foreign exchange income had exceeded outgo by $81.3 million. . . . In the closing months [of 1959] the [cost-of-living] index had remained stable . . . [and there was] some notable increase in production." Imports for 1959 totaled 2.433 billion pesetas while exports totaled only 1,532 billion pesetas, leaving a balance-of-payments deficit of 901 million pesetas, but this deficit was 283 million pesetas less than the 1958 deficit, and economists speculated that the trend had been reversed. The reserve of gold and convertible currency showed a marked improvement: In 1959 the gold reserve increased $10 million to $67 million while the convertible currency reserve rose from $4 million to $131 million.

Economists said that The Plan had stopped the inflation, but, according to Tamames, Spain still had to prevent a long-term recession. A series of reports issued in late 1959 and early 1960 by Banco de España, Banco Central and Banco Urquijo stated that during the 2d half of 1959 the rate of growth of the national income had fallen to 3½% and that in some areas production had exceeded consumption with the result that there were growing inventories. Some authorities noted with alarm that, in just a few months, several textile mills had closed and that there was an unusual number of bankruptcies among small firms. Salomon Wolff, writing in the January and February 1960 issues of *Swiss Review of World Affairs*, stated that while The Plan seemed to be working then, the reforms "touch only a few, and not even the most important, aspects" of the economy.

According to observers, living conditions improved throughout

1959.   Infant mortality dropped to 4.11 per 100 live births.   The
number of registered unemployed dropped to 94,805, the lowest
number since 1930.   (Foreign observers assert, however, that this
figure is misleading since one should add to the total unemployment
both the thousands of workers who were aided by the Instituto Español
de Emigración to find work in Western Europe, and the tens of thousands of workers who found employment in southern France illegally
during the harvest season.)   Income, in terms of the 1953 peseta, rose
to 10,600 pesetas *per capita* in 1959, while employed Spaniards earned
an average in current pesetas of about 25,000 ($418).   Average income
in Barcelona, Madrid, Guipúzcoa, Vizcaya and Álava provinces, which
accounted for more than 44% of Spain's industrial output, was more
than double the average income in the agricultural provinces.   Even in
semi-industrialized provinces such as Sevilla, Cádiz, Alicante and
Murcia, which produced 10% of Spain's industrial output, the average
income was 25% lower than in the 5 most industrialized provinces.
Only 34,550 people left Spain in 1959, while 19,100 Spaniards
returned; the net population loss of 15,400 was the lowest since the
Civil War.

According to Gonzalo Barroso Gippini in *España 1970* (a book
distributed in 1971 by the Information & Tourism Ministry), Spanish
families in 1959 had few comforts.   There were only 53 telephones
and 8 automobiles per 1,000 inhabitants; less than 2% of Spanish
families had refrigerators, less than 1% had TVs, about 60% had radios,
only about 51% had running water in their homes and 85% had
electricity.

In 1959 the government built 111,838 new apartments, about
10% of the need, as estimated by ex-Republican diplomat Elena de La
Souchere in *An Explanation of Spain*.

According to government reports there was an increase from 12%
to 14% in the number of children aged 11-17 attending school.   Only
554,400 children aged 10-16 were in high school during the 1958-9
school year.   There are no available figures on the number of children
aged 10-16, but government sources estimated that there were 2.6
million children aged 10-14 in 1959.   Of the 554,400 in school, only
133,000 were in technical schools.   Experts warned that (1) the years
of schooling were not sufficient to develop a population capable of
understanding the modern technical world, and (2) there were too
few children in technical schools to provide Spain with enough trained
adults.   Government sources stated that while there had been a steady
decline in the illiteracy rate, in 1959 11¼% of the population over
10 years of age (7½% of the males and 15% of the females) was

illiterate. The director of primary education, according to Elena de La Souchere, said in 1959 that 25,000 new schools were needed for children aged 6–12. If the minimum age of compulsory education were raised to 14, 56,000 new schools would be needed and 17,000 existing schools would have to be expanded. The director estimated that 30% of the school-aged population did not attend school.

Salaries for teachers were low. In 1958 10,000 teachers had left the profession, and in 1959 the government was able to hire only 3,084 new teachers.

Franco Bars Early Enthronement

In response to a growing demand for the restoration of the monarchy, Franco made clear that he would not permit the restoration of a Spanish monarch during his lifetime. Franco, 66, told Spanish monarchists that Spain already was a "monarchy" but that further agitation for the return of Don Juan, heir to Spain's last king, Alfonso XIII, or of Prince Juan Carlos, Don Juan's son, would not be tolerated. Franco's views were set out in a Jan. 14 letter to José María Peman, monarchist poet, from Rear Adm. Luis Carrero Blanco, Franco's chief aide.

In a 29-page Christmas/New Year's message Dec. 29, Franco, praising "the glories of our crusade" and "our revolution," spoke proudly of his accomplishments. He dismissed the whole question of the threat of bankruptcy, observing that solvency rested in the people of the nation and not in gold reserve. As for the form of government Spain had and would have, he asserted that the Spanish monarchy would be restored only as a continuation of the Falangist regime, its personnel and policies. Franco, denying that his regime was "provisional," asserted that it was the "normal and legitimate one" for Spain. He said history had proven "the inefficiency and futility of inorganic, formalistic democracy." He closed the speech with the traditional Falangist slogan "Arriba España!"

Monarchist leader Joaquín Satrustegui Fernández, 50, after a banquet held in his honor in Madrid's fashionable Hotel Menfis Jan. 29, had delivered a 15-page speech in which he attacked the "illegality" of the Franco regime. Benjamin Welles reported in *Spain: The Gentle Anarchy* that when the speech was over, "the banquet party broke into applause." (The government had granted permission to a group of prominent lawyers to hold a dinner meeting in honor of Satrustegui, a Basque industrialist who had studied law at Madrid University and Georgetown University.) Among the 90 or so individuals present were

José María Gil Robles, 61, leader of the Christian Democratic Party, Enrique Tierno Galvan, 41, a leading Socialist, who, with Gil Robles and Satrustegui, had founded the Left-wing monarchist Unión Española, Fernando Alvárez de Miranda, 35, socially prominent monarchist, and Antonio Menchaca, 39, described by Welles as "a hothead famed for his exploits in Franco's Civil War navy."

Within 24 hours, observers said, the contents of the speech were known to most government officials and opposition circles even though Information & Tourism Min. Gabriel Arias Salgado had ordered a news blackout of the meeting.

Arthur P. Whitaker asserted in *Spain and Defense of the West* that Satrustegui set his personal and business affairs in order in the hope "that the regime would give him and his cause the political boost of martyrdom by arresting him." Satrustegui and 4 Unión Española members (the Marques de Casa Arnau, Mariano Robles Robledo, Luis Benitez de Luzo and Amadeo Cardonello) were briefly detained Feb. 4 for questioning by the police. Satrustegui was fined 50,000 pesetas ($1,240) by the Interior Ministry Feb. 14. Tierno Galvan, who had spoken briefly at the Menfis meeting, was fined 25,000 pesetas. Meanwhile, according to Whitaker, the government began to attack Satrustegui's industrial empire but stopped when Satrustegui threatened to publish an account of its actions. Welles reported that Don Juan, on the advice of more conservative monarchists, broke with Satrustegui.

Theo Aronson reported in *Royal Vendetta* that the Carlists who supported the claim of Prince Francis Xavier de Bourbon Parma to the Spanish throne had repudiated those Carlists who, in 1958, had recognized Don Juan as pretender to the throne. (Carlists claim that all Spanish monarchs since the death of King Fernando VII in 1833 were usurpers and that the true rulers of Spain were the heirs of Fernando's brother Carlos, whom they call Carlos V.) 40,000 Carlists and supporters welcomed Francis Xavier's son, Hugo Carlos, and 2 daughters to the traditional Carlist rally at Montejurra in May 1959. Hugo Carlos, 29, assisted at a requim mass held in the church of the Irache Monastery, and he and his sisters then left the country.

Franco Vs. Liberalism & Leftist Opposition

Franco publicly criticized liberalism Feb. 18. Speaking before the First National Congress of the Spanish Family, Franco said: "Of all the evils that liberalism introduced in our society none were less than those affecting the institution of the family, the diminution of the discipline and authority of the father; the exclusion of the clergy from teaching with its resultant disrespect for divine law; the planting of hate and rancor in place of Christian charity; the abandonment of the children and the scandalous behavior of adults; the breakup of marriages through the implementation of divorce laws. . . ."

Liberal Roman Catholics announced in Madrid May 14 the formation of a clandestine Left Christian Democratic Party to work for the replacement of the Franco regime by a democratic government. The leader of the group was Manuel Giménez Fernández, 63, former agriculture minister in the Spanish Republic.

Dionisio Ridruejo, 43, a founding member of the Falange, had been convicted by the Spanish Supreme Court Feb. 2 of disrespect (*desacato*) of the Franco regime because, in an article in the Cuban magazine *Bohemia*, he had denounced the regime as repressive. Ridruejo was sentenced to 20 months in jail but was freed under a 2-year amnesty decreed for the coronation Pope John XXIII. Ridruejo, who had established the Partido Social de Accion Democratica in 1956, was still under indictment for anti-government activity arising from his demands for the restoration of civil liberties. Like other opposition leaders under similar indictment (*e.g.*, Tierno Galvan) Ridruejo was freed on his own recognizance. After the amnesty had freed him Ridruejo went to Valencia where, according to Arthur P. Whitaker in *Spain and Defense of the West*, he saw "some 200 callers [within 3 days] despite police regulations that permitted him to receive no more than a handful at one time." In the spring, in an interview with the Brazilian paper *O Estado de São Paulo*, Ridruejo called Spain a "political desert" and prophesized that unless something were done there would be a "national revolutionary protest."

Madrid dispatches reported the arrests May 28–30 of 20 young leftists charged with agitation for a general strike against the Franco regime. Those held were said to include Asst. Prof. Mariano Rubio Jiminez, 27, of Madrid University, Dr. Luis Martín Santos Rivera, 35, director of the San Sebastián Psychriatic Hospital, and Prof. Santiago Anton, 35, of San Sebastián.

Benjamin Welles reported in *Spain: The Gentle Anarchy* that in January several members of the opposition had begun discussing plans for a general strike June 18. According to Bernhard Schütze in *Rekonstruktion der Freiheit Die Politischen Oppositionsbewungen in Spanien*, the plan called for all "movies, theaters, bullrings and football [soccer] stadia to be emptied for a day." This strike, opposition leaders said, would not be illegal since there was no law that said people had to go to the movies, but by keeping people home the opposition to the Franco regime would become manifest.

When, according to Schütze, the Spanish Communist Party (PCE) announced support for the strike, members of the new Left Christian Democratic Party withdrew from the project. The Socialists refused to permit PCE participation in planning the strike, and when the PCE stated its intention to join, the Socialists dropped the whole affair. Members of the PCE, the Frente de Liberación Popular (FLP) and other opposition leaders, however, proceeded with organizing the strike.

But the general strike failed to materialize June 18. In the week preceeding the strike date the government had arrested 123 opposition leaders and had assembled extra police and security police in Madrid. Ex-Republican diplomat Elena de La Souchere, in *An Explanation of Spain*, described the failure of the strike as the "Waterloo of the mid-century generation. Its underground networks were very much subdued for the next 3 years its leaders in jail . . . or in exile." Apparently few Spaniards knew about the planned general strike until long after June 18, a date on which Spaniards filled movie houses, theaters and bullrings.

Among those arrested prior to June was FLP leader Julio Ceron Ayuso, 28, a Foreign Ministry official. The government said Ceron had been arrested June 16, allegedly for distributing strike literature with members of an extremist organization called Young Iberians. According to de La Souchere, Ceron had been in Geneva on government business during most of the time that the strike was being disucssed. She reported that he was tricked into returning to Madrid and was arrested at the airport. (In discussing the Ceron arrest with admitted revolutionists who knew Ceron, this editor was informed that Ceron knew that he would be arrested as soon as he landed.) The allegation that Ceron worked with the Young Iberians was denied by FLP members. According to private information, the Young Iberians consisted of 2 members and had no connection with Ceron.

The government brought Ceron and 16 alleged FLP members to trial Nov. 9 on charges of "provocation against the form of government." Among the 16 were Juan Masana, editor of the Catholic review *El Ciervo*, Ignacio Fernández de Castro, a young lawyer identified with the Catholic Action group and with the church's labor organization Hermandades Obreras de Acción Católica (HOAC), and liberal intellectuals Antonio Diez Yague and Manuel Gómez Ovejero who faced the additional charge of having collaborated with the New York-based anti-Franco publication *Iberica*. Each of the defendants had a lawyer, but, according to Welles, the "star" of the trial was Christian Democratic Party leader José María Gil Robles, who "left the army prosecutors speechless." (Sergio Vilar wrote in *Protagonistas de la España Demo-*

cratica that this trial marked the debut of Gil Robles as an active member of the opposition to the Franco regime.) According to observers, Gil Robles easily disproved the government's charge that the FLP was allied with the Communists; the defense called several priests who stated that Ceron was a good Catholic who had never expressed Communist views. Other lawyers called HOAC members to attest to the non-Communist attitudes of the defendants. The military court found all 17 guilty of "military rebellion" and sentenced them to prison terms ranging from one to 4 years; Ceron received a 3-year term. The case, however, was reviewed by the Special National Tribunal for Extremist Activities, and Ceron's sentence was increased Dec. 23 to 8 years. (He eventually served 3 years and 3 months of the term.)

In response to foreign criticism that most of the arrests were carried out in violation of the Spanish constitution of 1947, the government July 30 promulgated a "Public Order Law" that suspended the constitutional guarantees until the end of the "serious Communist threat."

During the late summer and fall the government reportedly arrested more than 700 people. Among those arrested was Simon Sánchez Montero, 44, described by Silvio Schaedler in the Dec. 59 issue of *Swiss Review of World Affairs* as being the chief of the PCE in Spain. (Sánchez Montero told Sergio Vilar that he had joined the PCE in 1936 and had been a member of the central committee since 1954.) Brought to trial, Sánchez Montero not only confessed to all charges but, according to Schaedler, used the trial to launch an appeal for a united front of opposition groups to overthrow the Franco regime. The prosecution demanded that Sánchez Montero be sentenced to 30 years in jail. The military court sentenced him Sept. 25 to 20 years and one day in jail.

Luis Lucio Lobato, who admitted to Vilar that he was a member of the PCE, was sentenced Sept. 26 to 14 years in jail. Luis Alberto Solano Madariaga, nephew of exiled anti-Franco leader Salvador de Madariaga, was sentenced to 3 years imprisonment for "military rebellion" by a Madrid court Sept. 29. Alleged PCE Central Committee member Adalberto Jiménez Lara was sentenced Dec. 1 to 23 years imprisonment for agitating for the general strike. 19 other alleged leftists were sentenced to lesser terms for strike activities.

The London *Times* charged Sept. 1 that the Franco regime was holding 400 political prisoners, many imprisoned since the 1936–39 civil war, in a prison near Burgos. Elena de La Souchere stated that in 1959–60 there were 357 political prisoners in Burgos alone while another 120 were in Carabanchel, 33 in El Dueso and other in Zaragoza, Valladolid, Ocaña, Puerto Santa Maria, and Alcala de Henares.

A protest against Spanish repression was delivered to the Spanish embassy in London Dec. 22. Among the 150 signers were Isaiah Berlin, Wolf Mankowitz, Sir Bertrand Russell, C. P. Snow, Sacheverell Sitwell, Dame Sybil Thorndyke and Graham Greene.

Opus Dei

A growing opposition to Franco's support of Opus Dei technocracy was noted by many observers in 1959.

Jesús Ynfante, in *La Prodigiosa Aventure del Opus Dei*, called Opus Dei the "Holy Mafia" and described the growing intellectual opposition to Opus Dei's control of the Consejo Superior de Investigaciones Cientificas (CSIC), the chief organ of scientific and historical research in Spain. (CSIC supports and publishes some of Spain's most significant scholarly works.)

Socialists such as Enrique Tierno Galvan, such moderates as Raúl Morado and liberal Falangists such as Pedro Lain Entralgo wrote articles (in newspapers or scholarly journals such as *Boletín Informativo del Seminario de Derecho Politico*) attacking Opus Dei.

Arthur P. Whitaker reported in *Spain and Defense of the West* that, when *Time* magazine Mar. 18, 1957 published an article asserting that the appointment of Opus Dei members to the cabinet meant a liberalizing influence, 25 intellectuals including Dionisio Ridruejo and Gregorio Marañon wrote a letter to *Time* denying this interpretation, but, "in 1959 they were still complaining that their letter had never been published." In articles published both in and out of Spain, Ridruejo attacked the ideas of the Opus Dei, especially the monarchist position of Opus Dei intellectual leader Rafael Calvo Serer, more frequently than he denounced the ideas of Franco.

Intellectuals, educators and newspapermen combined to oppose Opus Dei's alleged invasion of the educational and publishing fields. The opposition failed to prevent the establishment by Opus Dei of the quasi-university Estudio General de Navarra at Pamplona, called by some "the only private university in Spain." (Tuition there was 200 pesetas, or about $3.50, per month, but, according to Whitaker, "one student in 8 held a scholarship.") Opus Dei had residences in Spanish university towns, as it had in the U.S.

Opus Dei controlled La Sociedad Anonima de Revistas, Publicaciones y Ediciones, which had been founded in 1951 and was in competition with private and Church publishing houses. *La Actualidad Economica*, established in 1958, became the voice of the technocratic ministers and, as such, the most significant financial weekly in Spain.

Nuestro Tiempo, published by the Estudio General in Pamplona, and *Arbor*, published by the CSIC, became leading journals for philosophy and labor studies. Opus Dei-controlled newspapers such as *El Alcázar*, *Madrid*, *Informaciones*, *El Correo Catalán*, while failing to achieve the mass circulation of *Ya*, *ABC* or *La Vanguardia*, began to become newspapers representing the elite.

Industrialists and businessmen objected to Opus Dei competition. In 1956, with the support of the Opus Dei-owned Banco Popular Español, Opus Dei had established the holding company Sociedad Española Anonima de Estudio Financieros (ESFINA), which became the source for capital, according to Jesús Ynfante in *La Prodigiosa Aventura del Opus Dei*, for Opus Dei industrial and commercial expansion. In 1958 ESFINA took over Banca Pujol, Subirachs y Cia, changing the name to Banco Latino. In 1959 the holding company Universal de Inversiones was established. The so-called Andorra Trust (El Credit Andorra), established in the principality of Andorra, therefore, outside Spanish jurisdiction, was, after 1956, a dependent of ESFINA. The Andorra Trust became a vehicle for Opus Dei investment outside of Spain. (Spanish citizens cannot invest outside of Spain; non-citizens who are residents of Spain frequently invest in Swiss Mutual funds.)

The established church also began to object. In 1959 anti-Opus Dei articles appeared in publications controlled by the Society of Jesus and Editorial Católica, the publishing house directed by Bishop Angel Herrera y Oria of Málaga.

Church & Religion

A Spanish priest, writing under the pseudonym of Sabino Iturri, reported in the May 15, 1959 issue of the anti-Franco New York publication *Iberica* that indifference to the Church was growing in Spain. (In 1957 a survey by Catholic Action revealed that 90% of 15,000 workers described themselves as anticlerical, antireligious.) Iturri said that only 14,000 of the 105,000 people in Madrid's 8 largest parishes were "practicing Catholics." Other figures presented by the priest indicated that 52% of the males in rural areas were practicing Catholics, while in Barcelona fewer than 10% of the males in working class districts and about 20% in other parts of the city went to church.

Information & Tourism Min. Gabriel Arias Salgado appointed Bishop Angel Herrera y Oria of Málaga, Bishop Juan Hervas of Ciudad Real and Bishop Antonio Ona de Chave of Lugo June 23 to the 40-member National Committee on the Press. One of the purposes of the committee was to revise the censorship laws. Considering Herrera's debate with Arias Salgado when Herrera fought censorship in 1954, observers called the appointment of Herrera a rejection of the government's censorship policy. But Herrera announced in November that "the country is not ready to do without prior censorship," and in December he sent Arias Salgado a private note asserting that "the rectitude of the regime's censorship cannot permit it to be termed arbitrary."

In the midst of a July heat wave and the height of the Spanish tourist season, Archbishop Enrique Cardinal Plá y Deniel of Toledo cast an "anathama upon women who went about without sleeves and with low necklines." He declared that "public bathing . . . constitutes a prime danger to morality. . . . Mixed bathing must be avoided, since it almost always entails chance of sin. . . . Engaged couples should avoid solitude and darkness. . . . It is unacceptable that they walk arm-in-arm."

The editor Luis de Galinsoga interrupted a priest who was conducting the service in Catalan (the vernacular language of Barcelona) at the parish church of San Ildefonso on Sunday, June 21. Galinsoga, a Murcian who, according to Benjamin Welles in *Spain: The Gentle Anarchy*, Franco had forced the Count de Godo to hire as an editor of Barcelona's influentia newspaper *La Vanguardia*, objected to the use of the vernacular. When the priest insisted that Pope John XXIII had approved its use, Galinsoga, according to Elena de La Souchere in *An Explanation of Spain*, stomped out of the church yelling "All Catalans are shit [*mierda*]!" Catalan nationalists, Catalan Socialists and Catalan Christian Democrats united the next day to organize a boycott of the paper. The leader of the united action was Dr. Jordi Pujol. *La Vanguardia* had normally sold 140,000 copies daily, but sales fell quickly, and, according to Welles, youths began burning stacks of the newspaper "under the tolerant eye of local Catalan policemen." Advertising declined, and the paper faced bankruptcy. The Catalans insisted that Galinsoga and Gen. Felipe Acedo Colunga be removed from office (the civil governor of Barcelona, Acedo Colunga, in a speech Dec. 1, 1958, had called those who spoke Catalan traitors). Despite the boycott and disorder that continued throughout the balance of the year, Franco refused to discharge either official.

Father Ramón Sánchez de Leon, Superior of the Jesuit Order, had interrupted a public ceremony at the Madrid Chamber of Commerce Jan. 22, 1959 to declare that Spanish Protestants were "subversive, Masonic, immoral and mentally unbalanced." In September the English newspaper *Daily Telegraph* complained that both the Spanish government and Church made the sale of Protestant bibles almost impossible and that the activities of the Protestant Truth Society were hampered. Madrid Baptist minister José Nuñez Moreno was sentenced Oct. 17 to 2 months' imprisonment and fined 1,000 pesatas ($16.80) for illegally attempting to reopen his chapel, closed by government order in 1954.

Despite the fact that *legally* there were no practicing Jews in Spain, Benjamin Welles reported in *Spain: The Gentle Anarchy*, that "on Oct. 2, 1959 200 Jewish residents of Madrid met in a former ducal palace at 19 Calle Pizarro to dedicate their first synagogue in 467 years." 2 apartments had been purchased on the 2d floor of the building with funds obtained from the American Joint Distribution Committee, "the Conference on Jewish Material Claims Against Germany, and from local subscriptions." The synagogue had government approval although the edict of 1492 that forced Spain's Jews either to depart or to accept baptism had not been rescinded. Legally the 3,000 to 8,000 practicing Jews in Spain could not become Spanish citizens; some Jews who had arrived in Spain in 1938 were still on Austrian passports issued by the Austrian Republic before the Nazi takeover. Most of the 30,000 Jews who had reached Spain during the period 1936–45 used Spain as a stopping point to the Americas; just as in 1959 Moroccan Jews were beginning to use Spain as a way station on the road to Israel. A Sephardic Bibliographic Exposition (Spanish Jews are called Sefards) was held in Madrid Dec. 18. According to Welles, "more than $1 million worth of cultural treasures from 13 nations—including the Vatican—were displayed in . . . the National Library . . . [for] 6 weeks."

U.S. Relations & Other Developments

Pres. Dwight D. Eisenhower visited Spain Dec. 21–22, 1959. Arriving Dec. 21 at the U.S. Strategic Air Command's $120 million base at Torrejon, 13 miles outside of Madrid, Eisenhower left his plane, the *Columbine*, and greeted Franco. According to Benjamin Welles in *Spain: The Gentle Anarchy*, the President "shook Franco's hand somewhat stiffly." Foreign correspondents commented that there was no *abrazo*—the "formal embrace that," according to Arthur P. Whitaker in *Spain and Defense of the West*, "is customary among Latin peoples of Europe and America . . . on formal occassions." Franco said: "With profound satisfaction I have shaken your hand for the first time." Eisenhower read a brief statement in which he asked Spain to "join" the U.S. to achieve a world "free from aggression, from hunger and disease, and also from war and the threat of war." The President also saluted Spain as "one of the ancestors of the Americas." Then, according to Welles, Eisenhower and Franco "hurriedly inspected a mixed honor guard and climbed into Franco's Rolls Royce for the 20-minute drive to Madrid.

The drive to Moncloa Palace, where Eisenhower spent the night,

night, was a triumphalt procession. Despite the fact that Franco told Eisenhower that "we haven't paid our people to cheer," Welles noted that "trucks parked inconspicuously in the side streets attested to the Falangists' zeal in rounding up their loyal adherents." (The *Manchester Guardian* Dec. 31 quoted British MP Robert Edwards, who had been in Spain during the Eisenhower visit, as stating that the Spanish government had put 11,000 people in preventive detention to make sure they did not disturb the visit.)

Franco entertained Eisenhower the evening of Dec. 21 at a state banquet in the Oriente Palace. To please Eisenhower, the Spanish military band played "The Yellow Rose of Texas," which the President had once said was his favorite song. Franco, according to observers, offered the President an unusually warm and long toast. Franco started by saying, "Again I wish to express our gratitude for the proof of the estimation you have for us by visiting our nation." He listed some of the links that tied the U.S. and Spain: "from Ponce de Leon, Hernando de Soto and Brother Juniper Serra, the apostle of California, [to the names] of mountains, rivers and plains of your nation." He toasted Eisenhower and the American people for their "preservation of liberty in Western Europe . . . [from] the Communist yoke." He said the "2 countries are aligned on the same front for defense of peace and liberty." Franco concluded the toast by saying: "We are not able to forget the generosity with which the American people have accepted the sacrifices that destiny has imposed on its historic mission. Nor are we able to forget the generous and sincere friendship with which you have aided Spain. . . . I wish to express here, in the name of my country, our full gratitude, from the depths of our hearts, for the generosity and friendship of the U.S."

Eisenhower, U.S. Amb.-to-Spain John Davis Lodge, State Underscy. Robert Murphy, Embassy Counselor William Fraleigh and the President's son, John, joined Franco, Spanish Foreign Min. Fernando María Castiella y Maíz, Spanish Amb.-to-U.S. José María Areilza, Conde de Motrico, and the translator Jaime de Pinies for breakfast the next morning at the Pardo Palace. The Spanish government had flown in a 2-inch-thick steak from Kansas City for the President's breakfast. According to Welles, at first "a leaden silence hung over the room. . . . Franco was ill at ease." Murphy and Lodge told jokes, "the silence only deepened. . . . Eisenhower tried his hand with a Texan joke. Slowly the ice began to melt." The conference ended at 10 a.m.

A helicopter took the party to Torrejon later Dec. 22. Franco delivered a warm farewell. Then, before leaving Spain, Eisenhower gave Franco the *abrazo*, and, so that the cameramen could record the embrace, he did it again. The President shouted "Merry Christmas and A Happy New Year!" and boarded the *Columbine* for Morocco. Areilza went with him as his guest.

The 2 governments issued a communiqué that said: ". . . The talks, which covered a wide variety of . . . international matters of interest to both countries, were conducted in an atmosphere of cordiality and understanding. The President and the [Spanish] chief of state discussed the President's planned visit to the Soviet Union next year and confirmed their views, as expressed in their exchange of letters of last August that such consultations to improve the climate of relationships would be beneficial although a firm defense posture should be maintained. Gratifying progress was noted in the implementation of the economic and defense agreements signed by the U.S. and Spain on Sept. 26, 1953. These agreements are based on a recognition of the necessity for efforts on the part of both countries to achieve the common goal of world peace and stability. During the conversations Spain's admission to the Organization for European Economic Cooperation (OEEC) was mentioned with satisfaction, and the President expressed his good wishes for the success of the Spanish economic stabilization program. The conversations served as another indication of the friendly ties between the Spanish and American peoples and strengthened the bonds of cooperation that exist between the 2 countries."

According to Benjamin Welles, who was in Spain at the time as reporter for the *N.Y. Times*, the Eisenhower visit was "the brainchild of [José María Areilza, Conde de] Motrico, who had discovered [at his post as Spanish ambassador] in Washington that the American President was planning a world tour that autumn." Spanish Foreign Min. Fernando Maria Castiella y Maíz decided to visit Eisenhower while the latter was in London for the NATO meeting in mid-August to invite him to Spain. There was a slight problem: Castiella could not "just show up" in London, but getting an invitation to London was not simple. Castiella was still *persona non grata* in England because, among other things, of his views on Gibraltar (in 1951 Prime Min. Clement Atlee had refused to accept him as Spanish ambassador to England because of those views); and Franco, in an interview with the Falangist labor newspaper *Pueblo* May 1 condemned the British presence as "a symbol of a past that now has no reason to exist." Since the British would not invite Castiella to London, Castiella had asked Areilza to arrange the invitation to come from Eisenhower, and Areilza secured the invitation although British officials were said to have expressed annoyance Aug. 18 at the invitation. The British said that no Spanish foreign minister had been invited to Britain since the Spanish Civil War and

Castiella's visit might be marred by Laborite hostility to the Franco regime.

Castiella had arrived in London Aug. 30 and had announced that he had not come to seek entry into NATO, which, he said, was unnecessary since Spain was already involved in Western defense through its military ties with the U.S. and Portugal. It was also noted that there was a possibility that Spain, France, Morocco and Italy might become united in a French-sponsored Western Mediterranean Defense Pact attached to NATO. (During a 5-day visit to Italy June 23-8, French Pres. Charles de Gaulle had suggested such an alliance to Italian Pres. Giovanni Gronchi and Italian Premier Antonio Segni.) Castiella visited Eisenhower Aug. 31 at Winfield House in Regent's Park, the private home of the U.S. ambassador to Great Britain. The Spanish foreign minister gave the President this letter from Franco (the letter was made public Sept. 2 and printed in the *N.Y. Times* Sept. 3, but the official Spanish text of the letter dates it Sept. 3): "My Dear President, First, I wish to thank you for the sacrifices and efforts you have made to lead our Western world along the path of peace and understanding, and in particular for the aid and benefits that Spain is receiving from the United States under your direction. There are many people who do not fully realize that in the present situation lack of action, inertia and an exclusively defensive attitude would quickly lead to defeat, and that in today's situation all contacts are useful which seek to unveil the immediate aims of our opponents. As for the general and permanent aim of universal domination held by the Soviets, I know that such a great soldier and strategist as yourself always keeps it clearly in mind. For this reason I reject the view of those who, forgetting your record, are fearful of the consequences of your meeting with Khrushchev. . . . Your excellency is well aware that Western superiority, based as it is on the industrial power of the United States and its ability to adapt it to the needs of war, could be weakened if, at the time the Soviet Union completes harnessing its potential resources, Western Europe fails to reinforce its unity and its state of preparedness. I consider your presence and authority most useful in forging unity on our continent which, so easily tends toward disunity. I offer the hope, my dear general, that when the international situation will be able to permit it, in one of your trips, you will desire, with your wife to spend some time in our nation."

Eisenhower replied: "I am of course pleased to know that you think well of the planned exchange of visits between Mr. Khrushchev and myself and that you clearly understand the basic thought that I have in mind in this connection. I appreciate also your reference to the aid which we have extended to Spain in order to help our Spanish friends to assume certain responsibilities in the defense of the West. The agreements signed between our 2 countries in 1953 have produced good results for both of us. I am happy to have this opportunity to express to you my appreciation of the spirit of cooperation with which you have worked with us on the construction and operation of our joint bases. They are an important element in the common defense. I should like also to congratulate you on the bold new economic program already auspiciously begun and on your membership in the Organization for European Economic Cooperation [OEEC]. This constitutes another important link in forging the European unity to which you refer."

Eisenhower added the hope that he and Mrs. Eisenhower would "some day have the opportunity to enjoy the friendly Spanish hospitality about which we have heard so much."

After meeting with Eisenhower, the Spanish foreign minister had a private interview Aug. 31 with U.S. State Secy. Christian Herter, who had been present at the meeting between Castiella and the President.

Castiella and the Spanish ambassador to Britain, the Marquis de Santa Cruz, called on British Foreign Secy. Selwyn Lloyd Sept. 1. Their discussions covered a broad spectrum of subjects: (1) Spain's admission to the OEEC (2) the conditions of Spanish workers on Gibraltar (3) facilities for British tourists in Spain and (4) the rights of Spanish Protestants. The official communiqué from the British Foreign Office, however, said the discussions were held "in a cordial atmosphere" and that "all matters of Anglo-Spanish relations" were covered. The Spanish foreign minister paid a courtesy call on British Prime Min. Harold Macmillan at 10 Downing Street, and he left London Sept. 5 for Paris, where he had an interview with French Pres. de Gaulle.

Spanish circles claimed the Castiella visit to London and the exchange of letters between Franco and Eisenhower as a diplomatic victory. Madrid's monarchist newspaper *ABC* commented that the events proved that "from a military standpoint, the U.S. considered Spain the the most important of its allies in Europe, except perhaps the United Kingdom." Madrid's Catholic paper *Ya*, edited by ex-Foreign Min. Alberto Martín Artajo, remarked: "We may not be a great military or economic power, but no one can discount our mission as a bridge between Europe and Africa and Latin America and our unshakable brotherhood with the sole Asian [state] of Christian Western culture [*i.e.*, the Philippines]."

Castiella and West German Chancellor Konrad Adenauer in Bonn Nov. 10-11 discussed proposals for linking Spain to the European

Common Market or the rival European Free Trade Association. Also discussed, although not made public at the time, was the possibility of establishing bases for the West German army in Spain. This was reported to be the first visit to Germany of a high Spanish official since the Nazi regime ended.

At the invitation of Franco, Turkish Prime Min. Adnan Menderes and Foreign Min. Fatin Rustu Zorlu had visited Madrid Apr. 15–19. Zorlu and Castiella Apr. 16 signed a treaty of peace and perpetual friendship replacing the treaty of 1924. A communiqué issued Apr. 16 said that the 2 nations planned to cooperate on a broad spectrum of social and economic fields, that "diplomatic relations between them should be settled on this basis." A Spanish-Turkish statement issued Apr. 20 said that the 2 nations shared an "identity of views," and that their friendship constituted "one of the pillars of peace and stability in the Mediterranean area."

40 Spanish prisoners, including 35 soldiers, 3 women and 2 children captured during the Moroccan-Spanish fighting in Ifni in 1957, were released May 6 by King Muhammad V of Morocco. Crown Prince Mulay Hassan of Morocco called on Spain and France Dec. 24 to withdraw all troops from Moroccan territory by no later than 1963.

An oil exploration concession in Spanish Guinea, West Africa was granted Nov. 23 to an oil combine formed by the U.S.' Gulf Oil Co. and the Spanish CESPA firm. It was the first foreign oil concession granted by Spain.

Spain and Guatemala in Aug. 1959 had signed an agreement under which Spain promised to send a 3-year mission to Guatemala to train members of the Guatemalan National Guard.

Cuban Premier Fidel Castro in December gave the Spanish ambassador to Cuba 24 hours to leave the country and recalled the Cuban ambassador to Spain. The Spanish ambassador had interrupted Castro during a radio address when Castro had made an attack on the proposed Eisenhower visit to Franco. Observers noted that there had been a steady deterioration in Spanish-Cuban relations since the Castro takeover in January. (2 members of the Spanish Communist Party, Enrique Lister and Alberto Bayo, were employed by the Castro government).

Index

A

233